Sunshine

Sunshine

The diary of a lap dancer

SAMANTHA C. ROSS

ALLEN&UNWIN

SYDNEY·MELBOURNE·AUCKLAND·LONDON

Allen & Unwin
83 Alexander Street
Crows Nest NSW 2065
Australia
Phone: (61 2) 8425 0100
Email: info@allenandunwin.com
Web: www.allenandunwin.com

 A catalogue record for this book is available from the National Library of Australia

ISBN 978 1 76087 834 4

Set in 11.75/17.25 pt Sabon LT Std by Bookhouse, Sydney
Printed and bound in Australia by Griffin Press, part of Ovato

10 9 8 7 6 5 4 3 2 1

 The paper in this book is FSC® certified. FSC® promotes environmentally responsible, socially beneficial and economically viable management of the world's forests.

To Jeff Lindsay,
who knows my darkest thoughts and secrets,
and still endures the friendship . . .

And to Melanie May,
I know you're a shining star on the big stage in the sky

HEAT OF THE MOMENT

13 January ···

I punched a guy in the face last night. Violent of me? Yes. But there's only so much groping a girl can take, so I look upon it as aggravated assault.

I know the dirty old bastard wasn't visually impaired, as he had no difficulty in lunging for more than a handful. Like many men in the lap-dance room before him, he'd ignored the huge sign: NO TOUCHING THE GIRLS. Honestly, some people have such little restraint when faced with a jiggling pair of breasts.

The bouncers in the far corner were too busy to intervene—they were discussing important matters such as a forward tackle and where to locate the best buffet. They were quite satisfied that I'd handled the situation and that the pervert had made a speedy exit, without them having to lift a finger.

Though the bouncers at this club are sadly lacking in observational skills, they are most certainly capable of reducing most men—and all groping customers—to a crimson stain on the ground.

And rest assured, in a strip club the customer is *never* right. Place your paws on a girl in a non-touching club and you can expect a backhand from the dancer, or to be escorted from the premises by a heavy-handed security guard. In most cases, nobody bothers to call the police. Yes, it's illegal to smack someone, and yes, touching a dancer is a criminal offence—however, the cops don't want the hassle, so they're usually happy for the club to deal with these frequent incidents. Unless someone commits a serious sexual violation, we dancers are hardened enough to see wandering hands as pesky workplace hazards.

There's no law against verbally insulting a dancer—only against verbal abuse that entails a threat. But if you utter the word 'cellulite' in a strip club, you'll be out on your arse quicker than you can say 'ruptured testicle'.

When the bouncers come to our defence, though, I suspect it's less about protecting us than it is about their enthusiasm for bloodletting. Not surprisingly, the security here don't like us dancers much; if I made twenty bucks an hour compared to a hundred bucks per fifteen minutes, I wouldn't like me much either. In fact, ninety per cent of the staff in strip clubs—managers, bar staff, DJs and bouncers—are rather sour towards strippers. And the club I grace at present is no exception.

As an exotic dancer—or, without splitting hairs, a stripper— I travel frequently. Most of us do. From city to city, country to continent, we chase the cash, leaving when it becomes spasmodic or when we hit our boredom threshold. The money can go up and down depending on the time of the year and which part of the hemisphere we're in. And once we've spent too much time in one club, it shows. An unenthusiastic stripper is about as likely to make money as Taylor Swift is to remain secretive about a relationship.

I've started this year in Darwin, a city perched at the top end of Australia with metal-melting temperatures and a dedication to excessive drinking on New Year's Eve—hence the late diary entry.

One of the things a stripper can do, with admirable gusto, is party as though a zombie apocalypse will wipe us all out tomorrow.

I know that many people wonder why I take my clothes off for a living. They have lots of other questions too. Is a stripper a type of sex worker? Do we have boyfriends, *normal* ones? And why the hell am I in a place like Darwin?

It's true that the life of a stripper is full of melodrama. I hope my sanity remains intact in the year ahead, but I'll no doubt lose a little along the way . . . regardless of how I like to think of myself as 'Sunshine the Philostripper'.

HIGHLIGHT: Am finally able to write without alcohol poisoning shaking the pen.

DOWNSIDE: Ruined my manicure when I punched that dirty old bastard.

17 January

Darwin, though not exactly Melbourne, London or LA, does have a certain backward charm, and presents a more pliant and gullible style of customer than jaded big-city patrons.

Example? After a relatively slow start at the club tonight, with only a few hundred-dollar dances to show for it, I luckily wound up talking to a weathered old electrician. Who would have guessed at the wad of hundreds in his wallet? Me—that's who, because I saw them.

A good rule to bear in mind when patronising a strip club is never to show a stripper how much money you have while ordering a drink at the bar.

The below information is how a stripper operates at work. Or how I do, at least.

Once I'd spotted at least a grand in his wallet, my talent for manipulation kicked into overdrive. I began as I usually do: I set upon making him feel like the most intelligent man in the world, with the most interesting career—despite the fact that he screws in light bulbs for a living. '*Really?* An *electrician*?! What's the most fascinating thing that ever happened to you on the job? Have you ever been *electrocuted*?!'

I allowed him to tell me a longwinded tale while I calculated how much money I was likely to entice out of him. Another rule to remember is that people love talking about themselves; let a customer tell you his life story, and he becomes putty in your hands.

After that, I began phase two: I switched to making him feel like a king. 'Do you have your own business? I bet you do! A man like you doesn't look like he'd work for *just* anybody.' (A fair assumption, based on the cash he was carrying.) 'Oh, wait!' I laid it on thick. 'Let me guess, you probably have a *government* contract. You seem smart enough to land the big jobs.' Once I'd inflated his ego, I went in for the kill. 'Why don't you and I spend some time together in the back room?'

This, you see, hinted at a private, darkened space. Little did he know, another ten customers would be in there spending 'alone time' with the stripper of their choice in one large room. But by then it would be too late for him to back out, and nor would he want to, with all that naked flesh on display.

'I'd really like to do a naked dance—just for you,' I added, to imply how special he was.

This worked a treat. Now that the electrician thought I was attracted to him, he handed over a hundred dollars for a lap dance. I then hustled him out of a further two hundred bucks. How did I accomplish this feat? Simple: I asked if he'd like to extend the dance. But it's all in the *way* you ask. It might not work every time, but my method has a track record of success. *Always* end a lap dance while sitting naked on the floor while staring up at your customer with big, beseeching eyes; that way, you appear less calculating and more vulnerable while suggesting he part with extra money. And unless he's gay, what man can say no to a naked woman sitting on the floor at dick-level?

These days, both the spiel with which I enticed the electrician into the lap-dance room and my carefully orchestrated routine are second nature to me. Back when the big bucks first started rolling in, I sometimes felt a little ashamed over bleeding a customer dry, especially those susceptible to a lap dance or ten. Some patrons leave without a cent—not even a cab-fare home. But my guilt faded as I realised that nobody forces them to pay to see my vagina. They aren't coming to a strip club for guitar lessons.

Plenty of strippers, namely those new to the industry, have professed feeling the same remorse for draining a man's wallet. 'I feel so bad, Sunshine! He was so nice, but I took every dollar he had.'

'Yes, and if it hadn't been you, he'd have been just as nice to the next stripper.'

How would I have reacted had this man not been a local tradie, throwing a spanner in my working-class-hero hustle? Easy: I would have switched to sounding like a sexy tour guide, and even hinted at showing him the sights. A date to which I would never have shown up.

A stripper must think on her feet—or her seven-inch platform heels.

And that, my new friend, is how a hustle is done.

There are certain things you can trust in life, way more than a stripper who says you're special:

- Bangladesh tap water
- Mixed drinks from Bill Cosby
- Petrol station sushi

Signing off now, am exhausted after eight lap dances, seven stage shows and a serious case of alcohol poisoning.

HIGHLIGHT: A thousand more bucks to put towards savings.

DOWNSIDE: I now know a depressing amount about electromagnetics and alternating currents.

1 February

Barely drank a drop last night and have woken surprisingly clear-headed—drained, though. Only seven girls are working at the club right now, narrowed down to six due to one being a hypochondriac. As a result, I can only take one evening off each week.

I spend it with my boyfriend, Jim. We either lie on the couch watching movies and gorging food on a 'cheat day', or we sample dishes at previously undiscovered restaurants. Being a chef, Jim likes to explore new methods and flavours, and I like to eat— though don't always permit myself—so it's a win-win.

Jim is tall, dark and somewhat mysterious, and we've been an item for a little over four years, since before I became a dancer. In his freethinking way, he encouraged me to take the leap into professional nudity, and most of the time he's okay with it.

The moment we met, when our eyes locked across a nightclub, the electric current between us would have fried anyone trying to pass through it. Soon we were caught up in a conflagration of raw and primitive sex. We spent cold Melbourne nights in a hot tub, sipping on Southern Comfort along with each other. Within a week, we'd moved in together. Our nights were stolen by deep conversations on personal philosophies, religion, opinions shaped by our upbringings, cake preferences, demonic possession, and Team iPhone versus Samsung—discussions punctuated only by snacks and oral sex.

Within the month, we were having our first arguments, and our relationship has been turbulent since then. But our fights are an outlet for the passion between us, so they often lead to make-up sex.

Jim and I get each other. He's privy to my neuroses, insecurities, strengths and weaknesses. I know the secrets of his shady past, all the petty criminal elements of his teenage years. But lately he has a tendency to throw my career back in my face whenever his inner man-baby rears its head.

Today he'd gone to work by the time I got out of bed, so I decided to go shopping. What else is a woman to do with a fistful of cash and a sense of ennui?

As I made my way to the shops, I thought how it really is rather pretty here. It isn't anything like the cosmopolitan surroundings to which I'd grown accustomed, but in the past few months I've become slightly fond of Darwin. At first I planned to stay for a month; it's now been four. Whenever I become antsy and consider moving on, I think of the cash in this club and reconsider.

I'm here because an old and trusted friend, Harlow, called me up to share the love.

I'd been feeling stale in Cairns, my money drying up due to apathy, and my skin parched from binge drinking—in fact, I was on the verge of needing a liver transplant.

'On a good day,' I told Harlow, 'I contemplate faking my own death and moving to Mexico. And the rest of the time I feel like I've died of boredom and been resurrected by voodoo to perform on stage.'

'Oh dear, that lacklustre, huh?'

'Vending machines have more variety than I do. Seriously, Harlow, I sleep, work, drink, repeat. The only thing that distinguishes each day is the strength of my hangover.'

'And is your money dehydrating?'

'Like a stale crouton in the Sahara,' I said.

'Good!'

'Gee thanks, Harlow, how nice that we're celebrating each other's misfortunes. Should I be thrilled if your haemorrhoids keep growing?'

Her laugh rang down the phone. 'No, silly. Besides, they're only the size of lemon pips now. I mean *good* that it sounds like you're ready to move on. I've just spent a few months in a goldmine. But I have to leave—I've got a showgirl contract in Adelaide. You should come here and take my place. And because there's a few of us going, management will need more girls, so bring some friends. Hurry, though, first in undressed!'

'But where are you?'

'Darwin! Honestly, Sunshine, you'd be crazy not to get your arse up here. There's more money at this club than in a drug lord's offshore bank account!'

And so Jim, myself and ten pairs of stilettos hit the road. I was more than happy to have a change of scenery, and my boyfriend had never been overly fond of Cairns anyway.

Darwin is a small, strangely modern, shimmering city set in an expanse of desert and tropical rainforest in shades of ochre and jade. The swimming holes are aqua-coloured lozenges—of course, you can't swim in them for fear a crocodile will snack on you like a cheese toastie. And the temperature is *sweltering*.

At least the constant dehydration helps me achieve a heroin-chic look, which goes nicely with my deep tan and works a treat with my new pink Victoria's Secret teddy. I just purchased it for the criminal price of four hundred dollars. Funny, isn't it? The less material there is, the more the garment costs.

No doubt some pervert will be begging to buy it off my backside tonight. It's always advisable to purchase a few cheap G-strings to keep on hand in the likely event a customer asks to buy your underwear: the humblest two-dollar pair of Kmart knickers can go for one hundred bucks a pop.

Australian strip clubs are indeed a strange parallel universe. They might look different from each other on the surface, but they're all basically the same.

Upon arrival, your first port of call will be the reception area. Whether it's made of polished wood or smoky, tinted mirrors, you'll be greeted by a girl-next-door type, there to relieve you of a fifteen- to twenty-dollar entrance fee. This girl will be polite and not overly pretty, so as not to distract you from the real deal inside. If she can be bothered, she'll relay which and how many dancers are working that night—only she'll call us entertainers. For some reason, the staff never call us strippers.

You'll notice the foyer is adorned with signed pictures of Penthouse Pets past or still in residence, alongside a few arty depictions of half-naked women with impossibly beautiful faces, each staring down with a come-hither smoulder. Usually, a velvet curtain or dark passageway forms a barrier between the entryway and the club, hinting at the exotic delights inside.

Within these places of mystery, the lights are always dimmed. I don't know if this is for the dancers' benefit, to veil our flaws, or so the customers don't feel so exposed—I imagine it to be rather daunting if you're the first man to arrive at a club full of half-dressed, impossibly gorgeous women. I've seen a few patrons walk in at nine on the dot, look around and stop dead in their tracks. I also watch them consider walking out again—twenty-dollar entrance fee be damned.

Strip clubs are designed for partial cosiness, though. Most look like an expensive lounge room, with overstuffed sofas and plush carpet. There's also a slight elegance to the décor, either to pacify the rich or intimidate the working class into behaving; either way, it doesn't work well.

The inside of a gentlemen's club is almost never painted white, although I did see one during my travels. I simply walked right back out the door, not wanting the dimples on my arse to look like glorified moon craters. The customers looked more nervous than criminals in a police line-up.

Men like to hide in dark corners, which is why most exotic clubs are painted black. If you're an intelligent club owner, you'll colour the walls scarlet, subliminally suggestive of eroticism. The corners are softly lit to soothe and relax customers, while centre stage is a flashing neon rainbow that highlights the erotic experience.

The bar is usually tended by another generically pretty girl or three, who will charge an arm and a leg for a standard drink.

And at that bar, you'll *always* find the same kinds of men.

The Tight-Arse only drinks water or Coke and won't give the girls a cent, but he's the first to linger at the stage each time somebody *else* pays a dancer to get naked, staring intently enough at your vagina to catch sight of an ovary.

Then there's the Pity Party Guy. He'll sling you a twenty—if you sit for three hours listening to his story of woe. His wife has let herself go. (Never mind that *his* appearance makes Will Ferrell seem dashing.) His wife won't sleep with him. (No self-respecting woman would.) His best friend stole his business idea and made a million (I thought up the robot vacuum, not him!). Nobody respects him—not his family, not even the dog. His wife ran away with his best friend. They took the dog . . .

The Bastard. Beware of this one especially. He is in residence for one reason only: to insult the dancers. We symbolise every pretty girl who has rejected him, from the popular chick in high school to the hottest chick in the office—whom he once asked out and was given a reply along the lines of 'not if you were the last man on earth and I was already dead'. The Bastard is blind to his own shortcomings. He is surly and a blatant misogynist. He is unattractive in appearance and unpleasant in nature, yet he doesn't hold himself accountable for his many rejections. No, his lack of success with women is *our* fault—because we're all ball-breaking bitches, apparently.

The Boaster. He *loves* to tell you what a catch he is: how well his multimillion-dollar corporation is doing, how lavish his mansion is, how fast his speedboat goes. And all the while, the Boaster will flash great rolls of money that he will *not* spend. (Important note: any man who wants you to see the vast amount in his wallet has no intention of parting with it, because he's trying to impress *you*. Customers who have come to shell out big bucks pay *you* to impress *them*).

The Misguided Creep. Yes, he truly thinks you are his girl-friend and is desperately in love with you. Plenty of regular customers feel this way, but not on such a spooky level. The Misguided Creep will write you poems and bring you flowers and chocolates. I heard of one creep who would ask his favourite dancer to style her hair in the same way his ex-fiancée did. He even asked her to wear the engagement ring his ex had returned, *while* the dancer stripped for him. This great love affair ended when the dancer caught him lurking outside her car in an attempt to follow her home. Police were called, bans were put in place, and the Misguided Creep moved on to another strip club, where he fell in love with the next dancer who caught his eye. Nothing says 'I love you' like a restraining order.

Quasimodo. He has a hunchback, harelip, lisp, clubfoot, psoriasis, dermatitis, lazy eye . . . you get the picture. Quasimodo is by no means the worst of the lot and *will* actually spend money—unlike the other freaks. But he's hard to gaze upon. And you never know if you're more revolted by him or yourself, as you take his money in shamed pity while looking away. But what other pretty girl is going to spare him a glance?

The Dirty Old Man. No, he is not a myth. He is around seventy, with a leering grin and a filthy pair of wandering hands. His language is so suggestive and pornographic, it would make a pimp blush. The Dirty Old Man is usually only good for a twenty-dollar stage dance on account of his paltry pension. It's rarely worth the trouble or trauma.

Though many types of men grace strip clubs, and for varied reasons, those mentioned above can be found most nights of the week. The dancers are generally indifferent to these men and will only talk to them if there's truly nothing else to do. The usual suspects' faces and names may change, but the personas never do, no matter the venue, the city, the corner of the planet—whether the gentlemen's club is of the high-end variety, with an expanse of tasteful décor, or a budget-conscious variation, dark enough to mask the lack of expenditure.

Like the one in Darwin.

Walking into work this evening, I tried not to notice the dingy club in sad contrast to the pretty, balmy night outside. The black paint slapped against the walls doesn't quite reach the skirting boards in a regimented line. The disco lights are missing a bulb or three, and the stage, with its uneven surface, always feels like a deathtrap under my stilettos.

Tonight, an old Madonna song was playing softly in the background, and the mutants were already in formation at the bar, ogling scantily dressed girls. They were also lined up, awaiting a warm-up tequila shot. So I undressed for work, took my place in the line, and ignored the frugal freaks for as long as I could.

HIGHLIGHT: Forgot to eat, so stomach looks flat in Victoria's Secret teddy.

DOWNSIDE: Forgot to eat, so tequila hit me faster than a dog falls on an unattended steak.

15 February

I'm fortunate some of my closest pals from Cairns followed me up here. All strippers have a like-minded way of communicating, but certain private topics—like prematurely greying pubic hair and problematic flatulence—can only be shared with besties. Stripper acquaintances can spread secrets around a club faster than you can say 'genital warts'.

A good friend from Melbourne, Rowena, was already living in town when I moved here. Unfortunately I don't get to see her as much as I'd like; she is no longer stripping and is officially a day person.

Rowena is unusual because she met a rich older guy in the club—one whose looks didn't make her retch, whose conversation didn't make her physically sick, and whose touch didn't make her want to commit suicide. Now they're engaged, and she actually *likes* him. This is more rare than hot snow and benevolent dictators: strippers just don't go out with customers. But I approve of Rowena's fiancé because he'd never before been in a gentlemen's club and was forced into it by way of a work Christmas party. A once-only visitation can be overlooked. I also approve because he makes my friend happy. And because he bought her a really cool giftware and clothing shop in the city. It's where I get all my funky slogan T-shirts, and it's also great for last-minute birthday/Christmas/hens-party present ideas.

I'd told Rowena I would come by the shop this afternoon to browse and bring her coffee, and I'd invited the gang along to indulge in some girly chit-chat.

As I made my way out of the apartment, my neighbour's door suddenly swung open. He appeared in the doorway with a practised leer. I suspect he'd been waiting for the sound of me surfacing, which would have been creepy had he not looked like a bronzed surf god. 'Sunshine, glad I caught you! I bought you a little something.' He winked, all swinging-dick confidence.

A *little* something? I stared at the gift, unable to hide my confusion. 'You bought me a *bow and arrow*?'

'You said you love *The Hunger Games* . . .' He faltered, swinging dick shrivelling. 'I thought you might be the sporty type . . .'

Since I couldn't bring myself to sneer and leave him standing there with a fucking bow and arrow, I took the ridiculous gift and forced myself to say something. 'Thanks—I'll remember to take it with me to Panem . . . if I'm ever reaped as a tribute.' Probably not the nicest thing I could have said, so I fled.

It's the thought that counts. And he couldn't very well buy me anything romantic, like flowers, due to the fact that he also lives next door to my *boyfriend*.

What lies beneath the surface is that my neighbour has a thumping crush on me because of what I do for a living. A lot of the time we strippers encounter judgement and scrutiny from outsiders, but some boys simply have no idea how to act around us. Often their behaviour is nervous, awkward or full of bravado.

I took the archery set into town with me, intending to give it to Rowena in case she could sell it. The Mockingjay was a pretty popular character, after all, and someone might use it for a dress-up party.

When I arrived, Rowena was standing at her display window beside a young man who was scraping her painted logo from the glass. As I walked through the entrance, she announced, 'I'm having new signage painted.'

'Awesome.' I handed her a double-shot cap. I'd already emptied half of mine by tripping on my way out of the coffee shop. My clumsiness is legendary.

'And my new curtains arrived from Morocco, only five hundred bucks each! Look at the quality of the blue silk.' Row pulled the sparkly drapes all the way across the display window, blotting out the busy street and burning sun.

'Beautiful,' I said. 'Keeps it nice and cool in here too. It's *so* hot outside.'

'I know, but I can't let them stay that way—people won't know I'm open. I'll have to draw the drapes aside once the sign-writer is finished. Where are the girls?'

'Right here,' they called, as a trio of exotic dancers appeared in the doorway. They all arrived together, since they all live at the club's stripper house at the heart of town, a share house set up especially for out-of-town dancers.

Jade's incredible face led the pack. One of my very best friends from Cairns, she is charismatic, Eurasian and so unbelievably beautiful I often wonder why she isn't modelling instead of stripping.

'What happened to you last night?' she asked me.

'I tapped you on the shoulder and told you I was leaving early.'

'Oh, did you?' She frowned. 'I must have been drinking wine. Can't remember anything with chardonnay involved. Never tell me important stuff unless I'm drinking vodka.'

'It was hardly important,' Candy said from behind her. 'Sunshine wanted to get home and binge the last piece of hedgehog before Jim could. And Jade, your memory on vodka still makes a goldfish seem eidetic.'

Jade grinned. 'I'm not even going to ask what that means, so I don't have to pretend to remember it later.'

Candy gave one of her bemused, boisterous laughs. Almost six feet tall, my friend hails from the Pacific Islands; she has lustrous copper skin from her father's side with the chiselled features of her Scandinavian mother. She's serene, regal and wicked, and although she's a warm and empathetic soul to her friends, she works as a dominatrix when she isn't stripping.

Belle kissed my cheek in greeting while she glowered at her phone. She has rippling ebony hair to her waist, and her flashing chocolate eyes reveal a vivacious and somewhat erratic personality. 'My fucking ex again,' she said. 'Demanding child support from *me*, because *he* considers watching daytime soaps a valid profession.'

'I'm sorry to hear that,' I said soothingly. 'Perhaps he'll promote himself to *Studio 10*?'

'Highly doubtful. It's hard to absorb a news program after your fourth joint of the morning. How's Jim? Is he still smoking weed too?'

'Off and on. He waits until after work at least, which is why I needed to beat him to the last piece of hedgehog before his munchies kicked in. Mostly he's manageable.'

Jade was single, but Candy and Belle were here to take a break from tumultuous relationships. They were the ink to my tattoos, the sugar to my fairy floss, the melanin to my tan.

'Sunshine, why are you holding a bow and arrow?' Candy asked.

'Gift from my neighbour.'

'The same one who bought you a starting whistle because he misunderstood "Swarovski crystal"?'

'Yes, but in his defence I was pretty drunk and probably had my slur on.' I turned to Row and asked, 'Do you want it for the shop?'

'Thanks. That'd be great. Is this neighbour trying to impress you?'

'I think so. But he'll probably stop now, after seeing the bewildered look on my face. He went from cocksure to downward-dick in two seconds flat.'

'Speaking of dicks,' Candy called from over by the jeans rack, 'ask Jade where we spent the early hours . . .'

Rowena and I turned in tandem, while Jade giggled and shrugged.

'At the hospital,' Belle answered for her. 'Jade picked up last night—a totally gorgeous guy, hot as a Hemsworth brother—and guess who forgot to take her tampon out? The three of us were in casualty all morning, waiting for the nurse-on-duty to fish it out.'

I spurted the remainder of my coffee over Candy's white shirt. As she started thanking me for the inconvenience, Jade whined, 'But he had such a small dick! I had no idea it could be pushed in so far!' Lucky my cup was empty.

'When you say small, exactly *how* little are we talking?' Candy asked.

Jade thought about it. 'Not much bigger than the tampon, really.'

'Oh, I *hate* that!' Row cried. 'Isn't it just the worst? When you go home with a really good-looking guy and he has a big toe between his legs?'

'Yet he seemed so confident . . .' said Jade.

'I'd rather a smaller tower-of-power than a huge one, though,' Belle put in.

I nodded. 'True. Nobody likes a party-size penis.'

'Or a bent one,' Rowena added. 'I seriously dislike it when their cock is off to the side. It creeps me out—like a diviner looking for water or something.'

'But you don't want it looking like a chestnut either,' I said.

'What's a chestnut?' the girls asked.

'*Too* small. All ballsack, snake hidden.'

'Oh, I call that the fried egg,' said Row.

See? Stripper friends have our own way of communicating, without filters.

We were about to move on to more chaste subjects, like anal sex or bondage, when a shaken voice bleated from behind the closed curtain. 'Excuse me . . . I'm embarrassed. I think I have a chestnut.'

We'd forgotten that the poor young sign-writer was hidden in the display window. We all faced each other with a devilish snigger. Men were very rarely spared in our world.

HIGHLIGHT: Bought the best T-shirt with a cartoon image of Donald Trump's face and the slogan PRESIDENT? THERE WILL BE HELL TOUPEE.

DOWNSIDE: Even *I* blushed when they changed the subject to double-ended dildoes.

20 February

Some would consider my life to be luxurious; some would have a nervous breakdown if they tried it. It's an unconventional, hedonistic existence.

Usually I sleep all day, since I arrive home from work an hour or two short of when most humans are waking up. More often than not, I rise with the sun high in the sky, sometimes with the gritty dregs of alcohol still in my bloodstream. To treat my hangover, I lie by the pool as I mull over pressing topics, such as whether or not my toenail polish matches my tan, and if it truly matters. Drinking copious cups of coffee from a ludicrously priced machine, until I feel partially human, is another part of my regime. Then, if I can be bothered, I go shopping with the girls.

I always venture out on Wednesdays, because that's when the cleaner comes to spruce up my ocean-view apartment. Does that make me sound somewhat like a spoilt bitch? I loathe cleaning with a passion, and stripping is notorious for bringing out a girl's hidden shallows. Jim is committed to pointing this out whenever we fight. Sometimes part of my day includes either molten sex or a blazing row with him—usually between lunch and shopping. Exotic dancers don't always fare well with relationships, but I try.

I was raised to do so. Whether it be in relationships, career choices or personal beliefs, I was taught to strive. It's unfortunate that my personality comes attached with laziness, which I fall into whenever I'm given the chance, much to my folks' annoyance.

My mum and dad, who are no longer together, are lovely and generally easygoing, but otherwise like day and night. Mum was once a government caterer, while my dad was an engineer. My dad's religion is a dedication to working-class tradition: be honest, work hard, retire early and don't let emotions overrule your pragmatism or sense of humour. In contrast, my mum is extremely spiritual, less fond of working, and fierce in urging me to excel. 'If anyone ever tells you that something can't be done,' she often says, 'tell them it's rude to interrupt those who are busy doing it.'

They were both very proud when I finished my Bachelor of Business and went forth into a marketing career. I haven't told my dad that I'm a stripper; as far as he is aware, I'm the manager of an exotic club. There's no point in needlessly worrying him, which is exactly what he would do. I don't think he'd be disappointed by my choice—he's not overly judgemental—though he would definitely feel my degree was going to waste.

My mum, for all her open-minded, girl-power encouragement, actually burst into tears when I confessed my career change. It wasn't her fault: although she unknowingly supported feminist principles before her time, she also possessed the what-will-the-neighbours-think bias of her childhood era.

It was *her* mother, my nan, who nipped that attitude in the bud. 'Oh please,' she said, rolling her eyes as she scolded my mum. 'She'll probably be wearing more than they do in music videos nowadays. You can't raise Sunshine to strut confidently through life, then get upset about where she wants to do it. Besides, do you have any idea how much more money she'll make in her garter than in marketing?'

'How on earth do you know about that?' Mum and I chorused.

'Flossy next door told me Bessie up the road has a sister, Iris, whose granddaughter started nudie dancing a year ago. Calls herself "Peach".'

As my nan shared this gossip, my grandfather chortled. 'Don't you dare go calling yourself "Cherry".' He cackled at his own joke as he opened a Carlton longneck, standing in front of the fire in their cosy Melbourne lounge room.

My grandparents are a big source of comfort for me. They're also empathetic, jaunty and unperturbed by life's little setbacks, and they share a mischievous sense of humour.

Since that exchange, my mum has not only perceived stripping as a strong, liberated choice, but also, God help her, as glamorous! She keeps telling me about celebrities who dabble in exotic dancing: 'Rihanna is lap dancing in her new music video, and Kate Moss did pole dancing for an old White Stripes clip.' If only stripping *were* glamorous. Perhaps it is for some, but I have a tendency to grow apathetic towards my work.

I don't know if the problem is that I've relocated to yet another town fond of drinking and that some of my best friends are here to egg me on, or if I've just been dancing in the one club for too long. Whatever the reason, I'm bored out of my fucking skull. Again.

I've stayed mostly for the money. Wouldn't it be irresponsibly stupid to leave this kind of cash flow? On the other hand, I'm beginning to wonder what my sanity is worth.

I miss Cairns—that glitzy, tropical paradise. It's my adopted home, and it rivals Darwin in the great cash stakes. But I had to leave; I do occasionally recognise when something is bad for me. The real push came when I went all Jimi Hendrix and woke up choking on my own vomit after partying with rock stars. Some may consider twenty-seven to be the appropriate age to OD, but it's really not for me.

Why can't there be strip clubs in Amish communities? Or Navajo reservations? Or other dry areas? But in the life of an exotic dancer, the lines between work and celebration are often blurred by vodka.

In saying that, now that my hangover has worn off it must be nearing that time again.

Showtime.

HIGHLIGHT: Thank God housekeeping is coming today; the only thing I like to sweep the room with is a glance.

DOWNSIDE: Decided the fifty-dollar nail polish on my toes actually looks shithouse with my tan.

NO DRY LAND

If there is one thing that lifts the most despondent of spirits, pacifies the most extreme cases of restlessness and obliterates the severest monotony, it is the two most welcome words a stripper will ever hear: American Navy!

My thoughts of moving on have evaporated. My arse and hopes are firmly planted for the foreseeable future. Suddenly my mood is lifted higher than a stoned cosmonaut: a navy ship with more than a thousand marines is headed our way and will arrive in early March.

The boss, Dario, has sent a group text to his vast contact list of strippers, saying, 'Come and get it!' So they will be flooding in over the next week.

However, I've been dancing long enough to know I should gather certain information before I become overheated with excitement. To start with, where are these men coming from, and where are they normally stationed? If they're situated in Japan or Guam, forget it—both countries have ample strip clubs. If they've already stopped by Sydney or Melbourne, again, bad luck. Capital city strippers are ruthless and talented, and will have bled them dry.

Plus, in those places the lap dances are much cheaper; I suspect it's because there are more clubs per capita, and therefore more competition. The other question is, are they just on shore leave, and returning to sea, or bringing the bacon home to the States direct from Darwin.

All this information about the navy is strictly classified, but strippers are notoriously shady. Urged on by my fellow dancers, I rang the almighty Port Authority and pretended to be a local journo wanting to do a story on the brave troops. The girls often depend on me to glean such information, since I once worked as a receptionist. After some cooing and coaxing, I uncovered that the navy ship will be coming from the Middle East after having been at sea for three months straight, and the men will merely be on shore leave.

Fucking bingo! These troops won't have seen a woman without a burqa in almost a hundred days, will have ample tax-free dollars to spend and won't have to take it home to their families.

HIGHLIGHT: Might be time to start thinking about buying some real estate.
DOWNSIDE: Sometimes I miss being a receptionist . . .

1 March

The legion has gathered: the legion of strippers, that is. Our humble club of seven has ballooned to thirty-five.

Fortunately, another of my best friends is here! Unfortunately, I wouldn't claim some of the other new arrivals as friends with a gun to my head. It's impossible to forget these serial pains in the arse—especially some of the Penthouse Pets, the ones who choose to be egotistical, insufferable divas.

Most centrefold girls are also exotic dancers. All they've done differently to the rest of us is immortalise their vaginas in a glossy magazine, yet many of them carry on like they've released a number-one single. Us regular girls do our best to zone out their boasting, but sometimes it's hard to refrain from hissing 'Get out!' in an *Amityville Horror*-type voice once they arrive.

I was so relieved when, in the change room tonight, my lovely friend Aurora thrilled me by announcing she's just moved to Darwin with her boyfriend. At last! Then she shocked me as she stripped bare, smiled my way and asked, 'Do you like my new tattoo?'

It looks like she's wearing a onesie inspired by Ed Hardy— barely any of her skin will see the light of day again without extensive laser surgery. But I smiled and winked because I truly love Aurora; she's a ball of fun wrapped in a svelte frame, with the pursed lips and big innocent eyes of Betty Boop. Besides, it's rude to point out to someone that their new adornment could become a hefty-priced regret someday.

'Did you fly in from Queensland?' I asked her.

'No.' She grimaced. 'Melbourne. I'm on probation from the club in Cairns. Not allowed back until April.'

'Really? Why?'

'I stood on a guy's hand.'

'So?'

'With my stiletto. He needed five stitches.'

'Oh,' I said. Aurora can be a little vehement with men. 'Did he deserve it?'

'I always think trying to flick my nipple warrants retaliation. Oh, guess what?' She brightened. 'Tara wants to come up for a few days too—she was going to surprise you. But she has to stay in a hotel because the Stripper House is full.'

Indeed it is: full of debauchery and wickedness. Stripper lodgings are a great place to reside for fun and female company, but the wild times never stop and neither does the hangover. I try to stay away from them—after all, I can do just as well in both departments in my own home. Since I rent a three-bedroom apartment, and Tara is one of my best friends on the planet, I decided to message her and insist she stay with me.

'Awesome!' said Aurora. 'All the girls back together again. Let's make it a party!'

'As opposed to what?' I asked dryly.

HIGHLIGHT: All the girls together again.
DOWNSIDE: All the girls together again.

4 March

With the navy ship arriving tomorrow, we're in the calm before the storm. There's a frenzy of impromptu anorexia going on. And for those who can't bear to starve, there's always bulimia. My friends and I aren't quite that stupid: we're on a soup diet.

Under normal circumstances, I try to eat somewhat healthily before work—either that or McDonald's. But it's always wise not to eat too much of anything, since the last thing you want to sport while half naked is a food-baby.

And it's showtime again.

By eight, I'm fitting false eyelashes. This is the time when I indulge in gossip with the other dancers. Mostly we discuss earth-shattering subjects like which manager is the biggest bastard, and the merits of thin versus curvaceous bodies; because I have a big arse, and we're never happy with our natural attributes, I always argue the benefits of skinny.

As we get ready for work, ordinary pretty girls become show-stopping vixens with big teased curls or sleek straightened tresses. I favour a full head of hair extensions to imitate Elle Macpherson's honey-coloured lion's mane. Most dancers mimic the look of some sexpot or another, and I find the most popular are J-Lo, Gaga, Taylor and the timeless pin-up sauciness of Bettie Page. Our make-up is precise, our bodies shimmer with gold powder and glitter, and we don platform shoes that make us tower over any man who doesn't reach six foot.

It looks like magic, but it's all sleight of hand. We conceal perceived flaws with expertise and an almost pathological dedication. Rounded tummies are hoisted into corsets; cellulite is veiled by slinky evening dresses. In the first few weeks of my stripping career, Dermablend foundation was my best friend, since learning pole tricks will bruise your legs with more black splotches than on a dalmatian. Our best features—big eyes, plump lips, long legs—are enhanced in any way possible. It's all about concealment and artifice, and the bewitchery of make-up and push-up bras. There's nothing natural about physical beauty—not for a few billion people around the planet, anyway.

I vow each day that I'll look after the inside as well as I do the outside, and begin a fitness regime. But my promises often fall short, as it's just not easy to find motivation when you sleep half the day away. When it comes time to pound the pavement, I end up convincing myself that dancing all night and holding up my body weight while performing pole tricks is quite enough exercise. On a dreaded 'fat day', I starve myself so my body can look streamlined in a sequined bikini.

By nine on the dot we all file out to the main bar, where the DJ puts on the music. Usually it's a slow hip-hop beat and rarely one of our favourites—the DJs in strip clubs like us dancers marginally less than the bouncers do.

Then the lights are dimmed so low that a murder could take place in the corner and nobody without a pair of night-vision goggles would notice.

The bar staff, bouncers and even the manager look bored most of the night. A drunken customer once told our boss, Dario, that he has the best job in the world: looking at beautiful naked women night after night. He replied it was on a par with viewing the same porno over and over, and as sexually appealing as masturbating with sandpaper. Strip club managers are rarely favoured by dancers, and I avoid speaking to them if I can.

Likewise the bouncers. If asked a direct question, they try to think up a withering reply. This is fun to watch because bouncers are not always blessed with outstanding wit, while most strippers either have been, or develop it soon enough. I make exceptions for the Pacific Islander bouncers, though, as they're the most gentlemanly of co-workers. Plenty of security guards in Australian strip clubs are Maori, probably because they can look menacing but are truly sweet.

I sometimes wish Jim could be as amicable as those guys, but the gunpowder nature of our relationship doesn't feel wrong. Any perfect coupling would probably bore me more than a paint-drying documentary. Four years on, we can still enrage each other in a heartbeat or engage each other with one come-hither stare. I take our feuds in my stride, and they fizzle as fast as they erupt.

For example, this morning we had a ridiculous altercation over vegetarians—which neither of us are. I said that not eating meat but wearing leather was half-arsed; Jim shot back they were at least making an effort. It then escalated—vegetarians forgotten—into an insult trade-off. I called him a tucker fucker, the worst barb bestowed in the culinary profession at chefs whose food lacks flavour. He retaliated with the term 'slut', but after four years of stripping this insult is water off a duck's back. If I had a dollar for every time I've been called a whore, hooker, tart or mole, I'd have an even more ridiculous amount of money than I already do.

Being at work helps take my mind off our arguments. Just as well: many a dancer has been sacked for discussing her relationship with patrons. Under no circumstances are strippers, in any club on the planet, permitted to talk about their partners or spouses. Exotic dancers must appear unattached and available at all times.

When the men filed in this evening, I decided upon a Café Patron shot to relax me. It's not always easy to strike up a conversation with a stranger while you're barely wearing a stitch, so you have to ease into these things. However, getting drunk can hinder your ability to make money; you can easily spend too much time blithering shit instead of hustling for lap dances. I promised myself I would only have one shot, and maybe a few glasses of champagne. But when a man with yellow teeth and a leer sidled up to ask, 'How much to see your tits?' I knew there would be more shots to follow.

All girls are required to participate in the stage roster during the night: a rotation like any other, except with nudity for around ten or fifteen minutes. That night, a song by Fergie was my cue to take the stage.

Stage appearances are a good way to showcase yourself to the room. You can display a few pole tricks, and, if you're lazy like I am, include a slow crawl in the manner of a nymphomaniac jungle cat, while staring at the crowd with come-hither eyes. Plenty of strippers mimic sexual positions rather than dancing;

this is known as 'floor work'. For their onstage appearances, most strippers request down and dirty R & B numbers in which the singer croons about hitting that bitch's booty. However, a few rock chicks and goths ask for heavier stuff: AC/DC's 'You Shook Me All Night Long' is the hot favourite. If the DJ particularly dislikes you, he'll play something inappropriate and unworkable like 'The Devil Went Down To Georgia'.

Though I loathe being up on stage, there are a couple of benefits to doing a set. The first is the way you can make your presence felt in order to secure a lap dance afterward. The second is making money from a stage dance. Unlike during a lap dance, there's no contact. Men sit in a semicircle around the stage and tip the girls to take it off: twenty bucks for the top, and another twenty for the undies. I like to confuse them by saying, 'Let's just call it an even fifty.'

Unfortunately, patrons don't have to pay to sit around the stage, and us dancers still have to do our set if nobody at *all* takes a seat. There are some men who'll try for a free show by huddling as close as possible to a paying customer. And then there's the cheap groups of guys, who only need to tip forty between them. Though if they're not wily in strip-club ways they don't always know this, and I sure as shit don't share the information.

The best thing about stage dances is that you get to keep all the tips, without paying any commission to the club. Stage dances add up: you can sometimes make a few hundred from them by the end of the night. Australia has it quite good in this sense, at least compared to the US; as I learned when I worked there, they follow a stupid tradition of tipping one dollar bill at a time.

As I climbed on stage, a small horde of men took their seats and began waving twenty-dollar notes. So I removed my bra, hung upside down on the pole, and tried to ignore the litre of chicken-and-vegetable soup sloshing around inside me.

HIGHLIGHT: Barely any competition on the floor due to dancers fainting from malnutrition.
DOWNSIDE: Need carbs.

5 March

All the girls have left the stripper house to crash at mine, except for Aurora, who's happy in her own new apartment.

Before Jim headed off to work, he left me a surly letter professing that my friends are idiots. I can't defend them against this accusation.

Candy, while drunk, ate my night cream from the fridge on a sandwich—thinking it was gourmet mayonnaise—then threw up in the laundry hamper—thinking it was the bin. Belle fell asleep in the shower, which blocked the plughole, flooded the floor and soaked the laundry hamper. And Jade, for some bizarre reason, took a pot plant to bed with her; the potting mix caked in her hair and across my thousand thread-count sheets. She mumbled something about needing to 'connect with nature' as I woke her and the others gently with coffee, since we had a big day ahead. It wasn't easy to get them moving, as we'd painted the town various shades of crimson after work the night before.

I heard an exhilarated shriek from my balcony and turned to see Candy, topless, beckoning us all outside to salivate over the expanse of tanned American troops strolling down the beach. *'They're here!'*

Let me try to tell you about the kind of excitement a US Navy ship brings to a small city. The troops are everywhere you look: perfect specimens with flawless bodies and faces that rival those of Calvin Klein models. They have money to wipe their arses with. They are unfailingly polite and charming. They say things like, 'May I have the honour of a hundred-dollar lap dance, ma'am?' rather than the Australian mantra of 'Show me ya gash for a twenty?'

But first, my friends and I had to swing by the airport to pick up our fifth wheel, Tara, who'd taken a later flight from Cairns. I couldn't stop hugging my petite blonde best friend with her calming presence and hippy soul.

Then we had some serious lingerie shopping to do. We'd been waiting for Tara to arrive to join in the fun. The sales lady loved us—or, rather, the three thousand dollars we spent between us. She even overlooked the fact that Jade walked out of the change room stark naked (forgetfulness from lunchtime daiquiris) while contemplating what to try on next.

Costumes play a huge part in our profession. Some girls favour gauzy peignoir-style drapery, but most go for lingerie, bikinis, or teeny-weeny dresses made from either frothy lace or taut lycra. Black is a popular choice, but there's also plenty of white and fluoro colours so the outfits glow when they hit the backlights. All exotic dancers believe the right costume is necessary to profit. Every one of us has faith in a money-making favourite that we see as a talisman. Mine is a white two-piece ensemble, with a tube top decorated in cowgirl fringing and hotpants so tight you can see me digesting dinner.

We had our hair, make-up and nails done too, then we grabbed a quick dinner at a Greek restaurant in town, which came to no charge because the owner invited himself to join us and ogle our tits—we didn't mind. We then made our way towards work, full of excitement. And we weren't disappointed—they were lined up around the block!

One blond cutie with a southern twang that could only come from Alabama handed me a fifty-dollar note on my way through the door. 'Jus fur bein' born, ma'am.'

The staff attempted to fit four hundred troops in a club with a legal capacity of a hundred and fifty. Dario must have hoped the cops didn't show up, though from what I'm told, the police here will turn a blind eye for the price of a lifelong club membership.

I couldn't weave my way through the crowd to the bar, so I gave up and joined a table of marines. 'Welcome,' I said, smiling brightly in my almost non-existent bra and undies.

'How much for a lap dance?' a Californian demigod asked, throwing his arm around me and planting a friendly kiss on my cheek, which is allowed in all Australian clubs.

In a strip club outside of the lap-dance room, customers can hug you, hold your hand, brush a finger down your arm or give you a cheeky smack on the bottom—if you're okay with it. Inside the lap-dance rooms of Darwin, customers usually can't touch you at all. This, however, differs from state to state, and even from shire to shire. Sometimes it's up to the manager's discretion. In Queensland a customer can touch a dancer's breasts and legs in the lap-dance room, but not their arse. Sydney clubs are supposedly non-touching during a lap dance, but I've seen a few dancers there fail to observe this rule under the implicit promise of more money. Customers aren't allowed to lick dancers, and I don't know of any gentlemen's bars in Australia where a customer can grope genitalia, including their own. And though most touching rules constantly change for varying reasons between states, this rule I doubt ever will.

'Can I have a dance right now?' the demigod urged.

'Whoa, cowboy,' I said (for some bizarre reason, I take on the flirty drawl of a Texan whorehouse madam when the navy is in town). 'A lady needs a drink first.'

All seven of them stood for the honour. I grinned, pointed at the best looking one and announced that if he could achieve this herculean task within five minutes, I'd grace his lap first. He was back with a vodka and apple juice in under three minutes. I'm guessing he bribed the bar with a tip—a big one—because the staff were having serious trouble keeping up with drink orders. They were so busy they had to call in sisters, cousins, nephews, nieces and neighbours to help out.

I noticed Jade, over in a corner, performing a naked handstand to entertain the troops. This could only mean the private rooms were full up. Despite their name, these rooms are rarely private in Australia—unlike in the US, where there *are* personal booths for your viewing pleasure, but usually a different kind of transaction goes on.

Since I had seven marines raring to go, I put my name down on the lap-dance room waiting list in a snappy fashion. There just wasn't enough space for all the guys to get a dance. Dario was slinging white sheets in various corners of the club to create makeshift rooms. He even contemplated setting up the female toilet cubicles as lap-dance booths, until we shrieked at him: 'What gross disregard of hygiene do you think we'll put up with, you *animal*?!'

'The same neglect you all show when snorting drugs off a toilet lid,' he snarled back.

I got so many requests for naked dances that I couldn't keep up. I stole a pen and some paper from the bar, and began handing out ticket numbers, much like I was dealing with a queue at the supermarket deli.

My drink provider, a baby-faced marine from San Diego, had ticket number one. So when a space in the lap-dance room was finally free, I took him inside to start negotiations. Because the night was beyond busy, we strippers were able to bump up the prices. I told him it was $150 for a ten-minute dance, or $300 for twenty. He pulled out three hundred and asked if he could also tip me with some American dollars he had left over. Does Joan of Arc see visions?

I began the dance by taking off my bra and giving him a motorboat: a stripper term for jiggling your breasts lightly across a man's face in rapid succession. This is one of the only ways a stripper is allowed to touch a customer in the private rooms of the NT.

I then kneeled on the floor and arched my back over his knees, my hair trailing down to his ankles. Eventually, I slithered into the chair opposite, took off my undergarments and opened my legs in a flexed vee. See, a lap dance isn't a dance per se: it involves moving from one sexy pose to another, while leaning as close as you can to a customer without touching them in a sexual manner. A swish of hair across the face, a brush of a hand against theirs, but no stimulation of genitalia. I pretty much do the same succession of poses every time, each one a hint that another clothing item is about to come off. The talent is in the build-up. You want to leave the nudity to the last song, otherwise it gets really difficult and boring as you try to entertain them with something more than the main event: a view of vagina.

'Can you touch me?' the marine rasped.

'Nope.' I smiled apologetically.

'Can I touch you?'

'Nope—sorry, it's illegal.'

'Can you touch yourself?'

'Quiet, please, or I'll have to gag you with my hotpants.'

When it was time for me to sit on his lap, I was taken aback. We cannot, due to the law, actually sit on a person's lap; our bottom must be six inches from a man's crotch, which means we balance somewhere around their kneecaps to avoid their genitalia. Strippers, under no circumstances during a lap dance, can touch a man's dick in Darwin. But this marine from San Diego must have had a firehose tucked down there. This *thing* in his pants was coiled in every direction, like a giant Amazonian python. A manaconda!

I couldn't sit without making some kind of contact. In the end, I opted to stand and finish the dance, fearing the possibility of Dario popping his head through the door and seeing my naked bottom too close to the marine's inflated jeans. This would have resulted in a fine and possibly a ban from working the next few nights.

'God almighty!' I exclaimed once we'd finished, eyeing the marine's pants in wonder. 'I bet you never have a problem getting laid.'

'Actually, it's the opposite.' He sighed. 'Most girls take one look and run—I'm not real lucky.'

I found it hard to sympathise.

'Can I take a picture, or a quick video of you to prove you're real to the folks back home?' he earnestly inquired.

'Sorry again, but you can't even get your phone out in a club, anywhere in Australia. And showing the folks back home any film of me is a criminal offence with a two-year gaol sentence. But it's not the cops I'd worry about—the last guy who tried it was dealt with by the bouncers, and word on the street is he could only find his phone with a hospital X-ray. So you might want to keep that Galaxy tucked away.' I winked to lessen the sting.

While I was fitting in as many dances as I could before we closed at 5 a.m., I had no time to ponce about sipping drinks, so I simply didn't bother. The high I had from the thought of counting my money later was better than any shooter.

I'd barely seen my friends all night. I looked across the room and noted that Tara had stolen a naval officer's hat and was selling it back to him for a criminal amount. Charlotte, a Penthouse Pet, was telling any man who would listen how her dances are more expensive due to her 'celebrity status'. Candy was on stage selling her bra to the highest bidder, and the reserve was coming in at six hundred dollars.

I was giggling to myself when I came across Aurora guzzling water at the bar. 'This is like a lap-dance flash mob!' she said, panting. 'The marines want us to party on the ship with them after work, but I'm exhausted.'

I nodded as I was led away by an Adonis from Arkansas.

See? Sometimes we can act responsibly. And be sober. Sometimes.

HIGHLIGHT: Tipped the DJ a hundred bucks to play 'In The Navy' each time I got on stage, ensuring all cash and focus was aimed at me.

DOWNSIDE: I have blisters on my toes the size of US destroyers—pun intended.

6 March

'Did you sleep with any of them?' Jim fired at me before work tonight.

I regarded him coldly without saying a word. If he has to ask, he doesn't deserve a reply.

I'm a stripper, *not* a sex worker. In saying that, I don't feel an ounce of judgement for them—well, except the ones who sneak into strip clubs to steal away our clientele.

I just don't want to do sex work. Strippers generally make more money than sex workers, and meaningless sex with strangers goes against my personal values. I haven't indulged in many one-night stands; I'm not prudish, I just prefer to have a connection with an individual before the big event. It's probably my one value that could be deemed old-fashioned, and it was fostered by my parents.

To me, you choose to be either a stripper or a sex worker, and there's no grey area. If you perform any kind of sexual act with a man for money, you're no longer an exotic dancer because you have crossed that line.

Fuck Jim for asking me if I'd crossed the line. If I'm really being honest with myself, though, am I furious at his question because he struck a nerve?

Usually, the men who grace strip clubs are the kind I wouldn't speak to on the street. If they dared ask me the time of day, I would take off my watch and bludgeon them with it. But last night I was sorely tested. Who wouldn't be, if a young man with the face of an angel and Michelangelo biceps asked you to his hotel suite for a couple of thousand bucks?

Regardless, I loathe it when Jim acts all pissy, and it's getting more frequent. He's generally a laid-back soul; with the amount of dope he smokes, he couldn't really be otherwise. I've never minded that about him, as it can make him quite insightful when he offers mind-expanding, if not peculiar, perspectives.

I fell in love with Jim's charisma and his slow, unhurried persona. His aura and looks remind me of a long-dead rock star of the same name. But I'm not really sure what's happening to us lately. I feel awful about the way we've been speaking to each other.

Perhaps it's a phase caused by my irritation with life in Darwin. I tend to get snappy when I'm not content in my present and confused about my future, and it doesn't help when we both have a tendency to flare up without considering the repercussions. Not that there ever really are any—we have a bad habit of sweeping things under the mattress on which we're busy making up.

Doesn't every relationship have its shortcomings? We just find a way to accept them, because nobody wants to be alone. After a particularly gruelling shift, I find it more than welcome to have a man waiting at home for me who actually cares. Particularly on evenings when I've been groped, called names, been made to feel insignificant and worthless. It's a saving grace to have someone love you and see you as a person, rather than a vagina with a person attached.

And Jim works for a living. Not bad for the partner of a stripper, because plenty of them refuse to work. They watch us bring home the equivalent of a weekly wage in one night, and after seeing two weekly wages in two nights they decide that's ample cash for them to quit the workforce. All of a sudden, there you have it: another pathetic loser living off a dancer's money. I see it happen all the time. Shame on the girls who allow it.

It's risky to leave the kind of money we make lying around the house or in plain sight. It's just too tempting for partners, even those who work. And it's practically a handout if you're ever robbed.

A good way to conceal a wad of cash is to wrap it in plastic and put it in the bottom of a laundry detergent box. No thief would think of looking there. Most boyfriends think the laundry is where the cleaning fairies reside.

Another great place to hide money is in the bin, but only if you live alone and don't drink much. Never put money in the fridge or freezer: they're renowned hiding spots. One stripper I know used to buy KFC on the way home just so she could hide her cash under the greaseproof paper. When she *was* burgled, who'd have thought the thief would stop for a piece of hot and spicy while robbing the joint?

Quite often, we exotic dancers have a lot of money on the premises. How much, some may wonder? An established stripper on her A-game wants at least three hundred each Sunday, Monday and Tuesday; four on Wednesday, possibly five on Thursday, and between seven hundred and a thousand on Friday and Saturday. But this can only be expected from a good and established club— and remember, there are nights when we don't make a penny, even sometimes on weekends.

Also, take into account that all clubs charge us strippers a fee for working. We're never paid by the club itself—unless you're a performer willing to do a fifteen-minute show with choreography and Vegas-style costumes. Some clubs will charge a flat-out fee of eighty to a hundred dollars; others will take thirty to forty per cent of everything. So it's always best not to begin counting until your door fee is all paid up, in the annoying event that you have a night, or a few, when you've made zero; that means you're indebted to the club. A few places will let you pay off outstanding fees, and a few managers will even forget the debt if you let them touch your boob. Either way, you don't want your fees to accumulate during a bad patch in your finances, as no club ever lets it slide. Sort of like the strip club is the shopping centre, and we're the little shops paying rent.

Strippers are wise to hide their money from their partners but it's not a good idea to conceal it from the taxation office. Anyone who pays their own tax is a subcontractor; however, the police, liquor licensing officials or immigration officials can visit a club at any time, day or night, and demand to see a list of every girl on file. Mostly their visits are to ensure the club isn't hiring any illegals or backpackers working without a visa, but they'll also sometimes take down the names of every dancer and relay them to the tax office. So if you happen to be working without paying tax and the club gets hit, you're basically screwed.

HIGHLIGHT: Counted $2100 to hide in the bottom of a wholemeal flour packet.

DOWNSIDE: Wish I could allow myself five pieces of Colonel Sanders original recipe.

7 March

Last night I only danced for three marines, who each booked me for three hours at a time. Yet the money I made was equivalent to what it would have been had I done lap dances for twenty sailors. Plus, I've almost sold out of costumes, which are no doubt being displayed around the ship in a trophy-like manner at this very moment.

I don't like to think too much about the fate of my undies. I'd rather remain ignorant of their destiny and capitalise on their worth, 180 bucks a pop. This could be viewed as greedy and unfair, but I look upon it as entrepreneurial. No one can strip forever, I have my future to think about, and I *do* save plenty of what I make.

My ocean-front apartment is expensive, true, but who doesn't like to live in nice surroundings? Not to mention the feng shui factor.

My expensive lingerie is also a must, for all strippers need to look and feel their best in order to extract money. Beauty is a mindset.

Lots of dancers don't save a penny. They spend big on spray tans, nail and hair salons, personal fitness instructors, specially prepared, low-carb, high-protein, organic, free-range, macrobiotic, paleo home-delivered meals (with benefits cancelled out by their alcohol intake), custom-made stripper poles, self-commissioned portraits—you get the idea. I even met a girl who had a pair of diamond-encrusted stilettos designed for her . . . because she could.

There's lots of appeal in having cash to burn, beautify yourself or bundle away.

I used to worry about money much more when I was doing a normal job. There never seems to be enough to go around in the lower levels of the white-collar world, does there? You have to work ten hours a day as an underling in order to be the boss and work sixteen hours instead. I now call a normal job 'Just Over Broke'.

The pressures of a rigid office position also flustered me as I bustled around, tightly wound. I longed for languor, so I became a more shellac-coated, blasé but still slightly neurotic new version of myself. And while even Mother Teresa would grow used to the privileges of this lifestyle, it took a little while for it to fit me. It's not easy to shuck off the working-class guilt of a blue-collar background. I *still* neaten my apartment before the cleaner gets in, and I never fail to make her a coffee so she doesn't think I'm snooty.

But I'm not prepared to apologise for taking my clothes off or being lazy. I want a lot of money, and I don't want to do much for it. I'm know I'm far from the only one who feels this way, but most people wouldn't admit that particular truth.

After years of getting out of bed early in the arctic Melbourne morning to spend eight hours as a worker bee, I wondered why life didn't sit right. My boredom was almost religious, and I pondered, in agonised confusion, that there must be *something else* for me. At twenty-three, I left a firm that dealt with the riveting task of showcasing insurance, and became a marketing manager at a sports bar with a strip club attached.

I was witness to a brave new world. I watched the exotic dancers while enviously romanticising their lives. They slept all day and sashayed into work, unhurried, with a Starbucks Frappuccino, wearing expensive casual clothes much like the attire of celebrities when snapped at the airport.

I gaped as dancers pranced around in glittering costumes and costly lingerie, drinking champagne while chatting with rich customers, their laughter tinkling over the sexy music. I imagined how my laugh would tinkle too, if I were counting that kind of money at the end of the night. Plus I love a good sleep-in.

The self-indulgent nature of the work appealed to me like a spare million bucks. So the following night, I took a deep breath and went from manager to nude dancer. But, like every other ill-informed outsider, I assumed it was merely a case of taking off my clothes.

Ha. Ha. Ha. I had no idea of the debilitating self-doubt that stripping would bring, and the scarring lessons that required the formation of a new, impenetrable skin.

The first time you stand barely dressed on a stage in front of strangers is an occasion of acute mortification and crippling exposure. You're more naked than you've ever been, because the things you find loathsome about your body—the things you normally have the luxury of scrutinising in the bathroom alone—are now on show. *For the entire world to see!* Do my thighs wobble? Are my boobs too small? Can they see that pimple, that scar? Am I pretty enough, or are they wondering what the fuck a girl like me is doing up here?

You *must* overcome any embarrassment about showing your vagina to the public. The respectability you once wore is a thing of the past, and it's time to get used to men treating you however they deem appropriate. People assume if you strip for a living, you probably fuck for one as well. It's imperative you become resistant to sly looks when people find out about your job, deaf to the jealousy of other dancers when you make more than they do, blind to your friends' judgement, and understanding of your family's discontent . . . if you tell them the truth. Plenty of exotic dancers don't.

We all harden up under the repetition of cutting lessons. And the day comes when you shed the husks of your old values to make way for shinier, more flamboyant ones as you accept yourself as a sex object. You become self-possessed and immune to nudity. I no longer register things that would have once shocked me. I've seen more pussy than a vet nurse. I could have a conversation with a co-worker while she's dry shaving, legs askew, without noticing her bits staring me in the face. Whereas beforehand, I would have felt awkward around a room full of vaginas night after night.

Humans can grow used to any circumstances, and it helps that we strippers all share this outré reality. It also helps if you were born a bit different from most. I've always thought of myself as non-conformist, and my desk-job cohorts kindly referred to me as *neurotic* rather than *fucking weird*.

Of course, earning the big bucks serves as a kind of moral anaesthetic. That said, my morals are marginally greater than my costume supply right now. But since the club is opening two hours early to accommodate the marines, I have exactly twenty-three minutes to go shopping before work.

HIGHLIGHT: Favourite lingerie shop serves champagne.
DOWNSIDE: Already miss my peacock feather bikini . . .

8 March

Only one day to go before they hop back on their ship and sail away. I'm happy about that, in a way—I'm absolutely exhausted and feel like hell. The last few nights have passed in a haze of drinks. I've been dancing through twelve-hour shifts, then sleeping the sunlit hours away only to do it all again.

When I finally have a day off, I'm promising myself vegetables in abundance and hours of pure unintoxicated sleep. I won't just fall into a drunken stupor.

Why keep drinking? Because it's impossible to be the life of the party while sober, and the men aren't looking for responsible introverts. This job is too much of a mental challenge if you're not on the same drunken level as everybody else. Their jokes are no longer funny; their conversation seems stupid and lewd. And it's intimidating: try dancing naked and sober in front of a crowded room.

Once I arrived at work, Dario loomed over me looking smug and wearing a cruel smile. 'You can't have your day off,' he said. 'The Australian locals are complaining that the dancers have ignored them all week. We're opening Monday to keep them happy.'

I gaped. 'You've got to be kidding. *Nobody* goes out on a Monday! We'll be lucky to make five bucks. Come *on*, Dario, we're exhausted, we need a break!'

'Tough luck.' He grinned nastily, loving every moment. 'You've made more than enough in the last few nights. You're working Monday, and you'll be happy about it, whether you make a cent or not. I couldn't care either way—I know *I* wouldn't give you five dollars.'

'No doubt—I expect you couldn't afford a fiver on *your* salary.'

His face lost its sneer and became bitter; clearly, I'd struck a nerve. 'If you didn't have so many regular customers asking for you, Sunshine, I would have gotten rid of your arse a long time ago. You're a smart-mouthed bitch. Not even worth one dollar, let alone five.'

'And the rate of your sarcasm shows the price of your education. Do all strip club managers come from a long line of state schools and minimum-wage workers?'

His face went red as a tortured crustacean. 'You think you're so much better? Working as a *stripper*? Your parents must be *real* proud.'

'No. But my bank manager is.'

He finally lost it. 'Get back to fucking work. And be here on Monday, or you're fired.'

Dario didn't realise it, but he'd just made an important decision for me.

I got back to work with a smile.

HIGHLIGHT: Accidentally on purpose handed Dario my cash-machine deposit slip with my dancer's fee.

DOWNSIDE: Wound up drinking so much my urine sample would have needed a swizzle stick.

9 March

'I'm in love with a DJ,' Tara confided in the Uber on the way to work.

'But you've been with Justin for years!' I sputtered. I'd thought they were one of the very few happy couples I knew in the night-club world. And I really like Justin—he's a super-cool guy who seems a perfect fit for my way-out, hippy friend. The two look like they should be judges on *The X Factor*, with their long hair, leather pants, and T-shirts with left-wing slogans.

She shrugged. 'Can't be helped.'

'Wait till you hear about the DJ she's fallen for,' Candy chimed in.

When I heard the name, I was even more shocked. 'I thought he was gay!' I blurted, still shaking my head.

'Me too—he looks it,' Jade joined in.

'Well, he isn't,' Tara snapped. 'I can vouch for that.'

'You've already *slept* with him?' I asked. 'Does Justin know?'

'Oh *sure*.' She rolled her eyes sarcastically. 'I sent Justin a Snapchat straight after I took my undies off. *Of course* my boyfriend doesn't know—idiot.'

'Does the gay DJ have a big penis?' Belle inquired.

'Shut up. I don't want to talk about it anymore. I'm sorry I spoke.'

'That means "*no*".' Belle snickered.

We arrived at work ready for the evening ahead.

'Let's make tonight count,' Aurora announced in the dressing-room. 'It's their last night, and then it's back to dancing for the locals.'

This sounded about as appealing to me as a shooter of bile.

The atmosphere in the club was still crazy: the dances were nonstop, the drinks flowed faster than a burst water main, and the money was more excessive than Mariah Carey's ego. I had a devil-may-care attitude—after all, I'd soon be on another adventure, with more than enough cash to fund it.

'The marines have a penthouse suite for their last night, and we're gonna go party with them,' Aurora told me.

Another old friend of mine, Chloe from Melbourne, had turned up to work for the night, so I invited her along. Like Jade, she's an absolutely stunning girl you'd imagine would seek a career in modelling. If I could change my sexual orientation, she would be my first preference.

Getting to the party was a clandestine affair. Strippers aren't allowed to go to hotel rooms with customers straight after work, even if it's just for a slice of pizza and a spot of chit-chat. Under the law this is looked upon as prostitution, and soliciting from a strip club is highly illegal.

All the Ubers were busy, and we couldn't catch a taxi as cab drivers are notorious gossips. Walking would have meant changing into flat shoes, and I'm not only vain but also short. Aurora decided to collect her car and drive a gaggle of strippers while shitfaced. I was clearly drunk myself, as I piled into the car without a single thought about our limbs being strewn across the road. We were lucky to arrive safely.

The marines had put on a show. They'd rented out the top-floor penthouse with a 360-degree view of the city. So many people were crammed in that I was surprised the other hotel guests hadn't called the police. There was a seafood buffet that nobody was interested in, probably because of the *Scarface*-like mound of cocaine on the coffee table. Lap dances were being performed in each corner, and most of the marines were shirtless. Money was scattered all over the floor, along with more bottles of champagne than there are vineyards in France.

I spied Tara and Candy waving enthusiastically at me.

'Do a line with me?' Tara pleaded.

I hesitated. Some may scoff, but I'm usually careful with drugs. Alcohol hurts quite enough the next day, thank you very much, and I've never been a fan of the dreaded comedown. But I was drunker than I'd been all year, and my resistance was lost in a deluge of vodka and champagne. I was already going to feel like hell tomorrow—why not make it *utter* hell?

Jade appeared next to us, a rolled hundred-dollar bill in her hand. 'I can't remember who this belongs to. But I'm not giving it back.' Leopard spots had been drawn all over her body with a magic marker, and she'd clearly had help with those hard-to-reach places.

Belle, giggling with barbiturate-fuelled abandon, danced wildly on a leather sofa, her heels leaving so many pea-sized punctures that it looked like a shooting-practice poster.

Charlotte, the Penthouse Pet, was enthralling a group of marines with the gripping story of her naked magazine shoot. She'd even stopped by the Stripper House to pick up a few of the magazines in which she appeared as Miss September, and was selling them as signed copies. She kept insisting on how much classier centrefold girls are than us regular strippers—and I'm sure the navy boys would have believed her if she'd been wearing more than a sailor's jacket.

Aurora decided she'd become a human buffet, along with three other strippers. They lay across the kitchen bench, adorned with lobster and prawns, and charged the boys to eat seafood from their naked bodies. Suddenly, all the men had an appetite.

Tara and Jade disappeared into one of the rooms with three gorgeous boys for a different kind of smorgasbord, I imagine.

Without warning, there was a loud rap at the door. I cringed and looked for places to hide, thinking the cops had finally been called, and we strippers would be arrested for drugs, debauchery and solicitation.

Turns out it was only two naval officers from the ship, checking up on the boys. They radiated self-importance as they scanned the room, so I calculated that they must be quite high up in the pecking order. Perhaps they fell a notch or two down the ladder as they partook in a few massive lines of coke.

They singled me and Chloe out, plying us with compliments as they filled our glasses.

'I'm bisexual,' Chloe announced, causing one to choke on his single malt.

'I don't believe you,' the other officer challenged with a hopeful glint in his eye.

'It's true,' she insisted. 'I would do Sunshine in a second.' She gave me a laser-beam stare, and then I was the one choking on my drink. My friend was coming on to me! If I'd been remotely sober I would have felt uncomfortable, but I was far from it. Actually, I was flattered, and my imagination ran riot. I'd always been fascinated by lesbian porn, even though I'd believed I had no interest in having sex with women.

Exotic dancers are often treated as outsiders by mainstream society, so we don't tend to discriminate against minority groups. Our gay, lesbian, bisexual and transgender friends are just our buddies, full stop. It also doesn't cross my mind to kink-shame people or argue against alternative lifestyles—although I have been disturbed by some of my customers' preferences, such as the one who asked me to pretend to be a Third Reich woman while wiping my arse on his sleeve.

'I'll give you girls four thousand dollars to have sex in front of us,' one officer said.

Two thousand apiece!

Instead of turning him down flat, Chloe gave me a deep tongue kiss. My thighs went up in flames, and when she led me by the hand, I found myself following! Was I really about to do this? I *wanted* to.

We found a vacant room, and the two officers locked the door, pulled out a roll of cash and opened a bottle of Jack Daniel's. Unsteady on my stilettos and naturally clumsy, I knocked into the bottle and spilled half the whisky onto the floor.

'Just so you know,' Chloe said to the men, 'you two can only watch—no joining in.'

They nodded. Judging by their expressions, Chloe could have told them she was about to remove their kidneys and sell them on the black market, and they would still have given her an enthusiastic nod.

She peeled off my skin-tight Gucci jeans, which tore in the process. I didn't mind—earlier in the night I'd sat in a spilled bottle of black Sambuca.

And then I was naked and breathless on the bed. Obviously I'm no sheltered innocent, but I didn't know what to do—I'd only seen this happen in movies. Chloe really *is* bisexual, though, and had no problem taking the lead. She went to work on my vagina like a thirsty hiker. It was sweet and kind of . . . tame. I followed her example, and it wasn't what I'd expected; it doesn't taste bad down there, just different, kind of oily.

To impress the guys, we made a big show of it. Lots of moaning and groaning, licking and sucking. I was happy for the opportunity to see what all the fuss is about, but I'm definitely heterosexual. Although fingers and mouths are nice, I am a penis girl, and I like the primal hardness of a man's touch and body.

When it was all over, the officers stood up with erections the size of an aircraft carrier and thanked us politely. They imparted that it was time for them to go indulge in some sex for hire before returning to duty. We all wished each other well.

The minute they left, Chloe and I squealed, counting the money then throwing it around like confetti while jumping up and down. Then we finished off a bottle of champagne and lounged around on the bed chatting casually. I found this rather important, as we've been friends for years and I didn't want any awkwardness springing up between us.

But now I'm wondering if I've crossed a line. In all honesty, I probably would have had sex with Chloe anyway if she'd just asked me in my drunken state. And technically speaking, having sex in front of an audience isn't the same as having sex with the spectators, is it? On the other hand, in a roundabout way, I *did* have sex for money, didn't I? Or did I simply put on a show? And does it count as sex for me if the person doesn't have a penis? No—girls don't count because I'm not attracted to them.

That's the story I'm telling myself and sticking to. I put on a performance for cash with a bit more detail than usual. There, moral compass sorted.

HIGHLIGHT: Also pocketed some of the forgotten fifties festooning the floor.
DOWNSIDE: I will awaken with a hangover to rival a natural disaster.

10 March

'Where were you till eleven o'clock this morning?' Jim demanded.

'At Tara's hotel room,' I lied.

'She's staying with us,' he pointed out.

'Well, she *was* going to, but not only did you change her name to "Terror", you've been saying it directly to her face! She booked a room to avoid being in your vicinity.'

'Then explain why she's on the couch?'

'Fuck off,' I answered with all the venom of the guilty.

He looked at me, considering. 'Sunshine, I love you, but if you were drowning I'd throw you a brick.' As he left, he slammed the front door, and the sound skewered right into my hangover.

I'm dying. I wish I was dead already. I've been throwing up in twenty-minute intervals for the past three hours. Forget the natural disaster comparison—my hangover is of Armageddon proportions.

I could barely stand up to hug my friends goodbye when they called a cab to the airport. Candy, Belle and Jade have decided to go back to Cairns with Tara.

I will be lost without my besties. The sugar is gone from my fairy floss.

Before they left, the girls presented me with a silver ring boasting a giant Swarovski crystal. A completely unexpected, immensely cherished gift that is now a bit soiled—after I insisted on wearing it immediately but then had to stick my finger down my throat.

Fragile and shaky from alcohol poisoning, I thought I might cry as it dawned on me how much I'm going to miss my best friends. My amazing Tara, the unruffled hippy with a curtain of blonde hair, who should have been born in the Woodstock era; if you google 'laid back', you'll be presented with an image of her. My beautiful, feisty Jade: genuine, loyal, and able to start a party just by being in a room. My unique Belle, slightly scatter-brained, overtly hilarious, unashamedly loving. And Candy, the striking Pacific Island princess, sweet and nurturing as family, yet regal and staunch enough to work as a dominatrix when she's not stripping. Four of my closest friends, about to be a few thousand miles away.

But as they left, I stared at my new ring and smiled. Because if such rare individuals love me for who I am, I can't be all that bad.

I'm not always the nicest person. I'm brattish, unapologetic, a little indifferent and unafraid of confrontation, and I deliver sarcasm that wounds. Yet I agonise over whether or not I'm good. I have a theory about people: either you're born with a bad seed at the core and go through life striving to be nice, or you possess a good seed but have appalling traits. I hope I am the latter—scathing, but with a benevolent heart.

Right at this second, I both love and detest my best friends because they don't have to work tonight. How will I manage it? I can't even moisturise without throwing up. Nor can I stomach the thought of a coffee—and I am usually caffeine's bitch.

I'm only going to work because a stripper should never burn bridges. We don't have to give two weeks' notice or explain why we're leaving, but it's important for us to depart on good terms in the likely event we'll want to return. And we don't want word to spread that we're difficult and unreliable. Next time round, *two* thousand marines might arrive.

If I don't drag my sorry arse in, Dario will take it personally, badmouth me all over the country and never let me back.

5 a.m.

That sadistic, evil *motherfucker*!!! I cannot *believe* what he did.

At first the night was almost tolerable. My hangover was beginning to subside, so Aurora and I, being the last close friends standing, tried to stomach Mexican food before work. The restaurant owner brought over every dish on the menu—which was thoughtful but totally fucking stupid, since I was obviously hungover to the eyeballs, and Aurora is slightly bulimic. He announced that since dinner was on him, why didn't we all have a round of margaritas too? One sniff of tequila, though, and I was sprinting to the bathroom, head in the toilet bowl. Why can't a restaurant proprietor just let us strippers pay our own fucking bill for once, in return for leaving us the fuck alone?

In saying that, a final bout of vomiting did me good; my queasiness all but disappeared.

As I'd expected, the club was quiet on a Monday night, with only three customers perched at the bar. All the girls looked as bored and drained as I was. We appeared as I imagine people who've never visited a strip club envision us: worn and dejected.

The three customers were regulars, all there for a free look. None of the girls bothered to approach them, and Dario looked thunderous at our attitude. Honestly, I don't know what he expected when the girls were suffering from the DTs and needed a night off.

I perked up a bit when the bargirl handed me a note from Chloe, which said she'd left Darwin and hoped to see me again soon on our travels. I was slightly relieved—what had happened between us was strictly a one-off. Fun, but finished.

My brain felt like minced innards when the club picked up around midnight. A group of businessmen came through the door. One of them, Ray, was my Regular—a man who comes in predominantly looking for one stripper—until he finally realised I was never going to have sex with him, no matter how much money he handed over for lap dances, or how many gifts he bought me. Before that dawned on him, he was lovely towards me; now he's a prick, with an arrogance that all highly paid bankers seem to adopt.

I know I sound sour sometimes when I speak of the men who come in here, and the managers and other male staff. But this strange world of strip clubs hasn't once warped my opinion of men in general. I still like the boys plenty—just not the ones in here (except for the Maori bouncers, of course). But lots of strippers let this job taint their outlook, and some even become man-haters. Well, I guess when you're faced with a surly pig like Dario or a despicable twat like Ray, it's perfectly understandable.

Ray, along with his five friends, asked me and Aurora to do what's known in strip clubs as a lesbian show, except he called it a 'double growl-out'. The two of us sighed, listening to the Neanderthal bonhomie going on within the pack. 'Are we really going to see them bitches chow down on each other?' one charming banker asked.

The answer was no. Strip club lesbian shows are nothing like my experience last night: they're just an act. It's as against the law for us to touch each other's lady parts as it is for the customers to do so. So we simply pretend to perform oral sex on each other, with our long hair hiding the lie. To distract our audience, a lot of nipple licking goes on, a touch of kissing and a truckload of artificial moans.

Aurora and I were lying naked in the sixty-nine position, pretending to go at it, when I spied Dario watching at the lap-dance room entrance. He looked more put out than earlier, and I realised he was seething about us making money—he'd truly wanted the dancers to suffer, hungover, without earning a cent the whole night. But a lesbian double with two girls and six guys comes in at around four hundred dollars per dancer.

Aurora didn't know Dario was there and got a bit carried away. Her nose accidentally touched my vagina, and her finger accidentally brushed my anus as she pulled my legs open further. I sensed there would be trouble ahead.

'That was disgusting!' Dario screeched at us as soon as the dance was over. 'You touched each other for real.'

I tried to explain. 'It was an accident—'

'Shut up!' he screamed. 'I'm fining the pair of you three hundred dollars—along with your fee. Both of you are paying me four hundred *fucking* dollars!'

Exactly what we'd just earned.

I opened my mouth to object, but again he yelled at me to shut it.

Right then and there, I was prepared to quit while screaming, 'May the bridges I burn light the fucking way!'

I have no idea what freakish mind power Dario possesses, but he seemed to know this. 'Don't even think about not paying that fucking fine, Sunshine. Or I'll sack her!' And he pointed at Aurora.

The bastard had me over a barrel. He knew I was beyond caring about my job, but Aurora had just moved up from Melbourne to start a new life with her boyfriend. She couldn't afford to be made redundant, what with the need to eat and pay rent . . .

I had no choice but to pay the fine. What's worse, I couldn't even call Dario names while doing so.

To cap off the wonderful evening, Ray sidled over, looking smug. 'You would have been the perfect woman,' he said. 'If you had tits.'

HIGHLIGHT: When life gives you lemons, stick them down your top to make your boobs look bigger.

DOWNSIDE: Am a small B-cup.

BRIGHTER DISCO BALLS

'I'm leaving,' Jim announced late this afternoon.

'Me, or the state?'

'The state. This city. I've had enough.'

'Glad to hear it. Can I hitch a ride?'

His face broke into a broad smile. 'You're really coming with me?'

'Did you really think I wouldn't?' I said, pulling my suitcase out of the cupboard to prove it. As I began to pack, I didn't even complain that Jim had been using it to store weed paraphernalia, I just threw out his old bong. I told him about the fine last night, and about how Dario hates me. I added that I was ready to move on from Darwin too.

I did not tell him that I had sex with Chloe.

We talked long into the evening about where we might end up next. Maybe I should be calling my network of friends around the country to try to find out where the money is good. But there's a flaw to this method: strippers are notorious for being liars. If you're a good hustler—as indeed I am—then a fellow dancer, even a friend, might tell you an untruth. Unlike Harlow, they'll say the money is crap in their club, just to prevent you from making your way there. Not to worry, though, as I feel like a little adventure.

Jim was unusually jovial as we packed and discussed our plans. We also had a long-overdue chat about the state of our relationship. 'Maybe we can clean the slate?' he suggested. 'Write a new beginning for the next stage of us?'

I'm willing, although admittedly it disturbs me that he was prepared to leave Darwin alone. Not in an end-of-the-world way, since we've been apart many times when I've travelled for work, but I don't think a separation will do us any favours right now.

A road trip might be the perfect thing, though. Our relationship wouldn't be the first resurrected by a change of scenery, and Jim's always been fun on holidays. He's not only my partner but also quite a good friend. He can be a brilliant conversationalist and an empathetic listener, when he isn't so stoned that he abruptly wanders from the room, forgetting he was in the middle of a conversation in the first place. But hey, we all have our vices.

There was a knock at the door. Aurora stood there, beaming. 'I quit!' she hollered happily. I wasn't shocked: us strippers are extremely flighty because, well, we can afford to be, we're always seeking brighter disco balls, and we rarely live in leased apartments.

Beside Aurora stood her boyfriend, Ryan. He's friends with Jim, and I like him, despite the fact I wish he'd get a job and stop taking all of her money.

Each night after her shift, she goes home to him and hands over everything she made. *Everything.* One time while I was at her house, she showed me her new designer perfume. 'See what Ryan bought for me? And he treated me to a massage at the spa too—he's so generous!' When I corrected her, reminding her that *she* bought that perfume and *she* treated herself to a massage,

Aurora stared, blinked and mentally rejected the facts, then went on as if I hadn't spoken. Never underestimate the power of denial. Or ignorance.

Tonight, when Jim and I told the couple that we'd soon be on our way, they decided on the spot that they wanted to come with us. It turned out that like me, Aurora was only renting a resort apartment on a weekly basis.

'Where shall we go?' she asked.

'Jim and I are still contemplating. Maybe Melbourne?'

'Let's not—I've just come from there. Why don't you do the coin trick?'

When I'm stuck on my next location, I sometimes close my eyes and spin a coin across a map of Australia. Wherever the coin lands . . .

'We'll figure it out tomorrow,' I vowed. 'Because tonight, we're going to be busy.'

'Doing what?' they chorused.

I grinned like an assassin.

HIGHLIGHT: There are one million uses for superglue . . .
DOWNSIDE: My suitcase smells like hash oil.

12 March

I am evil. I am *brilliant*! The day I die, I will go out knowing I took advantage of how awesome I am.

First, I had Jim break into Dario's car. My boyfriend picked up this talent during his short stay in a correctional facility a long time ago; he was a guest there for three months due to his illegal substance cultivation skills.

I then placed a G-string under the passenger seat, where Dario's pathologically jealous girlfriend will definitely stumble upon it because I hooked them through the seat-positioning lever. And, of course, I changed the seat position so she'll think someone other than her (a stripper) was sitting there.

I then superglued a stiletto in the dead centre of the roof. I took care to bleach the sole and wiped it down beforehand, in case of DNA evidence and toeprints. Don't you just love the things *CSI* has taught us?

We spent the rest of the night opening a new Facebook account for Dario. We named his profile 'Dario "Buffalo Bill" Italiano' and listed his interests as 'Equal Rights for Serial Killers', 'Empathy for Incarcerated Klan Members' and 'Support Bestiality'. We then sent friend requests to every stripper Aurora and I could think of, along with a private message: *All strippers are intellectually challenged, have cellulite and need all the friends they can get, which is why I'm sending you this request.* I thoughtfully provided Dario's phone number. I also thoughtfully opened the account from an internet cafe, since you don't want such shenanigans leading back to your IP address.

I was in a Cheshire Cat mood when it came time to play spin the coin on the map. But sometimes fate steps in. My phone rang, and an old acquaintance, Liani, told me, 'I've just opened a club in Newcastle, and I'd love it if you'd come work for a while. Where are you right now?'

I smiled. 'On my way.'

HIGHLIGHT: Stiletto was Charlotte's from a pair I borrowed and forgot to give back.

DOWNSIDE: Liani was good fun as a dancer, hope she isn't a power-tripping boss.

14 March ··

On the road—almost. A sports car, I've learned, is not built to traverse the Outback.

The fastest route to Newcastle turned out to be the dirt path from hell: red dust as far as the eye could see, a barren landscape in which the skeletal trees looked hungry. It was ominous enough to make Wolf Creek seem like Disneyland.

On top of this, the road is a deathtrap. Kangaroos jump out of nowhere, right into the side of your car. And smash into the fender while damaging the radiator beyond repair. Thank you very fucking much, Skippy.

So the four of us have found ourselves at a roadhouse in a place I'll call Pisshole, Australia. A mechanic is bringing a new radiator from Darwin, but he won't arrive till tomorrow. Luckily, the roadhouse is also a hotel; unluckily, it's full of truckers who stared at me and Aurora the way Hannibal Lecter might gaze at a nicely marinated human liver. The boys had a beer and tried not to feel too uncomfortable as they were scrutinised by the rough crowd. I decided not to drink the house wine, because after the debauchery of the past few months I'm on a health kick.

Hungry, I approached the woman at the food counter. She had leathery skin and a wart on her nose, and she was bigger than any man there. I asked her, 'May I have a salad?'

'No salad here,' she answered with a sneer and obvious dislike for us 'city folk'.

'But it says on the menu that you have a burger with the lot . . . ?'

'So?'

'Well, doesn't that come with lettuce, tomato, cucumber and onion?'

'Yeah. What's your point?'

'Maybe you could whip me up one of those, minus the burger, bread and bacon? That would make a salad, wouldn't it?'

'Don't get fucking smart,' she barked, scaring the shit out of me. I'm sure my face turned the shade of nappy rash.

I didn't respond, as the situation now seemed tense. We'd drawn the attention of the locals, and she was much bigger than me. So I simply smiled at her and asked for a burger with the lot, along with a side order of deep-fried prawns, calamari rings and grilled fish.

A plan had come to mind. I am evil—I am *awesome*.

I took my dinner back to our room, where I'd noticed earlier that the ceiling is the type made of separate plaster squares (strippers are always on the lookout for good hiding spots). Each one of those squares can easily be lifted up. So after I'd eaten the salad from the burger, I stood on the bed and hoisted the beef patty and the seafood up into the roof. In a town where the temperature can reach fifty degrees Celsius, I can only imagine that the hot tin roof will soon smell like the buffet from hell.

HIGHLIGHT: My aptitude for vengeance.
DOWNSIDE: See above.

17 March

Two more days of driving have given me plenty of time to think. Who will be at the new club: nice girls, mean girls, stupid girls, smart girls? Mean and smart? Nice and stupid? Stripping takes all kinds, in contrast to the mainstream stereotypes.

There are always uni students, often trainee nurses and teachers, doubling as exotic dancers. In one night the job pays what everyone else makes in a week, which allows these girls to study most evenings without having to do tiring jobs like waitressing.

Some of the women I've worked with are wives and mothers who only dance one night a week to bring in a little spare cash. Others are lesbians who gloat at their ability to take the enemy's money while checking out pretty girls.

I once worked with a practising medical doctor who found she couldn't give up stripping. It can be a highly addictive lifestyle: an endless party, with the chance to make lots of friends and unlimited money.

There are also rock chicks and gothic princesses. There are fitness instructors, prison wardens, accountants and psychics. And there are, of course, a few women who dance for murkier reasons, having been to hell and back.

I'm very protective of Aurora, as she has seen true evil manifest on earth. In my opinion, exotic dancers like her are mainly motivated to do this job by something I think of as taking the power back. I came to this conclusion after listening to several strippers share harrowing stories similar to hers.

Aurora was once locked in a room for three days and repeatedly raped by a taxi driver, who is now in prison. She emerged not only determined to survive but also to weld herself together stronger than ever before, and she feels empowered by her sense of owning her body. She is the one who decides how she uses it, who can look at it and, most importantly, who can touch it. In a secure environment, men pay for the privilege of merely gazing upon her beauty while she commands respect. Any customer who doesn't show that respect winds up with a kick to the cranium from a stiletto and a covert beating from the bouncers as a finale. Each time she dances, she gains a jolt of power.

My friend Candy was abused by her uncle between the ages of six and thirteen. My pal Kristina was forced to watch her father masturbate in her presence from childhood. My buddy Jolie went through the horror of her brother hiring her out to his friends, every day after school throughout Grade Five.

Don't underestimate these powerful girls. They aren't being exploited in strip clubs—the only people being exploited are the customers.

For the vast majority of strippers, those of us with less harrowing life experiences, money is the main motivator. Many, myself included, see ourselves as relatively normal people who strip for a job.

There is also another dedicated category who are strippers in profession, attitude and lifestyle. These women take the job very seriously, just as dedicated athletes prepare for the Olympics. Every spray tan, fake eyelash, five-hour gym session and thousand-dollar costume is a form of training before they compete for the highest goal: Miss Nude World, the gold medal of the stripping universe. They hone their stage shows, along with their limbs, into a flawless and breathtaking spectacle in town and state competitions. Along the way they attract attention by appearing in various magazines and calendars, and gain up-and-coming titles such as Miss Exotic Angel and Miss Erotica. They might then become Penthouse Pet of the Year, and possibly Miss Nude Australia—perceived as the equivalent of winning silver if you don't take it all the way to the top. They're never seen without immaculate make-up and a full head of hair extensions, and they take a thousand shots to get their selfies just right. These glamourpusses live and breathe the stripping industry; they own what they do and make no apologies for their commitment.

Then there's the last tiny percentage of strippers: those who validate our mainstream reputation as bimbos. The type who think an IQ is an iPhone app. The type who will avoid thinking at all costs, and as soon as they have a genuine thought, it's stolen by their reflection in the mirror. The fact they were born pretty is proof of God's existence, because otherwise they'd be screwed.

Example? I once overheard a conversation between a dancer named Bambi and an exasperated manager.

Manager: Bambi, why are you late for work?

Bambi: My car broke down. I had to get an Uber.

Manager: What's wrong with it?

Bambi: Nothing—except it had an Indian driver.

Manager: Not the Uber, Bambi, your car?

Bambi: Oh. It ran out of petrol.

Manager: Why didn't you put petrol in?

Bambi: Not my job.

Manager: How so, pray tell?

Bambi: Because when I bought it, they told me it included on-road costs, a year's insurance and petrol.

Manager: So, you think the car salesman telepathically knows when you need petrol, and sends the fuel fairy around to your house to fill up your tank for the next year?

Bambi: Well, yeah. Why else would they have taken down my address?'

Manager: To arrange the finance?

Bambi: Don't sneer at me. You're just jealous because your car people don't put fuel in for you!

Manager: Neither do yours, evidently.

Bambi: (rolls eyes) I think you're bitter because you get paid collar-blue wages.

Manager: (gapes) I honestly don't know what to say. Actually, I do, but it isn't very nice.

Bambi replied with something that wasn't very polite either, and continued to run out of petrol for as long as I worked with her.

HIGHLIGHT: Most strippers are powerful, brave and smart. Must remember to buy a Smart car when purchasing next vehicle, to avoid pesky petrol costs.

DOWNSIDE: But it doesn't say a lot about the stripping world when Bambi's manager quit and went on to work with the mentally challenged . . .

18 March

'Sunshine!' Vegas greeted me with an inauthentic smile. 'How great to see you. How long are you staying?' This translates to: 'What the fuck are you doing here, and when can I expect you to go?' I hadn't seen Vegas for at least a year, maybe even two. She knows I'm as good a hustler as she is, so we've always had an amicable yet competitive relationship.

The new club looks good, housed inside a stately old building that also has a normal nightclub attached. On my first worknight, I could hear different music playing behind adjoining doors, and an adjacent public bar also pumps out a faint beat. The three tempos will take some getting used to, with a few migraines thrown into the mix, I imagine.

Liani is as down to earth as I remember her, and she's landed herself a rich older boyfriend who probably paid for the fit-out of the club. 'The girls have been doing okay money-wise, but nothing to get excited about,' Liani shared with me. 'I'm sure there'll be more cash coming in once the whole town finds out we've opened.'

Warning bells went off in my head. Shouldn't she have done a shitload of advertising before opening?

Then Charlotte the Penthouse Pet came stalking over. I didn't even stop to ponder how she arrived here from Darwin before me, nor did I really care. What unsettled me was that Charlotte, a world-class whiner at the best of times, looked genuinely pissed. 'The money here is *shit*!' Her petulance had the ring of truth.

Next to her, Vegas was nodding solemnly in agreement, and Aurora and I exchanged looks of trepidation.

But I'm still trying to stay optimistic—after all, the club has only just opened, and a couple of fresh faces may bring in a few more customers. It had better work out, because the four of us just booked into a furnished holiday home for a week at four hundred dollars a night. I left Darwin with over twenty-two thousand dollars in the lining of my suitcase, and I don't intend on pissing it up against the wall.

Things got worse tonight when the heavy doors to the adjacent bar opened, and two men walked in. I could sense the snide attitude radiating from them before they reached us.

'This is Mark and Reece,' Liani told me with a sigh. 'The nightclub managers.'

'Oh goody, more whores have arrived!' Reece sniggered.

Mark guffawed, while Liani and her boyfriend glared.

'Not much of a crowd,' Mark said to Liani, clearly not an innocent observation.

'Maybe your girls need to attract some clientele by standing on the corner,' said Reece.

Ha-ha, very funny. I've heard it all before, only wittier.

They smirked, and Mark said, 'We just wanted to drop by and introduce ourselves to the new girls.'

I stepped in. 'I'm so sorry, I've forgotten your names—did you say they're Dumb and Dumber?'

Mark looked at me incredulously. 'It speaks!'

I smiled sweetly. 'It also takes your eyeball out with a cocktail umbrella if you try insulting it again.'

He couldn't think of anything to say in retaliation, so he turned on his heel with Reece by his side. 'We've got to get back to managing a *real* nightclub,' he threw over his shoulder. 'See you tomorrow night—if you're still open.'

I turned to look at Liani with a question in my eyes. She sighed again and dropped into a nearby seat while I waited for the story to unfold. In her words, the owner of the building was forced to rent out the nightclub space to save himself from bankruptcy. He wasn't thrilled about leasing some of it as a strip club, yet had little choice as there were no other potential tenants in sight.

The staff from the adjoining bars were also ruffled by becoming neighbours to a club of ill repute; they protested to the city council, alongside various parliamentary members. What fucking hypocrites—I've stripped for dozens of politicians.

The bells in my head were clanging like an evacuation siren, and if I'm honest they still are. I've left behind a fountain of money to land amid a sulky penthouse pet, a hustler who can't wait to see the back of me, a club managers' mini-war and an alleged cash shortage.

HIGHLIGHT: Bar tab included for the first week!
DOWNSIDE: Sometimes I question my sanity. It rarely replies.

25 March

It's actually not too bad here. The club looked a little empty tonight, but that was mainly because the space is vast and only six dancers were working. And the townsfolk are becoming more curious, so we had about forty customers in this evening.

Liani is only charging the girls a five per cent fee to begin with. This is pretty generous considering some clubs take up to forty per cent—a serious amount if a dancer happens to make a thousand dollars in a night.

I landed a few fifty-dollar lap dances from a couple of the braver patrons, who said they'd never had an exotic dance before. Newcastle, despite its population nearing 400,000, doesn't seem overly taken with strip clubs. And the rules at this club are quite strict; not only is there no touching, but there's also no sitting on laps at all. So lap dances are performed on either a chair opposite the customer, or on the floor. It's also illegal here to give the customers a bird's-eye view. Once your G-string comes off, you must cover your bits with your hand. Try being graceful and sexy while attempting to dance *and* cover your vagina—awkward as hell.

Around eleven o'clock, a rather famous Australian rock singer slouched in. He carried a tobacco pouch full of white powder.

He booked out an entire lap-dance room, along with me and Aurora, for the duration of the night: a thousand dollars. He had four hours to kill before catching a flight. We sat naked on the floor for the remainder of the evening, helping ourselves to the goodies in his tobacco pouch and listening, awed, to the story of his life—a greater tale of debauchery than anything I could muster, even as I snorted a line off his trouser leg.

I hope to God he didn't run into any sniffer dogs at the airport.

HIGHLIGHT: Rock singer ignored Mark's and Reece's pens held out worshipfully for an autograph.

DOWNSIDE: I ignored promise to detox and kept waking myself with Richter-scale snoring from nostrils sticking together.

EVIL DICKS

All men have a certain degree of sexual deviancy—*all*. Any woman who doesn't acknowledge this is burying her head in the sand, or one of life's rare innocents (bless her no-nonsense cotton undies). Ask a man for his favourite sexual fantasy, and nine times out of ten he'll lie. On the odd chance he shares the truth, you should probably seek a good health insurance plan that covers the extensive therapy you're going to need.

Why are the particularly freaky men attracted to strip clubs? Do they truly believe the nature of our job means we're turned on by everything that turns them on? In my experience, strippers are rarely aroused by a patron *or* a lap dance—perhaps they would be if that patron resembled Ryan Gosling and spent money like the Wolf of Wall Street, but that just doesn't happen.

Regulars are indeed a strange species; however, they are the bread and butter of the stripping world. Tonight I got my first Regular here, a man nearing seventy. I call him Sea Monkey for two simple reasons. First, his daily four-hour work-out at the gym makes him smell of mould and iodine, and gives him the emaciated look of an anorexic crustacean. He also squirms around so much during a lap dance that his chair appears to be undergoing a seizure—until I shout at him to stay still.

You see, Sea Monkey was, sexually speaking, a late bloomer. Perhaps he also resembled a blanched prawn in his youth? But his first encounter wasn't until the age of eighteen with a female university professor. While not illegal, it was definitely unethical. Sea Monkey thought it was the best thing that ever happened to him. Nothing has compared to it since, or so he confided thirty seconds after we met. These days, he finds it difficult to become aroused by anything other than a stripper imitating the stern sound of that long-lost voice: 'Stop wriggling in your chair, or I'll make you revise your essay again! Don't you dare touch yourself, you naughty young man, or I'll send you out of the class!' I'm not a domineering person by nature, so I find the whole thing faintly ridiculous as well as nauseating. Sometimes I have to bite my lip to stop myself giggling. Or gagging.

But Sea Monkey has so far been good for at least two hundred bucks a dance, so while I'm faux reprimanding him on the outside, I'm inwardly paying bills or buying clothes on the inside, and remembering I have to vacuum the apartment.

Some might feel shock and revulsion at this tale, and question what kind of person would cater to such fetishes. Every single exotic dancer, that's who, or they don't last in the business. We strippers must be brilliant at switching off. A rather large part of our job is to be tolerant—in fact, perhaps this is *the* most important facet of stripping. Anyone who thinks exotic dancers simply ponce about naked is sorely mistaken.

I've seen girls with flawless beauty and reprehensible attitudes waltz on in and apply for a job with smug surety. Since these stunning creatures have always had an unfair advantage, and the whole world, *whole universe*, has never dared do anything but bend to give them exactly what they want, they imagine that stripping will be the same, if not easier. I sometimes feel sorry for them while I watch their egos get smacked around and flattened like pizza dough. But mostly I don't. These ill-informed girls truly think their looks will bring customers to them in droves, and that their task is little more than standing at the bar in lingerie, waiting for the money to roll in. It's almost amusing to see them experience rejection and self-doubt for the first time, as they come to understand that for once their looks didn't cut it. Many stunning girls, new to the business, are quite often unprepared to put in any effort and go home in tears after an hour or two, shocked and bitter that they didn't have what it takes.

Patrons aren't there simply for beauty; they require more effort. But what kind? You truly have to give them tolerance and time, unappealing as that may sound. Not too much time, though—some men will try to get away with talking to you for free all night if you let them. Nonetheless, it's important to master the art of seeming interested in their conversation and not chit-chatting for the sake of extracting money. If men just wanted to stare at a vagina, they'd do so on the internet. Never walk up to a customer and ask for a dance outright, as it shatters their illusions. If you approach in this manner, most men will whine that you're only in it for the money—which you are, but there's no reason for them to know that. Even mentioning cash in the first ten minutes can be a mistake.

In saying that, if a customer is shelling out like a lottery winner, do not leave his side for a second. When a patron is parting with big bucks, you can be sure the other dancers have noticed and will pounce. They'll wait until your back is turned then start working their own brand of magic on your customer before you can say 'lap-dance larceny'.

Moral of the story? Act like a gracious hostess, no matter how repulsed you feel. A lot of dancers don't realise that spending half an hour on some creepy old dude could earn you thousands in the long run if you acquire him as a Regular.

HIGHLIGHT: Sea Monkey gave me three hundred dollars.
DOWNSIDE: And a migraine.

30 March

Stripper financial insecurity: this is a term for *barely making a fucking cent*. Well, not the cash I'm used to, anyway. The money here still isn't great. I'm working my arse off for what we call a McDonald's wage—roughly three hundred dollars on average a night. For a weekday that's fine, but it's dismal for a weekend.

And it makes things tough now Jim isn't working. He hasn't even looked for work here. Perhaps he's taking a leaf out of Ryan's book, who *never* fucking works.

The vicious cycle is beginning again. Whenever we move to a new town, Jim loses the motivation to find a new job, then resents *me* for being the breadwinner—even more than I resent him for allowing me to be.

There was a time, not too long ago, when he was sympathetic about our financial responsibilities falling on me. After a particularly gruelling night, he would make me delicious food and stroke my head while he soothed my anxiety away. I miss those days. Now he makes snide comments like, 'What are you worried about? It's not hard to earn money when you show your pussy to anyone with a spare twenty bucks.' I protest, saying it costs a spare fifty.

Jim insists he has no problem with what I do. Apparently

he also has no problem with the two hundred-dollar seafood platters and hundred-dollar rounds of golf. But the moment our arguments become heated, I earn the insult 'dumb stripper'. He doesn't appreciate that this truly *is* work, and sometimes more difficult than most jobs.

Especially here. We dancers all find ourselves hustling extra hard to talk patrons into a lap dance. There are times when you may have chatted to a customer for a full hour, and he'll still say no. You can pull every trick out of the hat: cajole, lean over and rest your hand (with slight pressure) on his thigh, manufacture a throaty laugh at every dumb joke, and send him a come-and-get-it stare. Nothing.

But there *are* a few tricks to help your mental health with particularly difficult patrons. Try not to look straight into a customer's eyes—always focus on the skin between the eyebrows, which gives the appearance of a direct gaze. This creates a buffer to protect our sanity, because who truly wants to stare a dirty pervert in the eye? Never take a refusal personally; always convince yourself the reason they don't want you to dance for them is that they lack money or you're not their type. If you ponder it too much, you'll only wind up wandering the depths of self-doubt or even self-loathing. Know your worth, and do not let yourself fall into the trap of thinking, *Of course he wouldn't want to see me naked, I'm just not pretty enough.*

There are the customers who claim that fifty bucks is too much for a lap dance, and that they don't have that kind of money to spend. They'll then offer you two hundred dollars to come home and illegally have sex with them. Parasites.

Then there are the scumbags I have to deal with that aren't even customers. Mark and Reece have been popping in each night to torment Liani and throw a few pathetic insults our way. Vegas continues to ask me when I'm leaving, every hour on the hour. And Charlotte persists in whining like Veruca Salt.

Tonight, I stared in fascination while Charlotte took over half an hour to redo her make-up. She applied it carefully enough to earn her a job at the fine arts restoration department of a museum. Then she faced me and preened. 'Notice my eyebrows? You'd think they were real, wouldn't you? But I drew them on.'

'Remarkable,' I said, referring to her vanity more than her handiwork.

She turned back to the mirror and stared for a further five minutes, as I continued to watch her in astonishment.

'I mixed three shades of blue to get this particular cerulean— you can't buy this colour anywhere. See? Not just a pretty face.'

'Not even,' I replied.

HIGHLIGHT: If you held a nightclub manager underwater for long enough, he'd stop being an arsehole.

DOWNSIDE: Just learned that Jim found my money stash and took some to buy dope.

2 April

When the person you're supposed to trust the most helps himself to a thousand of your hard-earned dollars without an apology, you wonder if things can get worse.

I can tell you from experience, they most certainly can. And believe me, the dollars *are* hard-earned. Yeah, yeah, I know—some nights I do simply ponce about in lingerie for tips and take drugs with rock stars. But remember, some things in life are too good to be true, and there are some nights when *nothing* is good about this job, let alone true.

I'm not asking for sympathy. I'm well aware I took on a role that comes with the judgement of many people. Alongside it, we strippers deal with every twisted man who is determined to see a naked body in the flesh—one way or another. I'd much rather those sick motherfuckers come in and pay us, in an environment that's controlled, with girls who know how to handle their shit, than have the wack jobs assault some poor unsuspecting girl on the street. What a lot of people don't understand is that we're providing a *service*.

I once read that the rate of sexual assault is lower in towns with strip clubs than those without. I don't know whether this is true, but if you met some of the freaks we deal with on a nightly basis, you'd consider the possibility. But I understand that many people have no idea what we really do, and are prepared to look down on us anyway.

Sometimes, though, even I am unprepared for the depth of loathing directed our way.

Let me tell you how tonight's hell began. Liani, off sick with the flu, left us at the mercy of Reece and Mark, our managers for the night. It all started out normal, but then the jerks either got bored or envious while watching us make money, probably the latter. They opened the doors to the nightclub and let a crowd of critics come teeming in.

First came the girls. They'd heard we were here: slutty whores who had come to town to lead their men astray. You see, women who have never stripped for a living often see us as evil bimbos. Sometimes it's worse when they get a look at us in the flesh—then the hatred really sets in. They want a reason to look down on us, so they can become incensed when they can't spot an obvious one. You can see their eyes widen in disbelief, then narrow at our glossy appearance and articulate conversation.

Then comes the defiance as they reject what's in front of them. It *can't* be true. We *cannot* be normal and attractive. There *must* be something wrong with us.

The nightclub women surrounded the stage and podiums in groups, sneering and openly laughing as they condemned us.

'I think that one has cellulite!' was the first battle cry I heard.

Personally, I thought an angry mob of bitches bent on our humiliation could have done a little better. Cellulite? Big deal. Billions of other women on the planet have it too, genius.

But admittedly, I was shaken. This situation reminded me of the first time I stripped in public: the panic and insecurity at having my face, body and character scrutinised. Except this time, there was no doubt the stares were borne of contempt.

'Bet she doesn't really look like that under her twenty coats of make-up,' one spectator consoled herself, earning nods from her friends.

We dancers braved it out, swinging around the poles while shooting worried glances at one another. If the crowd turned, I didn't see security running to help us in a jiffy—not before we earned a couple of lumps and bruises, anyway.

When it was time for me to climb off stage, I didn't want to get down. But I took a breath, held my head high and walked past the hundred pairs of eyes watching my every move. I made my way straight to the bar, where Mark and Reece were sniggering along with the crowd. I was so shaken, I ordered a tequila without caring that they could see how badly I needed it.

The club was jam-packed, but not one patron was there to applaud or admire us. They were staring and pointing at the strange new species in their town. Any real customers had long gone, sensing trouble from the outset.

When I turned to survey the room, I saw a handful of women had followed me. 'So,' said a large, solid girl, 'you take off your clothes for other people's husbands?'

I couldn't avoid answering; this was an inquisition, and I was on trial. 'Yes,' I said simply, trying to maintain my dignity.

'And you're *proud* of that?' she cross-examined.

'Not necessarily. But I *am* proud of the fact that my profession has stopped a lot of husbands going to hookers instead.'

'How do you figure that?' she demanded.

'Because plenty of men feel less like they're cheating by getting a lap dance, than they would by sleeping with a prostitute.'

She snorted. 'And you're *not* a hooker?'

'No. We make more money than callgirls, and it's illegal in most of Australia to be both. Plus it's against the law to solicit prostitution work from a lap-dance club.'

The crowd leaned in at this revelation, reluctantly interested.

But the big girl looked unconvinced. 'Look, if you girls didn't take your clothes off, and prostitutes stopped having sex for money, then men would be forced to stay faithful.'

'They'd have affairs instead.'

Her eyes narrowed, and the crowd looked disparaging again. 'Aren't you a know-it-all?' she huffed. 'How did you become the expert on men?'

'Well, one of the things I've learned about male customers while working as a dancer is that they're driven by variety. And I think that applies to all men, to some extent.'

'So you're saying *every* man is *driven* by strippers and hookers?' she said, seething.

'I'm not saying that at all,' I answered carefully, aware of the hostile glares. 'Some men buy girly magazines, and some watch porn. Some just develop a crush on an actress or singer.

But every man will look at other girls, no matter how in love with his partner he might be. Men are primal, there's nothing we can do about it.'

The chick looked torn—but she wasn't done with me yet. And why should she have been? She was the bravest of them all, the first who'd dared interrogate us aliens, and she had an eager crowd supporting her. Plus, I wasn't doing a great job of endearing myself.

My grandmother always said, 'When you don't know what to do, do what you know.' Honesty was the best policy here, with a side order of humble pie; sarcasm would only get me killed.

The girl switched from making accusations to guilt-tripping. 'What do your parents have to say about what you're doing?' she grilled, making my profession sound on a par with being a small-animal torturer.

'My dad doesn't know, but he wouldn't be too happy about it. My mum just asks that I stay safe, save my money and show her how to work the pole.'

Some of the girls in the group actually smiled.

'I've heard pole dancing is great exercise,' one conceded, now I'd appeared moderately human and cracked a joke.

But the ringleader *still* wasn't finished. 'What about God? Do you believe in him? Aren't you scared you're going to hell? Don't you think your job is wrong in his eyes?'

'Well, I won't know till my expiry date.' I shrugged. 'But wasn't Eve created naked?'

The judge and jury looked taken aback. 'I suppose . . .'

I was getting tired of the third degree. 'Why don't we have a shot, grab a seat, and I'll be happy to tell you anything else you want to know.'

Fat chance of me getting a lap dance with this crowd anyway. No doubt if I approached a guy, he'd turn out to be one of their boyfriends, and they'd burn me at the stake by building a pyre around the stripper pole.

Our conversation flowed from that point, partly due to my relief that a stripper gang-bashing wasn't going to take place after all. The big girl, whose name turned out to be Penny, still had a million questions. She became riveted by my responses, and we wound up getting along rather well.

Looking around the club, I saw my friends had fared just as well by being themselves and were partying with the crowd. Thank God part of our job description is working the room.

Not everyone was swayed, though. One girl wandered by and shouted, 'Mole!'

Penny came to my defence. 'Shut up, you don't even know her. She's like, a *real* human!'

Wonderful, I'm nearly a person.

'So tell me honestly, Sunshine,' Penny said as she turned back to me, 'you're really not frightened that what you're doing is evil, or bad for women?'

'No and no. I believe there's a God, definitely, but I also believe there are much worse things someone can do than parade around naked—like beating another person as a release for anger, abusing animals, pretending not to notice the homeless, being vain to the point of ugliness, lying about being broke to avoid helping out a friend, judging people's weight, looks or job, and bullying anyone weaker, especially if it's for the benefit of onlookers.'

Penny had the grace to blush.

'All of those things are much more offensive than professional nudity. I think God is too busy to bother paying much attention to me when there are serial killers, rapists and paedophiles to keep him occupied. And don't even get me *started* on Donald Trump, or Woody Allen for marrying his own daughter.'

'What about the Me Too movement?' she asked. 'Do you feel you're letting the side down at all?'

'No. I feel the exact opposite.' The feminist in me tried not to roar, but I was on a roll. 'The first time I was inappropriately touched, I was only thirteen. A man came out of nowhere while I was looking at a Tamagotchi in Target and squeezed my non-existent boobs, right there in the fucking aisle without saying a word. The next time I was fourteen, and it was an old grey-haired guy who sat next to me and my friends at the circus. He tried to slip his hand between my legs. My dad went ballistic and said I was never leaving the house again. He didn't mean to do this, but his reaction made me feel like it was my fault, as though just by being a girl out in the world I invited men to prey on me. Since then, I've been groped, propositioned and sexually harassed by bosses, co-workers, so-called male friends and strangers. And each time it happened, I questioned *myself*. I wondered if I could have avoided it if I'd worn a higher-cut top or longer skirt. Because women are taught from a young age that *we* provoke men into committing offences against us, when the schooling should have been the other way around. Every boy should be taught from birth to control his impulses and reduce his sense of entitlement, and that there's no such thing as "asking for it" because of a fucking bra-top.'

Oh, I really was on a fucking *roll*.

'Then the Me Too movement comes along, and almost every woman on the planet has a similar story to share. We all just thought we had to put up with it, because men had gotten away with it for so long. But why wasn't commonplace harassment addressed *before* a bunch of rich white actresses spoke out?

I completely support the Me Too movement, I'm just pissed that it's a bit late in the day. And you'll probably smirk at a stripper pointing this out, Penny, but the SlutWalk movement was pretty much protesting the same thing for years before, only in mini-skirts. Because what we choose to wear should never be an excuse for abuse, rape, victim-blaming or slut-shaming.

'Strippers are very rarely anti-feminist. Isn't what we're doing a feminist act? Nobody is forcing me to strip—what I'm doing with my body is *my* choice. Everybody seems to think strippers are allowing ourselves to be exploited, when in fact I'm the one doing all the exploiting. The men who pay to see me could be saving up for houses, holidays or cars, but instead they choose to piss their money away on our nakedness. We strippers are also exploiting their gullibility and weakness, knowing they're powerless against our nudity and beauty. It might be anti-humanitarian, but it certainly isn't anti-feminist.'

I went on. 'There are those who say I'm allowing myself to be objectified, and there's a grain of truth to that, but I'm turning objectification into manipulation. And just because men know they're going to see nude women at a strip club, that doesn't mean they'll suddenly think every woman wants to get naked for them. They won't have a lap dance here, then automatically presume their sexy bank teller will shake her tits for them during their next transaction.

'And guess what else? Every single time I've been groped, propositioned or harassed, it was *never* in a strip club. It came from men like the CEO of the company I worked for as a marketing consultant, and my supervisor while I was in admin. I also get a lot more dirty comments if I forget to wear a bra to Woolworths than I do here. You know why? Because a strip club is the one place where the tables turn, and we dancers hold *all* the power. Our customers are transformed into the meek and helpless creatures *we're* forced to be in the outside world. See what I mean about turning objectification into manipulation?'

Penny stared at me like I'd just recited Shakespeare in Aramaic, a confused admiration in her eyes. She'd clearly realised that I'm something more alien and unbelievable than a woman displaying her genitalia for money: a stripper with a brain. Or at least half of one.

She hugged me goodbye and thanked me for changing her point of view.

But I *am* a stupid stripper. There I was, thinking the night would end on a good note. No such luck.

In order for you to fully grasp the following events, I must first explain how dancers' fees are paid. Some clubs will collect a hundred dollars from you at the beginning or end of the night. In clubs where a percentage of earnings is taken, the managers will calculate how many dances you've done during the night and ask for their cut once you've finished your shift. A few will request that you pay your percentage of each dance beforehand, in which case a desk is set up outside the lap-dance room with a receptionist taking money every time you go in.

In this Newcastle club, the gentlemen pay the receptionist at the door rather than the stripper. All of our money is placed in a cash register and then into individual envelopes, one for each dancer. We receive all our money at the end of each evening, minus the club's cut of five per cent.

When the club closed as usual at five this morning, us dancers sat around in the dark waiting for Reece and Mark to remove five per cent and hand over our earnings. They came out of the office muttering about having no time to calculate the tills, thanks to Liani's absence—could we all come back in the afternoon to collect our money?

I thought nothing of it. Exhausted, I collected my bag and headed for the door.

I'd like to go on the record in saying I am not as smart as I think I am, despite my practised feminist opinions. I would have made my exit if Vegas hadn't firmly said she'd wait for Reece and Mark to count our money.

Well, I decided to wait too. What else was I going to do except go home to Jim—who would probably be more stoned than a biblical character—and continue my health kick by eating fruit salad for breakfast?

So I sat back in a chair, Aurora in tow, and looked at Dumb and Dumber expectantly. They glared back at us with disdain.

'Go home!' Mark snarled. 'We don't have time to add up your money. We have a *real* club to run.'

'I don't see why not,' Vegas demanded, 'when there are only six of us. And thanks to you, we've had fuck-all lap dances to speak of—so it shouldn't take more than five minutes to add up the percentages, take your cut, and pay us.'

At that, Mark and Reece looked thunderous.

'We don't have enough cash here right now,' Mark suddenly spat. 'We had to pay for alcohol deliveries.'

'Not *our* problem,' said Vegas. 'We're subcontractors, so *you* don't pay us a thing. That money belongs to *us*—you had no legal right to spend it.'

I blinked at Vegas, stunned, and so did the other dancers. She was right: that money was already ours.

The two men shot her a look of loathing, then huddled in the office again. It was almost six in the morning. They appeared to be stalling, and I couldn't think for the life of me why. But Vegas clearly suspected something was wrong.

Reece appeared at the door with a new tactic: intimidation. 'Which part are you stupid sluts having trouble understanding? We can't fucking pay you tonight! Come back after lunchtime.'

God bless Vegas. She not only shocked the hell out of me, but she earned my lifelong respect as well.

When she stood up, she seemed to loom over them. 'I'll call the police,' she snarled. 'That money doesn't belong to you. Taking it for the club's purpose is *stealing*.'

I suddenly understood the seriousness of the situation.

The managers looked at us like they wished the gun restrictions had been lifted, then they retreated to the office again.

Vegas stalked over and rapped on the door. 'Five minutes,' she yelled. 'I'm calling the police in five minutes.'

The door was thrust open, and the bastards threw a calico bank-deposit bag on the floor.

And what do you know? Inside were individually marked envelopes with our earnings minus five per cent. When had they had the chance to sort out our earnings between shouting at us and managing a *real* club?

The men watched as we collected our envelopes, seemingly no happier that we had to get down on the floor like dogs to pick them up. Then they bade us goodbye by slamming the office door.

'That was . . . weird,' Aurora said on our way out.

'It was more than weird,' said Vegas. 'Something's wrong, just you wait and see.'

It was almost 7 a.m. and I was just too tired to try to figure out what that something could be. Not that I would ever, in a million years, have imagined the truth.

I ate a fruit salad and collapsed into bed, only to be woken an hour later by Liani knocking furiously at the door.

'*Those MOTHERFUCKERS shut us down!*' she shrieked in my face. 'They got a *MOTHERFUCKING* court order by petition! They padlocked the doors an hour ago.'

At first I was too tired and dazed to be anything but stunned by her fury. But then an incredulous chill crept over me.

They'd known: Reece and Mark had *known* that a court order was in effect, *and* probably the exact hour the club would legally be shut down. They had been stalling for time *so they could keep our money for themselves*!

Even as this dawned on me, I could barely believe it.

Mark and Reece had made it clear that they hated us for our profession. But they had so little regard for us as humans that they simply didn't care if we were unable to pay our rent or bills, or feed ourselves. Those thieves were prepared to steal our livelihood. They had also gone out of their way to destroy my friend's new business, no doubt leaving her in debt and with lacerated dreams of future ventures. She is a resourceful girl, and I know one day she'll find a way to rise again. But this is the kind of thing that leaves behind burning scars of rage, and my heart truly hurts for her.

I am in appalled awe. I am also pretty sure God disapproves of theft far beyond a naked body, and I for one wouldn't want to be standing anywhere near Mark and Reece when the lightning bolt hits.

HIGHLIGHT: Karma knows which nightclub you manage.
DOWNSIDE: Jobless.

COOL CHANGE

4 April ....

Thanks to Jim's dope-smoking habit and refusal to work, I'm down to sixteen thousand dollars in savings. It didn't help that we just travelled two hours down the road to Sydney, then changed our minds once we got there. The club I aimed to work in had fifty girls on the roster that night, all competing for twenty-dollar lap dances.

No sooner had I stepped into the infamous Kings Cross, than I was approached by a drug dealer offering me ice for a fifty or a blowjob. I politely declined.

The girls in the club, whom I mostly didn't know, gazed at me and Aurora with either disinterest or narrow-eyed competitiveness. I'll admit I was on edge too. Sydney strippers have the kind of confidence that would make a supermodel envious; their self-assurance is almost supernatural. I find them extremely intimidating, and I'm not easily daunted. These women will elbow you out of the way, without remorse, in order to chat with a customer you're speaking to. They aren't above threats or theft on a quiet night.

But there's good and bad everywhere, and one stripper—a vague acquaintance—kindly told me there had been no money in The Cross for quite some time. Apparently this was making the dancers slightly psychotic. 'You don't want to mess with the regular girls at the moment, Sunshine,' she said, looking nervous. 'The last new stripper who threatened their money had her drink spiked with a hospital-grade laxative.'

Right.

Aurora and I took one last look around the club, once luxurious but now going to seed, and walked out. Our time in The Cross was over.

Until the four of us figure out our next port of call, it's up to me to pay for a round of cheap, dodgy hotels, since the others are broke.

I was sitting with Jim in a communal barbecue area that looked like it would attract recently paroled individuals, when my phone rang. Tara and Candy were calling from my beloved Cairns. 'When are you coming back?' they asked. 'We miss you.'

'I'm not sure. Maybe tomorrow?' I looked at Jim hopefully, and he pissed me off by shaking his head. He has no inclination to return to Queensland, probably because he owes money there. And the people to whom he's indebted are not the sort who take kindly to evasiveness; they like to collect interest in a cracked fibula or dislocated jaw.

'Anyway, how are you?' I asked my friends, while shooting Jim a filthy look.

'Great,' Candy said. 'I'm stripping at the Pacific Club and still getting lots of dominatrix work. Think I might take a few weeks off for some headspace, though, after last night.'

'What happened?'

'A *Star Wars* fan wanted to be smacked around by a light-saber. Then he wanted it stuck up his . . . galaxy. It really fucked me up. I loved the force as a kid, I just never thought I'd use it this way.'

'I'm so sorry to hear that. But at least it's more innovative than a gerbil up the arse. So there's no shortage of freaks clamouring for your services?'

'You have no idea.' She sighed.

I smiled because my island-princess pal is as unique as she is unfazed. 'I miss you,' I blurted, filled with longing for my best friends.

'And I *you*, my lovely.'

'How's Tara?' I asked to stop myself becoming teary.

'You can ask her yourself, I'll put her on. Good speaking to you, babes! Don't stay away too long.'

Tara's voice replaced Candy's. 'Hi, sweetie, how goes it?'

'Okay. Suffering from strip club indecision.'

'Well, you should come back then.'

'I need a break from partying, and I never seem to control myself in Cairns. How are you, by the way?'

'I'm fine. Actually, I'm not really. I think he's cheating on me.'

'Oh no,' I said, genuinely upset. 'I can't believe Justin would do that! He seems so in love with you.'

'Not Justin!' she corrected. 'The *DJ*!'

'Oh,' I said, nonplussed. 'I thought he was gay?'

She huffed into the phone. 'I changed my mind. Don't come back in a hurry. I love you. Goodbye.'

I smiled at the silent phone, then I felt someone tugging on my arm. I looked up to see Aurora grinning at me. 'We just dropped a coin on Adelaide.'

HIGHLIGHT: Headed to the wine capital of Australia!

DOWNSIDE: There are people in the world who associate their sexuality with Jedi Knights . . .

11 April

Adelaide is like a slightly smaller version of Melbourne: glittering and cosmopolitan, with a fusion of contemporary, polished concrete and century-old buildings in shades of bluestone and honey-gold. As Melbourne has the MCG and Paris the Eiffel Tower, Adelaide has an institution known as the Wicked Pony Revue. It's been around for roughly thirty-five years and is a kind of Disneyland of strip clubs. Not only does it host Miss Nude World—yes, *world*—but it prides itself on the professionalism and high calibre of its dancers. No seedy underground den here: the Wicked Pony is a sumptuous wonderland of sparkling chandeliers, polished stages and mirrored fantasies.

Aurora and I have been accepted to work at this paragon of exotic clubs.

Madame Justina, the owner, and his manager, Ruby, run a tight ship. They maintain the club as a refined cabaret, rather than permitting an in-your-face, bump-and-grind style. Madame Justina, or Justin when not in drag, is glamorous and somewhat scathing like lots of fabulous gay men. I suspect that Ruby was once a famous King's Cross Les Girl, one of those dazzling transgender performers who dramatically lip-sync to classic tunes, wear make-up sublime enough to give artistry lessons, costumes that cause strippers FOMO, and probably fart glamour and glitter. Ruby runs the show with a no-nonsense demeanour that is perfectly understandable: it helps to adopt a take-no-shit attitude when you're in charge of a roomful of divas.

A great thing about Ruby and Madame Justina is their respect for us dancers. They appear understanding and empathetic with not a speck of judgement. Best of all, they actually like us—plenty of managers don't, which is pretty stupid if you think about it. Why dislike your commodity? If the club is the bread and butter, aren't we strippers the prosciutto, semi-dried tomato and triple-cream brie in the sandwich? I mean, who's going to come to a strip club without strippers? Or to meet a bunch of stroppy ones?

So the appreciation Aurora and I feel here is a welcome change.

There is a hierarchy, though. Madame Justina runs a dance school during the day, which I presume the cream of the crop attend to learn their extravagant stage shows. The rest of us are pretty much decorative pieces, wrapped around poles on podiums in various dark corners.

The money is somewhat steady, but nothing like in Darwin or Cairns. Damn Jim for not agreeing to return to Queensland.

Luckily table dances are encouraged here, as not every club allows them. A girl is paid twenty dollars to get naked on the customer's table for one song. Unlike in a lap dance, there is no close contact.

I did quite a few table dances last night, but only one lap dance—since the price at this club is somewhat exorbitant. Patrons are not only expected to pay around forty dollars just to enter the lap-dance room, but they have to fork out for the stripper as well.

I didn't think grinding on a customer's lap was allowed here, but I'm pretty sure I saw it happen. There are always one or two girls willing to break the rules for a few extra dollars. Personally, I've never understood how they can bring themselves to wiggle on some dirty old guy's erection. Gross.

When I got home, Jim wasn't in the best mood. And there we have it, folks: the cycle has begun again. After not working all this time, he's fallen into a depression and convinced himself he's worthless. Once again, I'm the bad guy for supporting us.

He actually slept in the spare room to avoid me. I tried not to find this hilarious, because although our tiny apartment—next door to Ryan and Aurora—was described as 'two bedroom', the ad should have read, 'second room would suit hobbit'. Jim's lanky frame hangs over the end of the bed.

It took me half an hour to get rid of the giggles before I could sleep.

HIGHLIGHT: Sweet dreams, Jim.

DOWNSIDE: Black holes will probably always remain a mystery, so too will the reason why women like me put up with their man being a douchebag.

16 April

It's a bit boring in Adelaide, and friggen freezing. Madame Justina asked if I would consider coming to dance classes, with the possibility of becoming a stage performer. Quite frankly, the weather is so arctic that I can barely bring myself to get up and go to the letterbox, let alone attend a class.

I hate being cold. I sleep all day, then get up, get ready, eat, and go to work. Rinse and repeat. I've had to take on six shifts a week, as I'm making no more than between a hundred and three hundred dollars a night—almost a normal wage, except I'm supporting two of us. I'm becoming surly and frustrated, and even my best manipulation skills haven't helped me crack a five-hundred-dollar night yet.

Usually I'm subtle and almost irresistible when acquiring lap dances. I have the gift of convincing men that they simply *have* to see me naked. This is by no means vanity talking; it took me a long time to hone my skills. Rome wasn't built in a day, and neither is a stripper's persona. You have to figure out which personality to adopt—one that suits you comfortably—in order to make the big bucks. I've created an alter ego who is approachable, a bit dry, a bit funny, yet sensuous. Like a femme fatale who tells jokes.

Some dancers choose to appear aloof, some exotic and some giggly, while others act like a schoolteacher, although it's always best not to intimidate patrons unless they ask for it. Some strippers hint at the promise of a covert meeting later (I guess we're all guilty of this from time to time), and others play the single-mother sympathy card, which I find as attractive as slime-based soup. There are some who can pull off unobtainable glamour and get away with acting like it's a customer's privilege to pay—or take out a second mortgage—for half an hour of their time. Others aim to embody sheer sluttiness and impersonate their favourite porn star. Some are friendly, some matey, others bossy, and a few meek and subservient. I know one girl who is steamier than a Brazilian rainforest and never even speaks; she just stares with those molten eyes as she points to a customer, and he follows as if in a trance.

Quite a few strippers play the bimbo, while for a few more this is not an act. But almost every stripper learns to 'dumb down' when they talk to customers.

It usually takes a glass of wine for me to shuck off my real self and morph into 'Sunshine'. Not every man likes an idiot, true, but if I were to show my true personality, I would be too intelligent for their liking. In fact, I remember talking to a patron once, thinking I was doing rather well and it wouldn't be too long before I lightened his wallet, when to my surprise he stopped me mid-sentence and said, 'Sunshine, you're a really lovely girl, but I'm going to go talk to somebody a bit dumber.'

As you can imagine, not all the stripper personas mix well. And the dressing-room of a club can sometimes turn into a war zone.

Lots of us are bullied when we start out. I certainly was. There are politics to learn and there is thick skin to develop. Becoming a stripper is almost like moving to a country with unfamiliar customs and laws.

One of the Stripper Laws is never to mention another dancer is married or in a relationship; it's clearly sabotage, to make the stripper less appealing to clientele, and it infuriates management. Likewise, don't ever approach your co-worker's regular customer, for the obvious reason that you are messing with their primary meal-ticket. Also, don't go so far as to scare new patrons (who are not regulars) into avoiding all other dancers, on the premise that you'll have them kicked out for not remaining lap-dance faithful. This tends to piss off the other girls enough for them to consider a shovel and a bag of quicklime.

And you also learn swiftly never to backchat or show animosity towards the head girl and her Clique, especially if it's your first night. A Clique of strippers can make *Mean Girls* look like a film about humanitarians. And there is *always* a Clique. Not long after you arrive at a new club, you find out who they are. They'll begin by ignoring you, then they'll snarl if you dare approach a customer who is there to see one of them. They often have the ear of management, so if you piss them off you'll soon find yourself accused of letting customers touch you. Or of undercutting: charging less for a lap dance than all the other strippers and messing with the club's set price—which, by the way, is the most serious breach of Stripper Laws, and looked upon as seriously as a criminal offence. Undercutting will not only earn you a tongue-lashing from everyone at the club, but quite possibly a few missing costumes as well.

Although I have never stolen a costume as punishment, I'm guilty of once throwing a girl's outfit behind a set of metal lockers. They had to be moved by two burly bouncers so she could retrieve the goods. I flush with shame every time I think of it, as that girl is now one of my good friends.

In Queensland I wound up with a reputation as a Mean Girl, and I've been trying to live it down ever since. I know that from an outsider's point of view, Mean Girls are usually seen as the most popular and privileged, but there is truly no fun in being a Mean Girl. It's awful when you greet a co-worker and watch them shy away from you. The girls who are not part of your Clique only want to be your friend because they fear you—and the partner of fear is dislike. So while girls are fawning over you, they can't stand you. Try going to sleep every night knowing you're seen in that light.

At least I'm never bullied anymore. And I never set out to be a bully either: my reputation as a Mean Girl arose from difficult circumstances.

I once became close friends with an exotic dancer who was crazy-infatuated with a world-famous DJ. When he toured Melbourne, she and I went to his show together and wound up at the afterparty, as strippers often do. The bash swiftly turned into an orgy, and my friend—we'll call her Demoness—thought she'd have her evil way with the unsuspecting DJ. I was ready to leave her to it, having no interest in swinging. However, it seems he likewise had no interest in group sex—or in my friend, for that matter. Instead he gave me a lifelong enemy by asking Demoness if *I* was single, and perhaps available for dinner. Honestly, you'd have thought I'd fucked her husband and sold her children into slavery!

Her jealous reaction, along with its repercussions, knew no bounds. But even with my penchant for revenge, I let her repeated attacks on me slide for some time. I ignored it when she told every customer I was married, another strip club no-no. I laughed it off when she rang all my friends and told them I'd been talking behind their backs. I took it in my stride when she hit on Jim. I defended myself to various managers after she spread rumours that I was both undercutting *and* touching my vagina during lap dances for extra money. I didn't even confront her when my car tyres were slashed, although I assume she was the culprit.

But when an ad appeared in the local paper with my phone number and an offer to 'Call Sunshine for a Good Time—Anal Preferred', I declared a fucking *war*.

Your opponent should never see you coming. I found it easy to take revenge on her because she gave no thought to her main weak spot. She was a UK citizen hoping to gain residency in Australia, and the rules stated she had to work in an office— which she had long abandoned for the stripping world, where she earned tax-free dollars. So I wrote an anonymous letter to the immigration department. Two weeks later, she was deported from our fair shores.

As the immigration officer escorted her to the airport, I waited outside international departures with a super-sized latte so I could wave goodbye, and so I could be certain she was gone.

After that, I became bitter for a while. My smart-arse shell became a spiked carapace. I wanted to keep other dancers away, particularly nice ones, lest I be fooled again. My tongue became a blade, and scrutiny a sport. The only girls I felt comfortable around were as intimidating and spiteful as I was.

It was a depressing period in my life, mostly because I shut out a lot of genuine friends and antagonised co-workers for fun, and I didn't like myself much. It feels awful to look back on those times, even though I'm not that person anymore. I may have a talent for revenge, but I am certainly not malicious by nature, and never without just cause.

I've since learned that the unfortunate episode with Demoness was unusual in the stripping world, because exotic dancers share a strong sense of camaraderie. Even while you're in the middle of an apocalyptic argument with another dancer—capped teeth bared, talons drawn—if an outsider dares intervene, you both swiftly turn on them. We can pick on one another, but nobody else can. We're all viewed the same way by those who condemn us, and so we're united by the outside world's judgement.

HIGHLIGHT: Must remember to send Demoness my yearly postcard with tropical beaches she can legally never step foot on again.
DOWNSIDE: Occasionally also still get calls for anal.

18 April

I'd believed my boredom was stemming partly from the professionalism with which the Wicked Pony is run. There's no drama here, I thought—and yet, soon after this crossed my mind, a small blaze broke out at work.

Aurora had just sprayed on some Marc Jacobs in the change room, when a showgirl named Titania sniffed the air and complimented the scent. 'It's my favourite. I won't wear anything but Marc Jacobs. I always have the biggest bottle in my locker—see?' Her face drained of colour when her open locker revealed no sign of her perfume. She turned on Aurora, enraged. 'You stole my perfume!'

My poor friend blinked in shock. I knew she had her own perfume and certainly hadn't taken Titania's. The showgirl's irrational fury probably meant that meth was involved.

'*Give me back my perfume, you beanstalk cunt!*' she screeched, on account of Aurora's tall, lithe frame. This was a bit rich coming from Titania, who I've named due to her titanic proportions.

Now, don't get me wrong, I have never judged a girl on her weight; that would go against the person I like to think I'm trying to be. Plus, I've seen some of the chubbier strippers clean up at clubs, taking all the money in the room. But it's difficult not to be mean to mean people.

When Titania called Aurora a few more anatomy-related names and slapped her face with a dirty G-string, I stepped in. 'Hey, stop that! My friend didn't touch your perfume. You need to apologise *right fucking now.*'

Titania's furious gaze fell on me. 'And who the *fuck* are you?' the showgirl asked, as though she'd never seen me before. And most likely, she hadn't—such is the Wicked Pony class system.

'Someone who can resist a buffet,' I calmly told her.

'*What the fuck did you say?!*'

It was a good thing that Ruby arrived to sort things out. 'What's going on here?'

Titania pointed at Aurora. 'This bitch stole my Marc Jacobs perfume!'

Ruby dipped down into Titania's bag and asked, in an ominous, mob-boss voice, 'Do you mean *this* perfume?'

'Oh.' Titania sniffed.

Aurora was sobbing in huge gulps.

'Sorry,' Titania said in a tone better suited to the words 'get fucked'.

I took a weeping Aurora to the bar and bought her a shot. Then I convinced a customer to buy another round of shots, and another. And another. I then found twenty bucks on the floor and used it to buy tequila for the two of us.

I hadn't earned enough to pay my bills, which meant I'd need to use my savings again. I felt like crying alongside Aurora.

I got her so drunk, she forgot the altercation and was in fits of drunken giggles. Then nausea hit her. But instead of taking her to the bathroom to throw up, I took her back into the change room. Where I gently led her to Titania's bag and told her to let it all out.

I am a brat. I am spiteful. I am irrational. I am loyal. I am caring. I am defiant. I am loving. I can be extremely superficial. I am selfish. I am giving. I am an actress. I keep it real. I believe there is one God. I believe in a thousand deities. I am smart. I am stupid. I rarely make sense. I love to give advice. I'm there for my friends. I like being alone. Sweet, sarcastic, superficial, philosophical, deep, questionable, erratic, Zen.

I am a stripper.

HIGHLIGHT: Finally, a bit of drama.
DOWNSIDE: Finally, a bit of drama.

20 April

Saturday night is my least favourite night of the week. Granted, it's the busiest. But it's also the evening when the children come out to play.

I'm talking about eighteen-year-old boys. And unless you strike gold and find a socially inept, obsessed teenager, the chances of extracting big money from a young man, especially a good-looking one, are practically zero. And a socially inept, obsessed teenager is a restraining order waiting to happen.

Some of the younger strippers love them because *'They're just so hot!'* Only a true imbecile would bother with a great-looking patron, usually because they're more vain than we are and refuse to pay for naked girls. Why would they, when it's so easy for them to hook up at a nightclub for free?

Groups of young men like to play a game: 'let's see if we can pick up a stripper'. Boys, be warned, there is only a slim chance. And strippers beware, if you're stupid enough to acquiesce, you are a bedpost notch that will propel him into legendary status among his friends forever. You will be talked about for years, perhaps decades, to come—the whore he picked up for free. Believe me, I've seen it happen.

I bet a lot of women wonder how their boyfriends act inside strip clubs. Generally, their behaviour is appalling. They snigger with their immature little group and try to get a free grope as you walk by. Somehow, just walking into the place turns relatively normal young men into smart-arse misogynists. One or two will always get brave at some point and have a lap dance—just a twenty-dollar one. Rest assured ladies, your boyfriend *has* had a lap dance at least once (or fifty times) despite what he's told you.

Tonight, like most Saturdays, the club was full of young fuck-tards trying to touch my arse and calling out stupid questions like 'How about a blowjob for ten bucks?' and 'Will you stick a vibrator in it for twenty dollars?' As you can imagine, my disposition was far from shiny. But I didn't bother telling security to throw them out, as the bouncers were struggling to keep up with the complaints from all the other dancers.

I was struggling to make a hundred bucks, since I don't give blowjobs or stick a vibrator in it for any amount going.

To truly top off my night, who should walk up the entrance stairs? Jim, that's who. And my boyfriend decided to act like the biggest fucktard in the place. He had shown up purely to ask for money! I gaped at his audacity, knowing he only wanted cash to score dope. At least this time I've hidden my savings in a place he clearly can't find: the air conditioner. I'm safe in the knowledge it won't be switched on during the early onslaught of winter.

I glared at Jim, my face burning, and responded to his request with words mostly beginning with F and C. I couldn't help myself.

Ruby gave me a warning look for arguing on the stairs but didn't say anything. She'd no doubt seen it all before; in fact, I thought I saw a glimmer of admiration in her eyes. Maybe she sees a lot of girls giving in rather than telling their boyfriends to fuck off.

As Jim skulked back down the stairs, frustrated and helpless, a biker strutted in. He looked me up and down. 'Beautiful!' he exclaimed, and I gave him a sexy, professional smile. 'Almost perfect!' he added. 'Shame about the small tits.'

Oh, for *fuck's* sake, why is everyone so obsessed with boobs? They're not *that* small! I've got a friggen B-cup! These morons carry on like I have the chest of a ten-year-old boy.

Morose, I was contemplating leaving work early when I heard a woman call my name. There stood an old acquaintance from Cairns, Amanda. She told me she was at the Wicked Pony to drink, not dance, as she'd recently given up stripping. Now that she was living with an Olympic swimmer, she had to quit: her boyfriend's sponsors wouldn't approve of a stripper girlfriend.

Amanda was standing with a guy so gloriously handsome— with bronzed skin, hazel eyes, sweet freckles and an amazing physique—he had to be the celebrated swimmer.

'It's so good to see you, Sunshine!' Amanda said. 'I didn't know you were in Adelaide!' All her sentences ended in exclamation marks, and I suddenly remembered her being a little too loud and a lot too vivacious for me, like someone intravenously fed Red Bull.

I smiled politely. 'I've almost been here a month. What brings you to town?'

'Oh, Chris is here to compete! A few of us tagged along to make a holiday of it!'

I turned to be introduced to Chris, whom I'd been looking at from the corner of my eye. If I'm truthful, I'd been trying my best not to stare, he was so wholesomely stunning. And, unfortunately, off limits.

'I'm Sunshine.' I shook his hand. 'I've heard great things about you.'

Amanda screeched like a hyena. 'Oh my God, you think this is my boyfriend?! You're so funny, Sunshine! Can you really see me going out with this nerd?!'

Personally, I wouldn't see a problem with it . . .

Amanda was still guffawing like a zoo animal. 'This is my old flatmate, Orion! I so can't believe you thought he was my type, yuck!'

Was she visually impaired? When her boyfriend arrived, I knew she had to be. He resembled some freakish amphibian, white and waterlogged, with the prune-like look of someone dunked in chlorine for too long.

Orion just looked uncomfortable. Now that I knew he wasn't Amanda's partner, my stomach filled with heat—in a way that hadn't happened to me in years.

'Are you named after the constellation?' I asked, to stop myself gaping.

He nodded and flashed me a smile, which didn't help matters; I wondered what it would be like to touch his skin.

'Are you from Adelaide?' he inquired politely.

'No, Melbourne.' I wanted to keep the conversation going. To keep his attention on me. Even as I wondered why. Jim and I have been doing it tough lately, true, but we always find a way to figure us out. And we will again, I'm sure.

Anyway, Orion didn't seem remotely relaxed or interested.

'So what do you do when Amanda isn't dragging you to places of ill-repute?'

My light joke earned me another smile. 'I'm a psychiatrist.'

My temperate cooled immediately, and I was stunned to find I felt unworthy of his company. Was it because I sensed he was assessing me, musing on what kind of socially maladjusted misfit belittles herself by stripping? I told myself I didn't care.

'It was awesome seeing you, Sunshine, but we have to go!' Amanda declared. 'We've got to pick up Orion's girlfriend from the airport!'

Of course he has a girlfriend.

'Oh, she didn't come with you?' I asked, for the sake of something to say.

Orion shook his head. 'She couldn't get off work until now. She's a nurse.'

Of course she is.

They waved goodbye, and I was annoyed to find myself feeling dejected. Even more so because I couldn't put my finger on why.

Until I did.

My career choice doesn't make me feel like a lesser person, but I'll never be compatible with someone like Orion. A regular person. A professional. Someone who probably plays tennis and has dinner parties that don't end three days later. Someone who doesn't find the antics of rock stars funny or commonplace.

Someone who would never go out with a stripper. And someone who would never ask his girlfriend for drug money.

HIGHLIGHT: I *did* think I perhaps saw Orion sneak a peek at my tits.
DOWNSIDE: My B-cup tits.

22 April

I'm normally a happy-go-lucky person, if maybe a tad jaded. I usually love life and being alive. If my cup is half empty, I'll refill it. But things are not going my way. My relationship, my job woes, the pokey little apartment and the crippling cold are all wearing me down.

When Jim is unhappy, he can be scathing towards me and his work ethic vanishes. Each day, he both insults and relies on me.

I feel like shit. My body is putting on weight because of the cold, like a whale armoured with blubber. At first I thought I was developing body dysmorphia, but I'm just getting fat. I want to eat salad, but the cold requires stodge. I'm more than happy to starve myself or throw up everything I eat. Who wouldn't, when their naked body is exposed to a hundred pairs of staring eyes most nights? Then I binge because I'm hungry.

I keep thinking of Orion, and how my fluttering behaviour might have seemed pathetic to him. Why not? It seems pathetic to *me*. Maybe he even laughed about it with his perfect nurse girlfriend. Then they probably went to bed at a reasonable hour. Not 5 a.m. They probably have nice, sweet sex.

I have no sex. Jim and I are just constantly bickering.

I can't even see my abs anymore. Each night, I climb up on the podium and wonder if the crowd is looking at my cellulite. I'm terrified that they're thinking, *She's too fat, why is she stripping?* Even though I am a rational person and know men love all body types, I can't help the irrational thoughts that bombard me, making me cringe about the way I look. I'm having a prolonged pity party for one.

Only a few months back I was confident and comfortable in my skin. I never used to let it bother me that I worked with spectacularly beautiful girls. I felt self-assured that nobody compared to me—not because I think I'm perfect, or even beautiful, but because there is only one me. Every stripper is unique, and we all have to remember this, otherwise we grow terrified of competition.

I'm in the midst of this now. The Penthouse Pets are suddenly attacking me, though they don't know it. When faced with their beauty, I see the lack of my own.

I was asked to do a test shoot for *Penthouse* last year, which seems so long ago. Obviously I was a lot thinner, yet I said no. And I would give the same answer now, if some partially blind photographer came along and inquired.

I don't object to shots of naked women in magazines. Some of this photography is beautiful, and the female form is a stunning sight (except mine). But that shit is around *forever*, especially in the age of the world wide web. I couldn't handle the thought of my dad, brother, uncles, cousins or, even worse, possible future children seeing my nether regions exposed in a men's magazine.

Though the money from a nude photo shoot would come in handy right about now.

When a club is going through a quiet period, we dancers suffer the most, and it quickly becomes a catch 22. We must be on our mental A-game to hustle well; we must sparkle, or we don't get paid. But when you've made zero night after night, a misery sets in that is obvious to all. Worse, after a while you go from being morose to desperate, and the customers will sense this and toy with you. There's no point going to work when you obviously don't want to be there: your tired indifference will not make you a single dollar.

The physical and mental strain can be overwhelming. Some days, I just don't want to get out of bed. Why go to the effort to maintain a perfect tan, nails, make-up and hair, all to sit looking pretty in a club for no financial gain?

After trying my damnedest, I only made $180 tonight, which will go on the gas bill. I *refuse* to touch another cent of my savings. I will *not* allow my financial future to bleed away from ill-luck. Nest eggs need to be protected, especially while they're not being feathered.

When I arrived home, I threw myself into a scorching-hot shower. I cleaned my body, removed my make-up and scrubbed the night from my soul.

When will things get better? Is my good luck fairy taking a cigarette break?

HIGHLIGHT: Gas won't get turned off.
DOWNSIDE: Ate pasta in fit of despair. Didn't let it stay in my stomach.

FRENEMIES

30 April ....

Exotic dancers can be easily misunderstood, or even misdiagnosed as bipolar, on account of our yo-yo emotions. I've been feeling a lot happier since I met a really cool chick from Ireland, Misha. She arrived at work the other night, stalked up to me and asked, 'Are you that gorgeous creature living in the apartment block my husband and I just moved into?'

In my vulnerable state, I melted like a super-sized cola slushy at the beach.

Misha and her husband, Joel, have relocated from Melbourne because he landed a job as head promoter for a nightclub.

'I noticed you down at the letterbox,' Misha went on, 'and I developed an instant inferiority complex after seeing you without make-up. Life just isn't fair!'

Misha gave me the shot of self-confidence I needed. She's fun and easygoing, and she never tires of complimenting me. And I never tire of hearing it.

I've also adored her husband from the get-go. 'Is this the goddess you've been telling me about, then?' he asked in his lilting accent when I invited them over for coffee.

Jim and Joel formed an instant rapport because they love old music and can chat about it for hours. Unfortunately, they both also share a huge fondness for marijuana.

Neither of the couple is physically attractive, at least not to me, but their charm makes up for what they lack in the looks department. Misha's larger-than-life personality is so sexy that she's been helping me out at work. 'I'm not dancing for you unless my best friend comes too!' she tells patrons. 'We're a double act.' The guys are mesmerised and can't bear the thought of not having her writhe on their laps, so they shell out for me to come along. It's amazing that she's flat-out busy on quiet nights while all the glamorous Penthouse Pets are complaining about the lack of money.

The only problem is Aurora. While Ryan loves the couple as much as Jim and I do, for some reason Aurora is dubious. She even warned me to be careful. I don't know if my old friend is jealous of my new friend, but she hasn't warmed at all to the Irish lass.

I don't get it. How can anybody that sweet, and willing to go out of their way to help, be remotely villainous?

HIGHLIGHT: New BFF.
DOWNSIDE: Older BFF with knickers in a twist.

8 May

I'm weighing up the pros and cons of having a boob job. I've noticed that girls with fake boobs have a habit of inviting people to squeeze, prod and admire their rack. They talk about the boobs openly and fondly, as though they are a zippy little sports car rather than an altered body part: 'Look how amazingly shaped my tits are! See how high and round? Come have a feel, check out how soft they are!' Can fake boobs ever feel like a true part of yourself? They are objects, after all, bought to be exhibited proudly.

Misha was horrified when I shared these thoughts with her. 'Why turn a lovely pair of mandarins into a couple of concrete cantaloupes?' she asked, groping one for good measure.

I adore my new friends. Thanks to them, I'm basking in the sunshine of life rather than dwelling in depressed shadows—even though it's so fucking cold in Adelaide, the sun itself no doubt finds Iceland balmy in comparison.

The money side of things is looking up too. Jim is doing some promotional work with Joel, helping to create hype for big nights with major DJs at the nightclub Joel practically runs. And with Misha's help, I'm finally averaging around four hundred dollars a night. I can work fewer shifts and have some semblance of a life again.

Jim and I are getting along much better. Each night before work, we take turns with Misha and Joel cooking dinner for one another. Then the boys drive me and Misha to work, where we remain joined at the hip.

Ryan hangs out with us sometimes because he also gets along with our new friends, but Aurora doesn't. She's distanced herself from me and has become tight with a beautiful but sour Indian girl, Floss. At work they huddle together whispering, their eyes flashing my way. Whenever I walk past, I hear Floss muttering cynical comments like 'she'll learn' or 'wait for her to find out the hard way'. Misha laughs openly in their faces. But although the situation is awkward, I'm having such a great time that I've decided to ignore it.

On our nights off, we visit a lot of groovy little cocktail lounges. Until now I had no idea Adelaide boasted such a glorious labyrinth of subterranean nightlife. The four of us soak up the ambience and drink experimental cocktails, then stagger home to chat for hours while Marvin Gaye and Otis Redding play softly in the background.

The couple do go on a bit much about how beautiful I am. I never thought I'd tire of it, but hearing it nonstop is slightly irksome, as though it's being enforced.

Oh well, life is pretty damn good if compliments are my biggest problem.

HIGHLIGHT: Am proud to be the type of person who makes friends easily and accepts all types.

DOWNSIDE: Jealous of Aurora and Floss. Traitors.

10 May

Misha pissed me off for the first time tonight.

A big movie star was in town, and I mean big enough that his face would probably be recognised in some parts of the outer solar system. I think of him as Cowboy, even though he's never done a western. Mostly he makes shit action movies that gross squillions at the box office.

Cowboy's real-life personality is as attractive as a weeping scab. He strutted into the club and surveyed it like a ruler casting an eye over his serfs. I've never been much of a fan, and this little act showed me he's an egotistical arsehole. Misha, on the other hand, clearly thought he was the duck's nuts and almost broke an ankle sprinting towards him while I ran the other way.

I guess my friend impressed Cowboy in some way, because she dragged me out of the lap-dance room to drink Dom Perignon, boastfully provided by Cowboy, with the two of them. As I sat down, he asked me not to look him directly in the eye. Seriously, did the dickhead think I'd never had Dom before, and that I'd be dictated to for a glass of bubbles?

Bored out of my skull by his self-absorbed conversation, I only stayed because he was handing us fifty-dollar notes as though they were pieces of chewing gum. In contrast, Misha was carrying on like an orgasmic groupie.

After listening to Cowboy's banal crap for a full hour, I began to think snorting my own vomit might be preferable. 'I broke up with my supermodel girlfriend because I couldn't indulge her primal desire for narcissistic procreation.' Why couldn't he just say she wanted a baby? 'Oh, I couldn't accept eighteen million dollars for my last movie—playing a corrupt cop challenged my advanced humanitarian standing and compromised my empathy for feminist values. I had to ask for twenty million dollars.' Apparently this hadn't bothered him the last twenty times he played a corrupt cop.

Then Misha leaned over to me and whispered, 'Listen up. He wants you and me to go to his penthouse. He'll pay big money.'

I frowned in disgust. 'No way. Not even if the Dalai Lama offered to drive us there.'

'Please? Come on, Sunshine! He wants both of us, *please* do this one favour for me.'

Cowboy watched us (perfectly okay for *him* to stare) with a bemused look on his smug face, obviously convinced we'd cater to his request.

'No.' I crossed my arms. 'I'm not having sex with that conceited piece of shit. I can't believe you would ask me to. I'm not a hooker,

Misha. Besides, Ruby wouldn't let us leave with him anyway.'

I wasn't sure if this was true. Celebrities, especially major ones, live by a different set of rules, and laws are bent for them. Management would possibly be *impressed* if we left to show Cowboy a good time; they'd be able to say, 'Our girls are so beautiful and special, even a big star like Cowboy is besotted with them.'

'We don't have to fuck him!' Misha pleaded in a furious whisper.

'What does he want to pay us for, then? I know it isn't our company—he's more than happy with the sound of his own voice.'

'He wants us to dress up like dolls . . . and lie on the bed without moving.'

'And?' I asked suspiciously.

'He wants to whack off over us.'

I stared at her in disbelief. 'You realise there's a word for that? *Necrophilia.*'

'But we don't even have to get naked! And he says he has costumes at home.'

'I'm *so* out of here.' I rose, repulsed, as Misha grabbed my hand.

'Wait, Sunshine! Will you just *listen*? There's nothing to be scared of! Cowboy explained he can't get an erection with substandard, urban ideals of fundamental sex. *And he's willing to pay us a grand each!*'

As I began to stomp away, I heard Cowboy mutter that she should just let me go, and that mediocre drones will always cling to their unremarkable comfort zone when faced with the boundlessness of an exceptional hierarchy. Or some such drivel.

'You're a twat,' I told him without ceremony. 'And after the misfortune of seeing one of your movies, what I'm *faced* with is how I'll never get those two hours of my life back.'

Misha was signalling like crazy for me to shut up. But I was on a roll and royally pissed off. Movie stars are no better than the rest of us, just more fortunate, and a pet hate of mine is their inability to remain grateful and gracious.

'And for the record, using big words to show off that you know them doesn't make you sound intelligent, just smarmy and pathetic.'

HIGHLIGHT: I walked off with the bottle of Dom.
DOWNSIDE: Why are all famous people perverted pricks?

12 May

Misha apologised profusely and even had a bunch of roses at the ready. I forgave her. Knowing what I know now, I should have stripped off the petals and flagellated her with the thorns.

I've repeated my mistake with Demoness. Why do I trust people so easily? Why do I assume they share my morals? Why do I keep making friends with freaks from overseas?

The night began wonderfully. It was Jim's birthday. We went out and ate seafood, washing it down with copious amounts of wine. Even Ryan and Aurora made the effort to come out with Jim, Misha, Joel and me. But after three bars and two night-clubs, Ryan and Aurora called it a night; they had no interest in what we had planned for the rest of the evening. As a birthday present, I was going to give Jim something he'd always wanted: a girl-on-girl show.

Misha was a very willing partner. We'd arranged it the week before, and I'd been nervous in the lead-up. Now, with at least twenty drinks under my belt, I was looking forward to it.

'Be careful,' said Aurora, hugging me goodnight. I was far too drunk to take heed.

The four of us bought a giant bottle of vodka and took it home. Sexy music was playing in the background as Misha and

I undressed each other. She licked my nipples and worked her way down my stomach to my thighs. The boys were sitting beside the bed with matching expressions of intense expectation—much like you see on a dog just before you throw a ball.

At first it was all passionate and lovely. I melted when Misha started licking between my legs, feeling like my body was made of hot liquid. I moaned helplessly as I grabbed her and kissed her with abandon. My experience with Chloe in Darwin had felt slightly put-on for showmanship purposes, but this girl was turning my body into fire. Returning the oral favour wasn't my favourite bit, as I'm not overly partial to the taste of girls, but I was happily caught up in the moment.

Then, as most naughty things do, it all went pear-shaped.

I felt Jim kissing my neck in amorous encouragement, which made me realise the boys had invited themselves onto the bed. It was supposed to be *girl-on-girl*! I wasn't crazy about this development—in fact, I was a little offended. Until shock took over.

Through a haze of alcohol I shook my head a few times, trying to grasp what I saw.

Jim was kissing *Misha's* neck. *Not* mine. Which meant that Joel was the one slobbering at me.

Before my eyes, Misha threw her head back as she moaned in abandon, gripped Jim's arse and pulled him towards her. My boyfriend didn't hesitate to accept her invitation, and I saw his dick slide into her.

I bolted upright, stunned to witness Joel naked and leering with a question in his eyes. I shook my head frantically, resembling a slasher-movie bimbo facing a murderer in a hockey mask. Scrambling away, I accidentally kicked Joel's dick. But he didn't care; he simply turned to watch the spectacle of his wife being pounded by my boyfriend.

The worst thing was that Jim and Misha never once bothered to check for my consent. They just assumed I was okay with what they were doing, and that I'd be merrily doing the same thing.

The sight of Jim blissfully fucking another woman—*without my permission*—was heartbreaking enough. But it was their intensity that shredded me; they were *immersed* in one another. Jim never meets my stare when we have sex, but I now understand the phrase 'locked eyes'. They were so taken by each other that they fell off the bed, knocking over our big bottle of vodka *without even noticing*!

My libido had withered and died. My head was spinning.

Jim picked her up without missing a beat and walked into the kitchen, where he screwed her on the bench. Joel followed, masturbating over the spectacle.

I have never been so sickened. I sprang from the bed, taking the vodka dregs with me, and locked myself in our hobbit-sized spare room. Sitting against the door, I tried to cry but couldn't catch my breath enough to sob. My chest heaved uncontrollably. This went on for hours—yes, *hours*. All I could hear were the animal moans of soulless sex, as Jim indulged in a threesome without a care in the world.

Nobody came knocking to see if I was alright. Revolted and nauseated, I couldn't even bear to leave the hobbit room to throw up. I used the vase.

Eventually, after what felt like a million years, they stopped. I could smell a joint being smoked, and I heard soft laughter and relaxed chit-chat. Then the front door opened, and they had a kissy-kissy goodbye: 'Oh, yes, let's get together tomorrow.' Jim yawned loudly and went to bed. I added 'incredulous' to my raging emotions.

I am appalled, disgusted, wounded. What kind of people *are* they? What kind of person is Jim? I thought I knew him, but who on earth is happy to let genital swapping go on without discussing it first?

It dawned on me, as I cried in that tiny room, that this probably wasn't the first time those vermin had preyed on someone like me. The compliments and instant camaraderie were all a ploy to lure their victims into non-consensual swinging. How stupid could I have been?

And I cannot believe Jim. How could he think it was okay to fuck that bitch in front of me? How is he okay with her husband wanting to fuck *me* in front of *him*? We've been through a lot together, but we've never had sex with other people.

Okay, there was Chloe, but that doesn't count. It was superficial, and I felt nothing.

Jim just cheated in front of my face.

In the past four years, I have seen plenty of things that have altered me and made me fear for humanity. But I have never been as shocked and violated as I am now. I've never been so changed.

HIGHLIGHT: Threw up the mud cake I had for dessert.
DOWNSIDE: Ran out of vodka. Those motherfuckers.

May 13th

I just stared at Jim in accusation, since I had no words.

'What?' he said, looking defiant.

This sent me off the deep end. 'It wasn't okay!' I shrieked. 'You allowed that to happen. *You!* I expected it from them—they're sexual parasites. But you went at it like a pig to a trough. You make me *sick*.'

'Do you want me to apologise for something I enjoyed? I didn't know you had a problem with it.'

'Really? Which bit made you think I was feeling all warm and fuzzy? When I locked myself in the spare room to cry, or when I threw up uncontrollably? Oh, wait, you didn't even *notice* I was gone.'

'I didn't know.' He sounded forlorn, but his ignorance made me feel even more ill.

'Get out of my sight. I can't even look at you.'

And that was true. But I *could* glare at Misha. I went to work early to avoid her, where I told Aurora everything.

'I *knew* it!' my friend said, enraged. 'That's why I was so frightened for you—I knew she was a fucking leech. Maybe she only wanted Jim to herself all along.'

Misha was welcome to him.

Floss, who'd also listened to the story, shook her head in disgust. 'Misha is impolite slime. It's never okay to impose yourself on people sexually. It doesn't matter that it wasn't forceful or abusive, it was cunning and immoral.'

But Misha, with her feisty personality, wasn't frightened off easily by our trio of glares.

'Can I talk to you for a moment, Sunshine?' The lilting accent I'd found so charming now offended my ears.

'No. And if you ever approach me again, my actions will make the IRA look like an angelic bunch. Plus, I'll lie and tell management you stole all my money.'

Now I know why all the guys in the club love her. Men can smell a slut.

HIGHLIGHT: Thought of the perfect Marilyn Monroe quote to tell Misha:

'Sweetie, if you're going to be two-faced, at least make one of them pretty.'

DOWNSIDE: Forgot to quote Ms Monroe to Misha.

INFLATED EGO

....

To add insult to injury, Jim has been spending most of his time at Joel and Misha's. He knows he isn't welcome at home, since I've coldly demanded he disappear from my view. I even used the words 'barbecue prong', 'eyeballs' and 'if you don't fuck off' more than once. But he could have taken refuge at Ryan and Aurora's apartment, couldn't he?

God only knows what he might be up to.

Needing to unscramble my brain, I ventured out into the frost-laden morning. The cold hurt my hands and face, but it felt like a good thing. Sometimes we need some physical discomfort to distract us from the agony in our minds.

It was strange to watch Adelaide come alive with rat-race normalcy, while I ambled along, trying to clear my tortured head. How sick a contrast life was sometimes.

I did my best to pull the nightmare apart. At the core, it seemed, was Jim's disregard for me. His selfish neglect of my feelings was the lowest act of disloyalty in my eyes.

I was also bothered by the three of them assuming I would engage in their thoughtless rutting. In fact, I felt violated by their expectation that I would join in. Even when I had expressed shock and outrage, they hadn't shown any concern for me, implicitly telling me to fuck off and let them enjoy their threesome. I'd wanted to shout, 'Everybody, stop! I'm repulsed by what you're doing! I'm not built for sex without a connection.'

As I walked down the frozen street, I realised that something else was enraging me. They'd somehow made me feel like *I* was the outcast—a prissy puritan. My morals had made me the odd one out. My boyfriend and our friends had brushed me aside.

And threaded among that rage was my self-blame for trusting Joel and Misha to have the respect not to overstep during the girl-on-girl scene I'd arranged.

I stopped suddenly at a pedestrian crossing, people brushing past me in irritation as I forgot to move. A stunned thought had surfaced, and my legs were unsteady, so I looked around for somewhere to sit and soon found a bench outside a clothing shop. I didn't feel the chill of the sleet falling on me; I'd turned from icy-cold to burning with rage. But was it directed at Jim or myself?

It had just dawned on me that subconsciously I'd been living under his control. Sure, he had followed me from place to place, letting me lead him to where the money was best. But along the way I'd allowed him to label me, even when I hadn't put any on myself. Every time he'd insulted my profession and belittled my character because of it, reaching for derogatory slurs, I'd let him. A part of me had believed that because of my job, he had some sort of entitlement to do so. Because strippers are looked down on by most people, I'd thought it was only to be expected—even by those who know me better.

It actually wasn't surprising that Jim had thought I'd be willing to get down and dirty in a foursome; some part of his mind thought of my integrity as non-existent. Maybe he'd even encouraged me to strip at the beginning so my morality would be loosened while he gained ammunition against me.

I work as a stripper, yes. But Jim has often treated me like being a stripper is who I am entirely. How could I have not seen it for so long?

Right then, on that bench in the pouring rain, I made the decision to show him what kind of woman I really was. One who *only* strips for a living—and, from here on out, lives by mighty ideals of her own.

The feminist in me roared. My body, my choices, my values and my profession. All *mine*. Not yours to stereotype anymore, Jim.

I'll start by doing something that's been on my mind for quite a while. It will seem to him that I'm wandering further down a clichéd path, but in fact this is a way for me to take the power back, while enhancing it.

For ages I've thought about having my breasts enlarged, but I haven't said anything serious about it to Jim because I know he'll be dismissive and call me a stupid stripper. In fact, I've been worried that everyone will label me a vapid tramp if I have a boob job. But now I realise I should only do what I think is best for me.

I've always wanted to have larger breasts. If I'd been happy with my bust size, the barbs from patrons about 'small boobs' wouldn't have mattered to me. I'm doing this because I want to become more appealing to myself, not to men.

Since making this decision, I've felt euphoric. I don't give a shit what anyone else will think about it, and this makes me feel in control again.

Fuck Jim, fuck Misha and fuck Joel. I'm going to turn myself into the most sexually confident being I can be—one who isn't afraid to flaunt the body she's always wanted. One who will make her own choices about how and when to be sexual. One so sure of herself, nobody will dare look upon her again with the expectation that she'll go against her principles by having meaningless sex.

And Jim will hate it. Good.

HIGHLIGHT: Glacial air made my skin go botox-smooth.

DOWNSIDE: Had to call out to a shopkeeper for help after my wet jeans froze to the bench.

20 May

'I've booked in to have my boobs done in three days' time,' I announced to Jim when he finally dared to come home.

He stared at me in disbelief. 'You're not serious?'

My cold gaze told him I was deadly serious.

'Can we at least discuss this?' he asked.

'I think you and I have pretty much reached a "do whatever the fuck you like" stage in our relationship. So, no.'

'But *why*?' he whined.

'A number of reasons, but your disgusting behaviour set it in motion. You left me stranded in a situation that made me feel powerless, and I've come to a decision that gives me full power over myself.'

He shook his head incredulously. 'You've entered a whole new spectrum of stupidity.'

'Wow. Who would have thought a stoner knew such big words?'

'Don't be a fucking smart-arse.'

'*There's* the Jim I know!' I clapped. 'You know what? I've been afraid of your opinions for too long, while you've clearly established that you don't care about mine. But you've also done me a favour—you reminded me that I don't bow to anyone's assumptions.'

'I can't believe you want to distort your body into some sick idealisation of what men want.'

I smiled, having anticipated this line of argument. 'Bullshit.'

'*Bullshit?* You're turning yourself into an inflated human fuck-toy! How do you see it as *bullshit*?'

My voice grew arctic. 'Like the fuck-toy you perceived me to be last week? The toy you were willing to hand over to another man? But that's beside the point. This is my way to take control while the world judges my preferences—including you.'

He gave me a nasty, mocking smile. 'Now *I* call bullshit. You're doing this to get back at me and so more men will notice you.'

'That's the exact response I expected. You express liberal views, but you're really just a misogynist at heart, aren't you? You assume everything a woman does is related to the approval of men, you stupid shit. If a girl chips a tooth and makes an emergency dental appointment, do you think the first thing on her mind is a *man*? I mean, it's not *really* an emergency, is it? Fixing a hillbilly tooth is cosmetic, right? But no girl with pride is going to tolerate looking at it in the mirror. And when we paint our nails, highlight our hair, wax our legs, tan our skin, buy new clothes, design our tattoos, make our noses smaller and our lips bigger, do you truly think the only reason is that we think *men* will appreciate it?'

Jim tried to interrupt.

'Don't speak. Women do these things for personal reasons in relation to how we feel about *ourselves*. The whole beauty-comes-from-within idea is a myth, probably created by men. *No* light shines from inside if the outside isn't shining too.'

He attempted to talk again.

'Didn't I tell you not to speak?' I snarled. 'Just so you know—not that I have to explain myself to you—I've always felt disproportionate. I want my boobs to match my hips, and improving on something I see as a flaw will make me feel better about myself.'

'I think you're about to become another walking-joke bimbo,' he muttered.

'Do you?' I debated. 'Well, men like you created the idea of the bimbo. You ram your beauty ideals down our throats—how small our arses should be, how large our breasts should measure and how taut our stomachs should appear. And when we try to meet these standards, you *still* try to take us down, and you're especially harsh if we don't go along with all your pornographic wishes. You call us uppity bitches for our troubles. So far as I can see, the only way women can win this war is by pleasing ourselves first. And that's exactly what I'm going to do—with a pair of double Ds.'

'And where are you getting the money for this?' Jim asked, self-righteous and surly.

I tried not to boil over. 'From the savings *I* earned. And before you ask—no, there's not enough left over for a penis extension.'

'You're being irrational,' he snapped, irrationally.

'No, Jim, what's irrational here is a *man* thinking he has a say in what a *woman* does with her own body. And the fact you even think you're *entitled* to an opinion. Next you'll be telling me abortion is wrong.'

'Well . . .'

I fixed him with a look much like I imagined Hillary Clinton gave Bill whenever Monica was mentioned.

He attempted to change tack. 'Don't I get any say in this?' he wheedled. 'I'll have to live with your body too. I mean, we're partners, aren't we?'

'That would imply a *partnership*.' I walked into the bedroom and grabbed my trusty dictionary; I like Wikipedia, but I love my grandmother's old book more. '*Partnership*,' I recited. '*An arrangement where parties agree to cooperate and advance their mutual interests.*' I shut the book with a snap. 'I had no interest in seeing your dick in another girl. So I wouldn't say we're partners. In fact, I'm not even sure I'd call you a friend, let alone my boyfriend. Come to think of it, the word "boyfriend" is almost an oxymoron, isn't it?'

'You're the *moron*!' he fired off without any ammunition.

I was serene when I said, 'And you're a cheating, untrustworthy, ignorant piece of shit.'

'Whatever.'

I sniggered as I left the room. The word 'whatever' is another way of saying 'bitch has got me beat'.

HIGHLIGHT: Scored two points by winning argument and selling Jim's weed at work.

DOWNSIDE: Half my savings.

22 May

Oh *God*! What am I *thinking*!? I'm turning myself into an inflated human fuck-toy!

I can't eat or drink as of midnight—doctor's orders. Not that I could eat. The thought of what I'm doing sends shock waves of nauseating adrenaline through me.

Okay, *calm down*! Just calm down. You're going to look *amazing*. No more small boobs and large bottom.

Misha knocked at the door, then stood there with an apologetic look and a bunch of flowers. It wasn't the right time to test my frazzled nerves. I stomped on the bouquet until it resembled a baking tray, and I told her to beat it before I called immigration. I've done it before, I'll do it again.

11 p.m.
What if I die under anaesthetic?

11.15 p.m.
Wonder if no food or drink includes an icy pole.

11.17 p.m.
In eight hours, I'll be a big-breasted beast . . .
  Or goddess?
  Or monster . . .
  Or Penthouse Pet!!!

HIGHLIGHT: Decided no food or drink didn't include a Weis Bar. All three in the box.
DOWNSIDE: *Fat* human fuck-toy.

23 May

Woot-woot. Whoa. Didn't realise *The Bold and the Beautiful* was a comedy. Characters hilarious. Wonder if it's time for another pain-killer? Remembered am supposed to be irate. But pharmaceuticals got in way. Also remembered I am a fairy. Was a fairy, I mean. When I was eight. In the garden. Found powdered cement-mix in shed and thought was fairy dust. Sprinkled it over garden. Mum came out and told me if I didn't stay outside for another two hours playing, fingers would set together forever. Stayed three, just in case. Selfish wench just wanted me-time. Wonder if it's time for another painkiller? Wonder if it will hurt to get up and wee? Why is Hollywood still allowing Woody Allen to live there and make movies after he married his own daughter? Why do people watch his movies anyway? They're crap. Visual Novocaine. Want to turn TV off and read. *Bold and Beautiful* no longer funny. Jim gone to get pizza. Hate Jim. Don't want pizza. Want hot cross buns. Ha! Just remembered Jim didn't get me an Easter egg this year! Hate Jim. What have bunny rabbits got to do with Easter? Want to read but can't feel brain. Have new Dexter novel. Is Jeff Lindsay best author on planet? Probably. Better to wait anyway. Words of world's wittiest serial killer best read without influence of narcotics. Does Dexter tweet? Do celebrities post on FB themselves? Is it still a selfie if someone else took the photo? Wonder how Orion and his perfect girlfriend are doing. Probly having perfect dinner parties with organic sun-dried capsicum and goat's fetta croquettes. *So* early millennium. Why can't spiders all be blue and pink and yellow. Less scary. Wonder if it will hurt to get up and wee? Hate Jim. Oh look! Time for another painkiller! Woot-woot.

HIGHLIGHT: Dexter is even *better* read on drugs!
DOWNSIDE: Would advise having a catheter instead of getting up to wee after four kilos grafted to chest.

29 May

I gather Aurora had visited me already, but my company had no doubt been comical under the influence of hospital-grade drugs. This time I was lucid enough to chat.

My friend sat by my bed and stared at my chest with a huge grin. 'What's new?' she said, and we dissolved into uncontrollable giggles. Her, because of my impossible cup size, and me, because I'm still higher than a NASA satellite.

My boobs are *mammoth*. I don't know what to think, so it's lucky I *can't* think properly.

I remember lying on the hospital gurney with a drip attached to my arm. At the crucial moment, just as the anaesthetic hit my bloodstream, my doctor leaned over and reported, 'I've just measured your hips again . . . and I think we should go a bit bigger.' That was the last thing I heard before oblivion claimed me.

I woke up with a pair of bowling balls grafted to my chest. I look like a carrier pigeon. Dolly Parton would be tearing off her wig in envy if she could see me. Oh God. Oh God. *Oh God!* What have I done to myself? Jim was right: I look like a blow-up doll. A beaten wife version. The skin on my earth-destroying comets is blue-black and shiny from being pulled tighter than anything Joan Rivers could have achieved.

Aurora insisted they're fantastic. They are hideous.

When Jim brought in some food, he tried not to look reproach-fully at my titanic chest. This is not all that bothersome, because I still find it hard to look at Jim full stop.

I will not admit I was wrong to him. I will not. Only to myself. When I'm alone. Crying hysterically.

HIGHLIGHT: Opioids.
DOWNSIDE: Will forever look pregnant in loose tops.

6 June ···

I didn't want to record the mental torture of the past week. But as it turns out, things are wonderful! The bruising has faded, and the swelling has gone down. I am the proud owner of a big, bouncy pair of double Ds! And I am the gatekeeper of my emotions again.

I still deeply despise Joel and Misha, but I refuse to allow them any more influence on my life. If I dwell on what they did to me, they win; by obliterating their memory and moving forward with new confidence, I do.

Plus I'll make damn certain I'm never again naked on a bed with more than one penis in the room.

Jim has a lot of making up to do if we're going to salvage our relationship. The one intelligent thing he's done is sever his friendship with the pair of maggots. He is acting his most attentive towards me, and he's the picture of caring, concern and companionship in front of visitors. He hasn't yet stopped sneakily looking at my new boobs as though they are an insult, though.

While I try to act blasé in the company of others, I can't lie to myself: I'm so goddamn *impressed* with my choice. I don't look anything like a pigeon, and I feel like sending my doctor chocolates. Even better, my bottom has shrunk and my waist is non-existent because I've been picking at my food.

HIGHLIGHT: My new melons outshine everything going pear-shaped!

DOWNSIDE: Know I will gorge a family-size pizza and Cadbury block as soon as appetite returns.

10 June

Aurora caught me preening in a car window this afternoon, and admonished me, promising to keep me grounded. 'If you ever become one of those vain, egomaniac bitches who think the world was created to worship them, I'll stab you to death.'

'If I ever become one of those vain bitches, I'll hand you the knife.'

What a great friend she is. She keeps it real, which is what I need. Because there are three of every person: the one you think you are, the one that others see, and the one you *really* are.

In the past, I've been guilty of what I call Stripper Attitude. How would this be defined on Wikipedia? Well, the page would probably read: *Pretty girls with ugly characteristics, due to repeated exposure to adulation.* In short, sometimes we think we're better than the average person, which is quite strange when the general public think the opposite.

Stripper Attitude can include a range of unattractive behaviours: a lack of respect for those less sexually overt (almost any woman who isn't a stripper), gloating over your lifestyle, and using your profession, along with your face and body, to get free drinks and party drugs along with coveted VIP entry to openings and backstage parties.

I've been guilty of all these things, and my tendency to cave in to external influences is the very reason it's important I take care not to become a big-breasted arsehole. I've long suspected the seeds of imagined superiority lie dormant in my soul; I just do my best to keep them dehydrated. It feels good to be the brazen, self-assured, uncompromising me again, but I'll use my new boobs for good. I'll make more money than ever and put it away for the future. They're an asset, not an excuse for me to act like a self-centred bitch.

I was mulling this over when my phone rang. Tara, Candy and Jade were calling to see how I was feeling after the operation, bless them.

'Text us a photo of your tits!' they chorused.

I obliged, or rather, Aurora did. (I have decided it cannot, in fact, be called a selfie if another is snapping you; it's a self-helpie.)

Where would we be without friends? Regardless of my brattish flaws, I know I'm not a complete monster thanks to how strongly I feel about the people I love.

This has led me to another revelation—Adelaide seems to be the place for them. Putting my foot down has inspired me to put it forward too. I've realised how much I miss *all* my best friends, and where I need to be.

7.32 p.m.

Despite still finding it hard to look at Jim for too long, I stared him down tonight. 'I'm moving back to Cairns.'

He made a face like a smacked arse and looked as though he would start an argument. Which would have gotten him exactly nowhere—I've made up my mind.

'With or without you,' I added.

Then my phone rang.

When I hung up, he lost his glower at the sight of my expression. I felt all the blood drain from my face as the mirage of Cairns faded from importance.

I'm not going anywhere but Melbourne. My grandfather just died.

DOWNSIDE.

11 June ··

> *Better by far you should forget and smile*
> *Than that you should remember and be sad.*
>
> CHRISTINA ROSSETTI, 'REMEMBER'

It only took an hour for me to pack my humble belongings this morning, then another half-hour to hug Aurora goodbye, and half a second to stick up my middle finger at Misha. It's roughly an eight-hour drive from Adelaide to Melbourne. I barely said a word to Jim during those hours. I didn't particularly want him to come with me, but he insisted on driving the whole trek so I didn't have to do it myself. Plus, we technically still *are* a couple.

In the past month, I've experienced a foursome fuck-up, major surgery and the loss of my grandfather.

Now here I am in Melbourne, mourning with my family. Well, I was, but since it's midnight, they've all gone to bed. I've been walking around the darkened house like a wraith, memories of my grandfather spearing my heart.

I considered sneaking out to do a quick shift in a club to take my mind off things. I'm not being callous, it's just that there's not much I can do for my family in the late hours, and the carnival atmosphere of clubs can help me feel better. Sometimes the music is louder than my thoughts.

But I've decided against it, remembering how much I loathed working in this town. The club always had too many girls on the books—I was once rostered on with ninety dancers in one night. Plus, like in Sydney, the girls here are so competitive that some will take your eye out with a pair of nail scissors if you so much as look at their Regular. Not that you can blame them: cheap lap dances promote a cut-throat atmosphere.

I have a strange relationship with this big, gritty city. There's beauty in its heritage-listed buildings, and in its cafes down graffiti-splattered laneways.

Some say Melbourne is the height of trendiness. No sooner has a bar selling rosewater ingested from a gold-plated oxygen mask become the place to be, it's already outdated. Melbourne—always ahead of the fads, or willing to make up its own.

I'm allowed to talk ill of this metropolis. I was born here, you see, and some part of me will always belong to it.

I did need some alone time, so I tiptoed out of the house and drove to the city, where I found an all-night cafe. I sat outside alone while the wind whipped its icy tentacles against my skin.

As I sipped my coffee, I began to cry. And nobody looked at me. It wasn't that nobody cared; it's just that in Melbourne, all forms of self-expression are permissible. Being yourself in public is celebrated, whether it involves screaming madness or a mohawk worn with a business suit.

My city, my home town, treats me with respect: it allows me to sob with grief and has the courtesy not to comment.

HIGHLIGHT: The waitress covertly wrote 'Tomorrow, the sun will shine again' on my serviette.

DOWNSIDE: And so it shall, minus one of my favourite people.

13 June

I wish I had gotten to see my grandfather one more time. He was full of merriment, equipped with a Dean Martin style, and the teller of fascinating stories. And I honoured him today by telling my favourite. I offered to deliver his eulogy because no other family member was up for the job; their sorrow was too raw.

I rarely wear black, so I borrowed a pencil skirt, overcoat and leather gloves from my mum. I looked like a sad spy. I wish I could also borrow all her grief and never give it back. I can't imagine what it's like to lose a parent: the loss of a grandparent is heart-rending enough.

There were so many people at the funeral that if my grandad had seen the gathering, he'd have suggested a party.

After I thanked everyone for coming, I said, 'As you all know, my grandfather loved the ocean. So much so, he changed his birth certificate to say he was sixteen, in order to join the navy when he was only fourteen. He once told me about the time he was at sea for almost six months during the Second World War. As the ship finally sailed towards the London docks, all he could think about was a bottle of rum, and a girl or three—sorry Nan, he hadn't met you yet.'

My grandmother gave a fond smile.

'When he docked in London, my grandfather bought his bottle and a girl for about a shilling. After he finished both, he thought he might fork out for more rum and maybe another girl—sorry, Nan. But just as he bought and opened the next bottle, Germany began to bomb London. Grandad looked around for shelter, and all he could see was an old train carriage. So he ducked underneath and watched, sipping rum as parts of London were destroyed. Then he passed out drunk and missed the rest of the show. The next morning he awoke and climbed out from underneath the train. He said that London was in a terrible state—but *nothing* compared to his hangover.'

There were smiles through the tears.

Some might ask if my story was fitting for a funeral. Yes, definitely. He would have been happy I'd told his tale. My bloodline boasts a bawdy, inappropriate sense of humour, passed down through the generations. If I'd talked about his tragic loss, Grandad would have scolded me to 'stop your whingeing'.

I did, however, cry plenty before the service. I wiped my nose with Mum's black leather gloves, causing the dye to run. I delivered the entire eulogy with a Hitler-type moustache—which no one thought to point out.

My grandfather would have laughed his arse off.

HIGHLIGHT: Aunt Bett got stuck into the sherry and provided entertainment by throwing a *Playboy* magazine in Grandad's plot.

DOWNSIDE: Glove dye also gave me Frida Kahlo eyebrows.

15 June

Though my family were in mourning, they couldn't keep their eyes off my boobs. My mum couldn't keep from giggling hysterically whenever she thought I wasn't looking, while the rest of my relatives were clearly wondering why I suddenly have such huge assets. And Jim hasn't refrained from scowling at my breasts as though they are a separate entity; say, for example, a particularly nasty chihuahua I insist on carrying around at all times.

When those we love leave us (or, in the case of Jim, piss us off without an end in sight), we go on as best we can. The tears are drying into memories, and my family have assured me they're going to be okay. They told me that I didn't have to stay, knowing how I feel about Melbourne and sensing all is not well with Jim and me. I also suspect they wanted me to return to pure northern shores so they'll have somewhere to go on holidays.

It was time for me to go back to the sun. I'd been cold for too long.

Jim and I had agreed to have some much-needed time apart, so he's been staying with a cousin across town. So today I flew to Cairns without telling him. Some might think this heartless of me, but it should be put in context. The night after my grandfather's funeral, Jim was seized by the urge to create a new nickname for me: 'Plastic Spastic'.

When I arrived at Cairns International, I breathed a sigh of relief. How I love this exquisite tropical haven. Lush palm trees dance in the floral-scented air, and the humidity caresses your body like silken honey. Mountains thick with emerald rainforest are offset by jewels of purple bougainvillea, fiery hibiscus and blazing yellow wattle. The city cups a trove of nightclubs, bars, restaurants and shopping centres, all fringed by the azure Pacific Ocean.

Jumping in a cab, I headed off to Tara's apartment where the girls were waiting for me: Candy, Jade and Belle, plus another good friend, Charlie. They greeted me by poking my boobs. I had to physically remove Charlie's hands as she went somewhat overboard, to which her natural exuberance makes her prone. I've known her for years, a bouncy girl with curls, freckles and an antenna for listening in on other people's business.

As girls often do, we began by gossiping about our relationships.

Belle had a custody battle on the horizon. 'Can you believe that shit?' she spat. '*He* sleeps until three in the afternoon and thinks marijuana is a secondary source of oxygen, yet the court awarded him custody of our two kids because *I'm* a stripper!'

'Unfortunately, I can,' I commiserated.

'Bullshit, isn't it?'

'Utter,' I agreed, turning to Tara. 'And how about you? Did you work things out with Justin?'

'She did the opposite,' Jade answered before Tara had the chance. 'Now she's seeing the DJ.'

'And apparently, he's *not* gay,' Candy said with a smirk.

Tara exploded. 'Do I look like a friggen *dude*?'

I was floored. 'I can't believe you left Justin for a DJ who wears make-up.'

'Justin and I just grew apart. Look, let's talk about you instead, Sunshine, I haven't seen you for months. How's Jim?'

'What can I say? If you and Justin grew apart, me and Jim put an entire canyon between us.'

'And a few thousand kilometres, evidently.'

'He hates my boobs,' I revealed.

'*What*?' they cried in mutual outrage.

'How can *anyone* hate these massive puppies?' Candy said with reverence. 'I can't think about anything but grabbing another handful.'

'Can you think about what we're doing tonight instead?'

HIGHLIGHT: Jim will be more pissed than a mosquito in a mannequin factory.

DOWNSIDE: Might have to dislocate Charlie's fingers before the day is through.

17 June

My friends are evil. A merry band of demons. Am still drunk.

HIGHLIGHT: Drinks bought for me all night.

DOWNSIDE: Forty of them.

18 June

My hangover is still smarting.

We began at a Mexican bar called Cacti, where we drank tequila as an appetiser. We then went on to the local nightclub, Coconuts, and indulged in shots for dinner. For dessert, we invited the entire club back to Tara's for a party.

I'm now wearing stilettos in bed and have acquired an unmentionable tattoo.

I also have a vague memory of partying with a semi-famous comedian—well known in the business for swinging both ways—and pickpocketing his bag of coke. I'm pretty sure I dragged the girls into the bathroom at Coconuts and snorted the lot, then giggled as I placed the empty baggie back in his pocket. 'You should be illegal, Sunshine,' I recall him saying, exasperated.

Yet I have no remorse, as I'm not a great fan of Comedian. He's the type of person who offers to take the bill up to the counter at a restaurant after a dinner party, just so he can pocket the tips intended for the waitress. And the type who sleeps around knowing he has a venereal disease—he passed one on to my friend.

The coke I stole was a bit strong, though. My eyes had no irises left, so I looked like a demonic possum. But you can rest assured I will not fall once more into the Cairns Trap.

People here drink alcohol like no other place I've ever lived. They blame it on the heat, as it rarely gets cold in these parts. But really, it's lack of control and sheer debauchery, simple as that. Cairns attracts a plethora of somewhat freakish people. Barely anybody I know is actually from here; they have gravitated towards this hedonistic place with little regret over leaving home. Most residents of this town have large, eccentric personalities and an inappropriate demeanour, which is partly why I'm so comfortable here.

Most of my friends work in the hospitality industry and night-club world, and night workers live to party. Like me, they sleep all day, work all evening, and relax with a beverage or ten in the early hours. Drugs also play a large role in this neck of the woods, along with celebrities who are usually passing through to vacation in the famed Port Douglas, an hour up the road.

It's easy to get caught in the party-hard snare. However, if one sets one's mind to it, the goal of clean and healthy living is also easily achievable. In this climate you can pretty much live on fruit and salads, which is what I intend to do, and there are many spectacular walking tracks through the rainforests, yoga classes on tropical beaches, tai chi lessons in the botanical gardens, and places to swim in the Pacific.

So there's no need for me to fall headfirst into the Cairns Trap. Me and my new boobs are on track to fulfil our mission: make plenty of money, buy some real estate, save for a business.

I shall forget the fact that strippers are rarely expected to pay for drinks in bars and clubs, but always expected to show up.

HIGHLIGHT: Am looking for my own place tomorrow.
DOWNSIDE: Jim has called 117 times.

ALL THAT GLITTERS

I've moved into a two-bedroom furnished apartment in a resort. It's beautiful and has maid service, and I only have to pay rent from week to week, without signing a lease or forking out for the usual exorbitant resort prices. This is known as permanent holiday letting and quite easy to obtain if you're in the know.

No sooner had I unpacked my clothes and costumes, than there came a knock at the door. When I opened it, I froze in shock at the sight of Jim. Finally I managed to screech, 'How the fucking hell did you find me?'

'Your Find My Friends app.'

Oh, I'd forgotten to disable it.

'Please, Sunshine, give me one more chance,' he begged. 'I know I didn't support you enough. But I love you—I'm *in* love with you. I promise, I'll never have sex in front of you again. With *anyone* else again, I mean! If you'll have me back, I'll be the best boyfriend any girl ever had. I'll do *anything*.'

'No. *Fucking*. Way.'

'I just drove three thousand kilometres, thirty-four hours straight, *for you*. Just to tell you how I feel. Doesn't that mean anything?

I scrutinised him in the doorway as I thought about it. One more chance?

'Don't throw away four years,' he said. 'Please.'

He *did* drive all that way—I'm guessing immediately after he'd found out I'd left—without stopping, just to tell me he loves me . . .

We *do* have a four-year history.

Am I an idiot? I don't know.

'I'll do anything,' he repeated.

'Okay. You can start by calling every restaurant in town until you find a job. I'm not supporting your dope habit again.'

HIGHLIGHT: Going after the girl you love is very *Jerry Maguire*.
DOWNSIDE: Or *Sleeping with the Enemy* . . .

28 June

I'm on a roll. Jim and I went swimming at a secluded cove all morning, then ate mango and papaya for lunch. For dinner, I wolfed down an organic goat's cheese and rocket salad, and I've also drunk a healthy three litres of water. I feel sparkling for my first night back at work.

The Pacific Gentlemen's Club is slightly old-fashioned and a bit seedy, with its red velvet décor and disco strobe lights. That said, compared to the other even more dingy clubs in town, it is also a bottomless well of money: the vast amounts that go through this club would make a counterfeiter jealous.

There's a casino not too far away, so we're continually graced by high rollers. There are bored tourists looking for a distraction and able to afford it. There are visiting celebrities with more dough than they know what to do with. There are farmers who have contracts with major conglomerates and dollars to burn.

There are cashed-up mine workers stopping over on their way home after working the gold and aluminium mines in Weipa or Papua New Guinea.

And there are my new breasts.

Look out, Cairns, here I come.

HIGHLIGHT: Ready to get down.

DOWNSIDE: Hopefully not weighed down, since my boobs feel kinda heavy.

30 June

Money, money, money! Oh Lord, I'd almost forgotten what it was like to make copious amounts.

Me and my boobs were a hit! The customers' eyes were on stalks like those of crazed cartoon characters. They watched, mesmerised, as my breasts weaved and jiggled in front of them, battling with their inner perverts not to reach out and touch. One guy sat on his hands during a lap dance, revealing that he didn't trust himself.

See? I made the right choice after all. I'm happy with myself. They're happy with me. Everyone's happy!

Best of all, I only had one shot for the duration of the night. I did, however, also deliver one slap.

A patron was chatting to me at the bar, saying how he couldn't possibly pay for a lap dance because it would be unfair to his wife. He wasn't here for *that sort of thing*. What are you here for then, shithead, the fucking electrical department? The camping aisle?

All the while, his hand crept up the back of my thigh, inching its way between my legs. No doubt he'd have revoked his status as a faithful husband had I offered him a free dance.

Disgusted, I smacked this freeloading groper. '*NO TOUCHING!*' I spat as the girls looked on and cheered.

They thought the incident called for a round of shots; I agreed and promised myself a single drink wouldn't become plural.

The only people who didn't see the humour were my bosses, Sebastian and Hugo. 'Oh, *great*,' Sebastian huffed. 'Sunshine's back with Attitude Boobs.'

'I would have thought that was obvious when you let me in the front door.'

He huffed again. 'I won't be putting up with your bullshit this time around. You can't just smack customers whenever you feel like it!'

'He was groping me! Isn't this one of the few non-touching clubs left in Queensland? Should I have *let* him fondle my arse-crack?'

'No. But you shouldn't handle it yourself, that's what the bouncers are for!'

'They're all busy playing on TikTok.'

Sebastian and Hugo both gave me scathing looks before sashaying away. Since neither of the club owners are kings of wit, this is how they handle any situation where they have no retort.

No matter what their facial expressions are, they're never pretty. Sebastian, an abnormally short, thin redhead from Ireland, was once a manufacturing wholesaler and reminds me of an irate gnome. Hugo, his sidekick, is rotund, bleached-blond and has the goggle-eyes of a dumbfounded goldfish. He's likewise scornful, but no less stupid, and worked a lifetime in our local council office. Which is why they're out of their depth in the nightclub world after buying this club. They're not only afraid of strong women, but think we're a bunch of lying, manipulative princesses. If one of us had a migraine, they'd refuse to believe it, and would rather make a stripper stay at work with a blinding headache and have her drop dead from a brain embolism the next day than lose out on her fee. I have christened them the 'Dickhead Duo'.

Aside from the slap, I didn't give them any more reason to complain. Three quarters of the way through the night, I was in possession of so much cash I had to put it in the club safe. Some girls like to display their earnings in an obvious place, so they look as though they're busy and popular. One way of doing this is to stick notes in a fan-like creation held with rubber bands on the wrist or looped around a garter. The less showy dancers opt for carrying a clutch or purse. I keep cash in my shoe; platform stilettos are now made with the option of having a slot in the side. Tonight, though, my shoe storage space didn't cut it.

My happiness was overwhelming after I'd done around twenty lap dances. All my friends did roughly the same, along with half that amount in tequila shots. Except Candy, who downed at least fifteen; my island-princess friend was drowning her sorrows after a nasty argument with her boyfriend, Jay. He got his revenge by going into her wardrobe and pissing all over her clothes, even the designer labels. Why do strippers never go out with normal people?

My friends gave me a hard time over my sobriety, but I think my health pact is the smartest thing I've done in a long time. It always helps to begin work without a hangover. I'm taking things seriously this time around.

'Sho, are you like, ever gonna drunk again—*drink* again?' Jade corrected herself with a slur.

I smiled at her stunning Eurasian features; even after imbibing litres of alcohol, my Chinese-Dutch-English friend was one of the most beautiful creatures I'd ever seen.

'Of course I will,' I told her. 'Just not every night—I'll have a massive blowout on my birthday in two weeks, okay?'

She nodded and gave me a lopsided grin. I noted, with mild irritation, that she still looked gorgeous. It's hard work when all your friends are beautiful; it really takes special effort not to let the side down.

HIGHLIGHT: Nobody told Sebastian about the toilet paper hanging out the back of his slacks.

DOWNSIDE: Turning twenty-eight in two weeks.

5 July

At last, Jim is gainfully employed! The bills are no longer mine alone to pay. Now all the money I make in Cairns will mainly belong to me!

I've only been back a week, and some of my Regulars have heard of my return.

Now, as I've mentioned, a Regular comes into the club to see you, and you alone. These patrons are financially desirable, but generally they are socially inept creatures who have rarely, if ever, had a girlfriend. They often think you *are* their girlfriend, and you'll play along for as long as you can milk it—or until your own sanity blows a fuse. Regulars are a test of psychological strength. For starters, you have to *look* at them, and it usually ain't pretty. One Regular I had a few years back resembled Quasimodo. He would paw at my hands with pathetic hesitance, his fingers like sweaty slugs. It took everything I had to hide my revulsion, as I do with almost all of my Regulars.

These customers are a reminder that we strippers are not just paid for nudity, but also tolerance. The way you keep a Regular coming back is by masking your true feelings at all times, pretending an interest in them and their lives, and acting like you're a little bit smitten with them too.

No easy feat. Sometimes I think I would rather eat offal.

It was almost a relief when I became too old for Quasimodo, who wouldn't have a dance with any girl older than twenty-four. I do miss the guaranteed four hundred dollars, though.

Tonight brought the return of the Bug-Man. He loves entomology, studying creepy-crawlies in his spare time. He also wears specs that rival magnifying glasses, giving him the appearance of an over-eager praying mantis.

During his visits, I smile and lean forward in faux fascination at his tales of monstrous spiders and rare caterpillars. Bug-Man has never had a relationship to speak of, and I'm quite safe from him ever asking me home—as so many Regulars do—since he can't get it up. He confided in me that he's visited sex workers many times over, and his penis just won't work. Yet that doesn't stop him trying to grope my breast while pretending to trip over. It's quite fitting that he's into entomology, because when he puts his clammy hand in mine on the way to the lap-dance room, it makes my fucking skin crawl.

Since the Pacific Club allows open-leg dances, he inspects my vagina as though it's a new species. He also buys my underwear—every single time he visits. This can get pretty annoying if I've run out of cheap G-strings and have to sell my favourite costumes. I do add on a couple of hundred dollars to recoup losses: with a pair of undies sold and four lap dances, Bug-Man is usually good for at least six hundred dollars.

Oh, and he once bought me a gold grasshopper pendant with two-carat diamond eyes. It sits in my bedside drawer with all the other shit patrons have given me, which I would never use or wear. I don't want to sound ungrateful, but at least six of my friends have had *their* Regulars buy them a car. Another friend hustled an apartment. And at least five had their boob jobs paid for.

HIGHLIGHT: Won't see Bug-Man for at least three weeks.
DOWNSIDE: Must remember to clean out all the shit from bedside drawer.

7 July

'You should wear a dress, hotpants don't suit you.' So said Sebastian as I began work tonight. Thankfully, there was no sign of Hugo that night.

'Really? Why is that?'

My boss, due to his inability to relate to women, is as subtle as a terrorist attack. 'Because your arse is the size of Tokyo.'

This was how I began my night: with the world's most unattractive club owner insulting *me*.

'And your tan looks orange,' he added for good measure.

Well, great. There's nothing like being compared to a landmass-sized Cheezel to make you feel sexy. You'd think it would be common sense for a manager not to insult the girls at the beginning of the night.

My shift was painfully slow. A few apparent customers turned out to be the 'just looking' type, lonely or simply cheap. These guys keep you talking as long as possible without spending a cent, then become surly when you've had enough.

I'd been chatting to a guy for around fifteen minutes and, sure enough, when I suggested a lap dance he became insulted. 'I knew you were talking to me for a reason! You're just in it for the money!'

I gave him a calm, slightly condescending smile. 'Strippers don't sit around a club in a bikini all night out of kind-heartedness. We have to get paid somehow, don't we, sweetie?'

'But you were only after my cash all along!'

'Let me ask you a question. What do you do for a living?'

'I build swimming pools.'

'Oh goody,' I said. 'Because I need one. Would you mind coming over tomorrow and building a pool in my garden out of the kindness in your heart?'

'Bitch.'

'Inarguably, but at least you see my point.'

It was almost a relief when Comedian sauntered in. 'You stole all my coke the other night,' he declared by way of greeting.

'Keep your voice down,' I hissed.

Sebastian was eavesdropping nearby, as he always does with celebrities, even minor ones. This particular owner, you see, is gullible enough to be impressed by them. He's also older than most of the nightclub crowd; he's part of that ill-informed generation who believe drugs are tools of the devil. He thinks one puff of a joint will lead to a full-blown, skin-scratching heroin addiction, and he doesn't grasp the meaning of recreational use. If he knew the dancers at his club indulged, it would send him into a frenzy of ignorant fear and he'd sack us on the spot. Fortunately he's naive enough to think cocaine is an exotic fairy dust confined to the far reaches of Colombia. Whenever a stripper emerges from the bathroom unaware of a bloody nose, Sebastian is honestly convinced it's caused by sinus problems.

Neither Comedian nor Sebastian—picking his teeth in the corner while pretending not to listen—were appealing conversational partners. In fact, I'd have chosen to talk to the Yorkshire Ripper over both, but Comedian won. I led him to the other end of the bar as he kept whining about his coke. 'Did you have to steal *all* of it, Sunshine?'

'Yes. And I wouldn't leave your pockets unguarded, or I'll take your wallet next.'

He suddenly grinned. 'See? That's what I love about you. Personality and spark! Want to snort a line?'

'No thank you,' I said primly. 'I'm not doing drugs anymore.'

'But are you doing any less?'

I peered at him, not liking what I saw. He may be a celebrity, but he's also a freak.

'What do you want?' I inquired sharply.

'I'm glad you asked. What are you doing for the next week? I thought we could have sex and get married, and then I'll let you divorce me and take all my money when you find out what a jerk I am.'

'I already know you're a jerk. The other night you told me Australia is the Alabama of the world. I'd hoped it was a declaration that you'd piss off back to Britain.'

'Well, it *is* the Alabama of the world—only worse.'

'I take it back, you're not a jerk, you're an arsehole.' I yawned. 'So how much to get married?'

Why do famous folk never believe they're being rejected?

'I'm not the marrying kind.'

'But you are the judging kind. You don't like me much, do you?'

I shrugged. 'You don't cause a big enough impression to dislike.'

'Everyone *else* is a fan,' he said with a grin.

'That way of thinking is a sure sign your meds are working. But don't take it personally—it's not me, it's you.'

'Alrighty then,' Comedian said with supreme confidence. 'What's wrong with *me*? Delight me with your stripper acumen! I can't wait to hear the observations of a girl who makes money out of enticing erections.'

'Well, from what I've seen so far, you're an egotistical, morally retarded bastard. Being a dick won't make yours any bigger, just so you know.'

'Why all the labels and name-calling?'

'Because you gave my friend the gift of *crabs*. If it had been anything more serious, she would have taken out a contract on your diseased arse.'

'Did you know, sexually transmitted crabs are officially an endangered species? It's because everybody is into waxing. You know, boasting a Brazilian or husking the corn.'

'Has anybody ever told you that you're not remotely funny in real life? And that your entire personality is a cry for help?'

'I think I love you.'

'Piss off.'

God save me from celebs.

HIGHLIGHT: Comedian's eyeliner had run down his face in Alice Cooper rivulets by the time he left.

DOWNSIDE: Sebastian and Hugo won't look at any of the brochures I hand them about holidaying in Syria.

9 July

Had the most wonderful day lying on a tropical beach with all my friends, turning my skin the colour of Scotch. But our fun was slightly dampened when a mother stalked over from where she'd been sitting with her kids. 'I just want you to know, you girls are disgraceful!' she spat at the sight of our bodies, clad only in G-strings, before she ushered her children further up the shore.

I felt slightly bad, as I tend to forget most people aren't as open with their bodies and bits as we are. (Stripper Attitude, remember?) But the offended mum sent the other girls off into gales of laughter. They threatened to remove their bikini bottoms too; I put a stop to that by informing them there's a hefty fine for public indecency.

'So, you must be happy now Jim is working full-time?' Belle asked, tying her shampoo-commercial hair into a topknot. I tried not to notice her lack of cellulite and concentrated on happy things.

'I'm over the moon,' I told her. 'He even seems to like this job—he's enthusiastic about going each day.'

As our conversation flowed, random and risqué, it dawned on me how less interesting my world will be when I eventually stop stripping. Normal people don't talk about the things we do in such an idle way. For example, Charlie began a lazy conversation about masturbation, and Belle casually shared how her tampon had got stuck the night before last. We clucked at her for cutting off the string, which is just asking for trouble; most strippers roll the string into a little ball and tuck it inside while we perform.

Candy announced she thinks Jay might be addicted to porn, since he loves to copy every position in his extensive collection— when he's not pissing on her clothes, that is.

I almost felt bad my relationship was going well for once.

'Hey,' said Tara, suddenly sitting up, 'isn't that the new girl from our work?'

We all leaned forward to watch the beautiful blonde coming our way. I wanted to hate her; she looked like a jungle cat with aquamarine eyes and streamlined muscles. But she approached in such a meek manner and with such a sweet smile, I held off on the dislike. After all, if I despised everyone in the industry for their looks, I'd lose about a hundred per cent of my friends.

'Hi, guys,' she said.

'Aliah, isn't it?' Jade asked. I admired her for remembering, as we rarely bother to learn any new girl's name—too many come and go. Plus, because my little group is the Clique in our club, we're not easy to approach.

The girl nodded shyly when we invited her to sit down. She surprised and impressed the gang by instantly removing her top.

'Where are you from?' I inquired.

'A tiny country town in New South Wales. I came here because I heard Cairns is wild, but I haven't seen any evidence of it yet. The girls I've talked to so far at work think taking drugs and drinking alcohol are on a par with consuming the blood of a homeless child.'

The poor girl had only struck up conversations with the club nerds; yes, there are stuffed-shirt strippers too. Aliah needed some proper friends to introduce her to Cairn's nightlife. Plus, any stripper with her inappropriate wit was a woman after my own heart.

However, we've all done our time as the new girl. Each of us had to prove ourselves worthy. There are tests to overcome and curveballs to catch.

'What do you think of Sebastian and Hugo?' I challenged.

'What a pair of wankers! Hugo told me my tattoos remind him of bathroom graffiti. Fucking imbecile! I don't understand why it's legal in some places to cull animals for fur, but not okay to cull men for their behaviour in general.'

'You mean like starting wars, waiting for us to pick up after them, rape, abuse, and coming up with the idea to cull animals for fur in the first place?' I put in.

'Precisely. Do you think Sebastian and Hugo are misogynists?'

'No. They don't hate all women—just strippers,' Candy said.

'So they treat every dancer the same way?'

The girls nodded. 'Pretty much.'

There were, of course, a few other clubs in town any of us would have been welcomed at, but they were dilapidated, seedy and less well known, without even a trickle of the money that went through the Pacific Gentlemen's Club. None of us girls would have worked at those with a switchblade pointed at our kidneys.

So there was nothing we could do but tolerate the Dickhead Duo.

'There was this one time,' Tara shared, 'when I'd been doing lap dances for the same guy all night. This dude was running a credit card tab, and I'd made about seven hundred dollars off of him. Just as he left, Sebastian swiped his drink tab but forgot to add all the dances. When I asked Sebastian what the fuck we would do, he said I'd earned plenty of money in the past, and sometimes you just have to take one for the team. Thanks to our bastard boss, I lost the entire seven hundred—a whole night of earnings, *gone*.'

Jade nodded in disgust. 'I remember once he wouldn't let me get off stage to change my tampon.'

'What about when Hugo sacked Riley for not showing up to her shift?' Belle reminded us. 'It turned out she'd had a car accident, and he *still* didn't rehire her because he didn't want to admit he was in the wrong.'

'When I got kicked out of my apartment for having too many parties, Sebastian gave me the number of a homeless shelter,' Candy said. 'I give him almost five hundred bucks a week in club fees, and he couldn't care less whether or not I had a place to go.'

Everybody turned to Charlie, waiting for her to dish some dirt.

'What?' She blinked. 'They aren't awful to me at all. They even let me leave work early to drive two hours down the road so I could catch Brett in bed with that air hostess.'

The girls tried not to look sour, but nobody likes a fence-sitter.

I had no such privilege. 'Sebastian once asked me if all strippers wind up with a venereal disease. And a couple of nights ago he called me fat.'

This provoked a suitable number of shocked gasps.

'You're not *fat*!' Tara raged like a true friend.

'I know,' I said. 'My arse hasn't been this small since I first discovered bulimia.'

'Bulimia's back in a big way,' Aliah joked. 'What a prick Sebastian is. Hey, why don't you girls come to the Roman Bar before work tonight? My fiancé is the manager, we can drink for free.'

We all said we'd love to.

'Great,' she said, 'I'll get him to save us a table. Um, is that mother over there glaring at us?'

I nodded. 'Because our boobs are out.'

'Prude. Your boobs deserve their own parade, Sunshine. If I had a pair like that, I'd never put them away again.'

I adore the new girl.

HIGHLIGHT: Another place to drink for free.
DOWNSIDE: Shut up, liver, you'll be fine.

11 July

I'm pleasantly surprised that Jim is enjoying his job so much. Each afternoon as he gets ready for work he seems more enthusiastic than I've seen him in years, maybe because he's head chef at a seafood restaurant and finally making great money.

Strangely, he also appears more insecure than ever too. He keeps asking if I'm going to leave him or if I've ever cheated.

Why is he contemplating these things when we're getting along the best we have in years?

I mulled this over at the beginning of the night while I sat sipping a lemonade and waiting for the club to fill. I'm quite proud that my health regime is ongoing. I was impressed with myself last night for only indulging in a two free-drink maximum before work at Roman Bar.

Aliah proved to be a kindred spirit with our Clique, and the girls bought her a gram of speed to tell her so. Nothing says 'I accept you' like mutual drug taking. And her fiancé, Guy, is a charming and cool dude.

As I finished my lemonade, Charlie brought her bouncy curls, freckles and exuberance over and sat next to me at the bar. We chatted about my upcoming birthday party. Then she switched to the thing I consider her least attractive interest: malicious gossip. 'Did you hear that so-and-so has been sleeping with bikers—plural—at their clubhouse? And so-and-so is doing her best friend's husband? And so-and-so is a full-blown heroin addict now. And—'

'Stop!' I cut her off because for Chrissake, who the fuck needs that kind of negativity? I like gossip as much as the next girl, but only when it's fun and full of mirth, not damaging. I also like Charlie, I truly do, but her love of spreading rumours makes her resemble a soufflé with fishhooks: delicious and fluffy, but filled with dangerous barbs. I have to be careful which secrets I share with her.

A bucks party came teeming through the door, and I suddenly thought listening to Charlie's gossip might not be so bad.

All the girls groaned in tandem. Bucks parties are rarely a stripper's favourite thing. They arrive boisterous and rude after drinking all day long, often dressed in stupid outfits, with an awful pack mentality.

For any woman who has wondered how their men act on a stag night at a strip club, the answer is simple: APPALLING! Oh, you might get the one supposedly nice guy who will apologise for his friends' behaviour, but more often than not he is using that approach as a ploy to get laid.

A large group on a stag night rarely equals a lot of money; they are there to spend all their cash on alcohol, and on the buck. If you're the lucky girl they choose to entertain the man of the hour, they'll all throw in money for you to dance for him. It might be just enough for you to take him for a personal lap dance—or they'll raise a bit more to see the buck humiliated on centre stage.

Yes, ladies, it is more than likely your fiancé has been stripped naked, whipped with his own belt, made to wear lipstick and tied to a pole while a couple of strippers suffocate him with their boobs.

And the crowd goes wild.

But before the show takes place, they usually have another form of entertainment in mind. They're pack animals on the hunt for humiliation, and they laugh in drunken companionship while one or two of them play 'let's try to degrade the stripper'. Generally, this is done with a few scathing observations and a couple of crude insults. The party look you over and judge whether you're pretty enough, skinny enough, *good* enough to be the privileged dancer who gets naked for the buck. And if you're not, they'll try to belittle you until you feel suicidal.

Curiously, one of the worst behaved and most lecherous is always the father-in-law to be (on either the bride *or* groom's side). He will try to grab your boobs roughly or poke at your vagina while shouting out charming phrases such as '*Show us your pink bits!'* for the benefit of the crowd. He is also always the one most likely to be thrown out first.

Even more curious is that the buck is often the most reserved—probably because by that time of the night he's a drooling mess, so sedated by alcohol he wouldn't know if we were giving him a lap dance or performing a colonoscopy.

There is only one thing I find worse on a bucks night than a perverted father-in-law, anaesthetised buck and pack of insult-hurling drunks: the Cheating Groom. The most despicable kind of man I've encountered in all my years of stripping. *The one who asks you for sex right before he's getting married!*

No matter that he's about to walk down the aisle and swear undying monogamy to the love of his life—he wants one last fuck before he has to put up with the same vagina for the next few decades. And apparently if it happens *before* he exchanges vows, it doesn't count.

There are more of these grooms than you'd like to think. Can you imagine finding out the man you married had sex with a stripper right before the big day? Personally, I would think it grounds for a quick divorce. But lucky for the bride, no stripper I know would indulge such a vulgar request.

Many an exotic dancer has been in tears over the offensive antics of bucks parties, which is why I was staggered to find Orion among this one. He tapped me on the shoulder, smiling down at me with those amber eyes. And sexy freckles. And golden tan. 'I thought you were in Adelaide?'

'Orion!' I managed. 'What are you doing here?'

'I live in Cairns. But if you're asking *why* I'm at this club, I had no choice. My co-worker is the buck.'

My opinion of him further ballooned when he gave a little grimace. He wasn't comfortable, and I adored him for it. He's clearly not the kind to degrade strippers.

Not that he'd go out with one either, because of his perfect nurse girlfriend and their dinner parties.

We chatted for a bit about this, that, and antipasto—which I brought up.

'I'm not overly partial to it,' he confided.

Hmm, does that mean he's not giving dinner parties with the nurse anymore? Or do they cook curries? And why am I even wondering, when Jim and I are getting on better than we have in years?

Orion peered more closely at me. 'You look different,' he mused, clearly trying to pinpoint what the change might be. His eyes slid to my chest and, I kid you not, he blushed to the roots of his sexy, messy hair.

I tried not to look bemused. Or smitten.

His eyes darted this way and that. 'I remembered I have an early start,' he stammered. 'Just had to put in an appearance for my friend. So, um, I'll be heading off now.'

'Okay.'

'But . . .'

I looked at him expectantly.

'But . . .'

I began to frown in bewilderment.

'But I just want to say you look pretty tonight—no, *beautiful.*' He said this all as one word without a breath between syllables. Before I could say anything in return, he went from pink to red and left without turning another sentence into one long word.

I stood there for what seemed like a long time, suddenly oblivious to the bucks party and my surroundings. I was confused and ecstatic, spinning and grinning. A big, stupid, moony smile plastered on my face. Had I heard right? Could a respectable psychiatrist find a dysfunctional stripper pretty? No—*beautiful*? Had he truly been appreciating my outside, rather than analysing my inside?

Charlie came running up to me, looking breathless. 'Wow! Who was *that*?'

I opened my mouth to say, *That's what heaven looks like.* But then I remembered who I was taking to, and thought better of it.

HIGHLIGHT: Pretty sure Orion had a quick peek over his shoulder at my arse, too.

DOWNSIDE: Had to wax the buck's hairy bottom on stage at father-in-law's request.

15 July

5 a.m.

It is early morning, and I write only an hour after I left my bizarre birthday party. I am high sky. Sky high. Flying. On ecstasy. Drug, not emotion. Well, maybe a little of that too.

What a bush! Bash, I mean.

Get self together, Sunshine!!!

5.07 a.m.

Right. Have splashed cold water on face, and am sucking on ice chips.

Did drugs, obviously. But was one-off present to self. Just this once. Health kick again tomorrow. Worth it—am skinny from dehydration and looked a million bucks in thousand-dollar Gaultier dress.

Nope, still fuzzy. Will go make a coffee. No worries.

5.45 a.m.

Better. Caffeine has hit my bloodstream. My birthday was . . . weird.

It began magnificently. About two hundred folk turned up, and everyone made the effort to wear blue, my theme. Everyone has white parties, don't they? Break the mould, that's what I say. Don't go the beaten track, walk your own path and leave a trail!

Oh God, drugs are still scrambling my brain. Concentrate!

Right.

My friend Clay certainly broke the mould, painting his entire body blue to imitate an Avatar. He looked amazing too, until his loincloth was ripped off and his pink dick dangled in contrast.

All my best friends—Candy, Tara, Belle, Jade and Charlie—got together with Aliah and her fiancé, Guy, to arrange the giant shindig in my honour. Shucks.

The sweethearts did the restaurant up like an ice castle, with faux snow along with polystyrene icicles that looked so good some of the acid-taking guests tried to eat them. My favourite part, though, was the giant slushy machine dominating the room, filled with vanilla-infused vodka. And my next favourite bit was when Candy tried to hop in the tropical fish tank.

I felt bad for Guy, who had put on an extravaganza of titbits—such as crayfish mini-pancakes with garlic aioli, prawn dim sum, and barramundi spring rolls with banana dipping sauce—yet everyone was too wasted to eat.

Lots of nightclub owners and managers showed up, each bringing me a bottle of something alcoholic. I can't decide whether this was an extravagant or cheap gesture, since the booze probably came from their own stock. At any rate, with this amount of alcohol in my possession I could open a bar and not have to order stock for a year.

My friends bought me various trinkets: jewellery, perfume, scented candles, and mobile-phone covers with bling. All except for Jim, who bought me *nothing*.

'I forgot,' was his weak excuse.

'How could you forget?' I seethed. 'It's not like today crept up on you—you've known my birthday was coming for a whole fucking year.'

I thought I saw a ghost of a *shrug*. Instead of appearing apologetic, Jim just seemed preoccupied. He was glued to his phone all night, probably immersed in TikTok like every other person on the planet. Maybe he resented that all the attention was on me?

I didn't have time to think, or argue about it, as Tara materialised from the thick of the party and grabbed my hand. 'You'd better come with me.'

She led me through the overcrowded dance floor, past the jam-packed tables and onto the terrace, where we pushed aside a group of coke-snorting girls to find Candy and Jay huddled in the corner. They were giggling in a way that only Class-A narcotics can evoke.

'What are you pair up to?' I asked. 'Why do you look like you've been naughty?'

Candy went off into more gales of crazed laughter, and Jay grinned. 'We sort of spiked your drink with ecstasy.'

I thought of the little blue pill, wrapped with a tiny bow, that Belle had given me as a pressie, and shrugged. 'Cheers. Now I can sell or save this one for later.'

'I told you she wouldn't mind,' Jay triumphantly told Tara. 'Ray from GuitarBar also has a gram of coke for you, and Zack the bouncer wants to give you a sheet of acid.'

How thoughtful. Now I could set up as a drug dealer in my new overstocked bar. Party on.

I honestly didn't mind being spiked this once, as Candy revealed it was the type of ecstasy tablet I'd been about to swallow anyways.

Until the drug hit me in a mad rush, that is. I shakily walked back to Jim. He was still preoccupied with his phone, seated alone at a crowded table. 'Can you take me for a walk?' I asked. 'This pill is a bit strong. It's coming on ferociously.'

He shook his head without looking up, barely registering me. I thought about snatching the phone away to investigate the cause of his rudeness, but intense waves of MDMA were pulsing through my bloodstream. I had to get out of the jam-packed room.

The first tendrils of a strong ecstasy tablet are like the world's most intense roller-coaster, bound for heaven and hell. There are gut-clenching waves of nausea, and expectant fear as your mind falters. Then it whirls like a spinning top, fast enough to fling all the fear and crazy thoughts away—if you can hang on tight enough. Immediately after, euphoria sets in and the planet is a fascinating place, where all humans are beautiful and everything is Zen.

I sat down in the park opposite the Roman Bar, sinking into the grass and thinking how the air smelled like a Midori cocktail while I gazed at the stars. Often my mind goes on a tangent while on drugs, and I wonder about obscure and ridiculous things. Why can't we all just get along and have a universal religion? Why won't the rich share their money evenly with the poor? And why can't I paint like Monet or sing like Adele? Or be tall?

Tonight as I stared up at the sky, I pondered if aliens are perhaps a future version of *us*. Are we coming back to check on ourselves through a time warp, to ensure history is unfolding as it should? Are those bald, elongated-eyed beings an advanced form of humans? Pleased with my cleverness, I then thought how lucky I was to have such a crowded party. And how it would probably be impossible to invite the whole gathering back to my two-bedroom apartment—I'd need a thirty-bedroom house.

I'd like to live in a house. With giant palm trees in the garden and stone gargoyles on the roof. You never see gargoyles in Queensland, do you?

In the midst of my musings, I suddenly thought I must be hallucinating. For there, on the pathway that fringed the park, strolled Orion.

Perhaps he was my real birthday present from the universe, in lieu of Jim giving me nothing.

He ventured over with a smile. 'Hello.'

'What do you think of gargoyles?' I asked, as though it was a perfectly normal greeting.

'As a pet or roof feature?'

'Feature.'

'I'm quite partial to them. I come from Melbourne, so I kind of miss their architectural presence.'

I grinned. 'Me too!'

He grinned back, looking down at me cross-legged on the grass. 'Can I ask why you're here in the park, alone on a Saturday night?'

'It's my birthday.'

'Happy birthday. Have you decided to spend it by yourself?'

'No, that out-of-control party across the road is mine, I took drugs . . .' I said before I could stop myself.

He raised an eyebrow at me.

'I needed some headspace when my pill kicked in,' I blathered. 'I know you probably think I'm an airhead, dysfunctional stripper, but I don't really indulge very much, not anymore. I'm trying to be healthy and eat less carbs. And I *was* sitting here thinking deep things. Did you ever wonder if maybe *we're* advanced aliens . . .' I trailed off, realising how drug-addled and ridiculous I sounded. 'Anyway,' I said, smiling brightly, 'what are *you* doing in a park alone on a Saturday night, instead of having antipasto dinner parties with your normal nurse?'

Immediately I thought, *Oh God, Sunshine, shut up! You sound like you need therapy.*

Orion stared at me with a bemused smile. 'I was once sacked for working in a hospital dispensary and sampling the medication. I've done my own share of drug taking—but I used to ponder dinosaurs, not aliens. And I think I already mentioned, I'm not a fan of antipasto. I'm walking out here alone because I needed to clear my head too—the nurse and I broke up.' Then he shocked the hell out of me by leaning down to kiss my cheek. 'Enjoy your birthday, Sunshine.'

I went back to my party in a floating daze. Then, across the room, somebody screamed, '*FUCK YOU! GET YOUR FUCKING HANDS OFF ME, YOU PIECE OF SHIT!*' I sighed, unable to pretend that drama wasn't unfolding. I dragged my mind from thoughts of Orion.

Elbowing my way through the crowd, I found the girls in a circle looking stunned. Aliah, in the middle, was practically foaming at the mouth. Our new friend, normally sweet and serene, had her fists clenched as she faced her fiancé with murder in her eyes.

I put a gentle hand on her shoulder. 'What's going on?'

Aliah whirled my way. 'This *fucking* bastard, he . . . he . . .' She broke down before she could finish.

Belle and Tara threw protective arms around Aliah. They each shot Guy a venomous look over their shoulder as they led her away.

Frowning in confusion, I caught up with them in the female toilets, home to all late-night drama.

'I just can't believe it.' Aliah was sobbing.

I stared quizzically at Tara, who softly filled me in. 'Guy slept with a seventeen-year-old behind her back.'

'What?' I gasped. 'But they're *engaged*!'

'Thanks for pointing that out, Captain Obvious,' Tara said.

Christ on a cracker! Calling Guy a fucking bastard was *generous* on Aliah's behalf. I'd probably have reacted by performing an on-the-spot castration.

'What am I going to do?' she said brokenly. 'I never want to see him again . . . I need to get out of here.'

I made a split decision. 'I'll take her home,' I told the girls.

I'd had enough fun and dramatics for one night. I was feeling very drunk, exceptionally high and slightly sick—I had no more party in me.

Hustling Aliah through the masses, I found Jim where I'd left him and filled him in.

Bastardly behaviour was clearly on the rise tonight, as he shot us a cold look and raised a sardonic eyebrow. '*Another* psycho-drama? *Really*, Sunshine?'

I was lost for words.

And so here I sit, after listening to my new friend cry herself to sleep, watching the sunrise on the day I was born. Happy birthday to me.

HIGHLIGHT: Twenty-eight. Orion. Orion's freckles. Orion's single status.
DOWNSIDE: Jim. Bastards. Drugs. Twenty-eight.

18 July

Jim has decided against coming home, because he wants to avoid our new heartbroken flatmate; he's staying with an apprentice chef from work, his new BFF, Jack. I've assured Aliah she can stay as long as she'd like, since that's what a spare room and a friend is for.

Her pain is gut-wrenching to watch as she goes through every emotion, from self-persecution to recollecting her wedding plans. She says she can't forgive him, and I don't blame her. I wouldn't either.

I was more than surprised when she said she wanted to come to work with me tonight. 'I can't stay here alone and think. I'll either feel tempted to call him, or hang myself from the shower rod—one or the other.'

Sebastian and Hugo noticed but didn't comment on Aliah's red-rimmed eyes. The Dickhead Duo neither cared nor wanted to bring up personal topics, which they regarded with the same icky discomfort as picking up puppy shit.

I know this from experience. Our bosses are notoriously fussy about letting us go home early, and would expect a dancer to stay even if her leg fell off due to advanced leprosy. However, every girl who works here knows that uncomfortable subjects are their downfall. We simply tell them we have our period, including the gory details, and watch them recoil in disgust and wave us away as though we're infected with, well, advanced leprosy.

As Sebastian pretended Aliah wasn't looking like she'd lost a limb, he turned to me. 'Do you know of a Penthouse Pet called Soleil?' he asked, clearly excited.

'Yep, why?'

'She's just moved to Cairns, and I've convinced her to work here.' He looked about to burst with self-congratulation.

'I'm not sure you'll feel so pleased with yourself once you meet her,' I told him. 'She's probably here due to being sacked from every other club in Australia.'

Sebastian cast me a look that translated to *what the fuck would you know?* and stalked away muttering to Hugo about sour grapes. He could not be further off the mark: if I were anything like Soleil, I would pay for my own lobotomy and pray they scoop out all the narcissism.

I know I give some Penthouse Pets a hard time, but there are quite a few I rather like, who have a self-deprecating sense of humour beyond even a normal dancer's capabilities. Soleil is not one of them. She's self-absorbed to the point of hurtfulness and possessed of a callous ignorance about everyone but herself.

A few years ago I tried to engage her in a serious conversation. Admittedly, I had an agenda: I wanted to if see there was any semblance of an empathetic human in there.

I commented on how awful it was that millions of Jewish people had been tortured and murdered by the Nazis. Soleil replied that continuing to talk about it would ensure the horrible business would never go away. 'How is the world supposed to forget about the Holocaust, Sunshine, if you all keep bringing it up?' I wasn't sure if I was more shocked by her mentality, or that she knew the word 'Holocaust'.

Tonight I smiled as she strutted through the door, sure that Sebastian was about to learn his lesson. Until now, our stupid boss had assumed the girls working for him were the epitome of high maintenance. This belief was about to be shattered.

I openly giggled as Soleil sashayed over and handed him a list of demands.

'What's this?' he asked with a blank stare.

'My rider, you know? All celebrities request a list of stuff before they arrive at a venue to perform.'

'Celebrity? I thought you just appeared in *Penthouse*.'

'Yes, silly, but it was a *celebration* issue. Anyway, I need certain things in order to achieve my best for the club—while the club achieves its best for me. Mi casa, su casa, you know? Have you stocked organic coconut water? I'll need electrolytes in my system before I get ready. Oh, and this will be the last time I come in at nine, I have to be allowed two hours for creative grooming, best if I do that at home. Did you get my text?'

He shook his head in a daze. 'I haven't checked.'

'Oh, well that explains why you haven't installed lavender oil dispensers, they're necessary for me to relax. Never mind, we can start properly tomorrow night. Now, my midnight grazing platter can consist of any local fruit available, even though I prefer free-range mangoes and Amazonian papaya.'

Sebastian's eyes were bugging out so much, he looked like a helpless insect that has just seen a very big arse about to sit on its face. He shot me a look of loathing as I sniggered again before I left him to it and joined my friends at the bar.

The girls were crowded around Aliah, attempting to lift her spirits. But to no avail.

Soleil flounced over my way. 'Hello, Sunshine. I wasn't sure if it was you. Where did the rest of you go? Are you starving yourself or taking Duromine? Keep up the good work either way, girlfriend, skinny suits you. How have you been?'

'I was great until one minute ago.'

'Why, what happened a minute ago?' she asked, wide-eyed.

When a Regular of mine came in, some of the girls snapped to attention, though none approached him. Another rule of the strip club world is *do not* try to steal another girl's Regular. Not that you have much of a chance: they're obsessively smitten with the dancer they're here to see. Personally, I don't mind too much if another girl performs for one of my Regulars when I'm busy on stage or dancing for someone else, but some strippers take it very personally indeed. A friend of mine once smacked me with a hair straightener for getting a quick fifty dollars from her main money source while she was indisposed with another customer. We all try to keep our Regulars as long as possible.

Some of the girls at work tonight were clearly wondering when this particular Regular would tire of me and notice them. It's no secret that he's absurdly wealthy, having made a killing out of the tech industry. I don't know how exactly, because I rarely listen to a word he says. Nor would I be able to hear him if I did, since he mutters like a child cursing under his breath.

Tech is tall and gangly, with elbows and joints jutting out like Mr Burns from *The Simpsons*. Tonight, he jittered nervously and asked me for a dance without preamble, then ushered me to the private room with a clammy hand. 'Are you going to show me your pussy?' he asked anxiously.

'Did you see it last week?'

He nodded.

'Then let's assume you'll see it again tonight,' I replied sarcastically.

I did the same lap dance I always do. Leg on chair, throw head back, kneel on chair, toss hair. Stand on chair, bend over, remove top, sit down, arch back. Smile, pout, fling hair around a bit more, strike a pose, remove underwear, shake arse. Then I do the entire dance in reverse, as Tech had booked me for a whole half-hour.

'Do you like sex toys in your pussy?' he blurted, shaking with arousal that revolted me.

This is the main reason I don't listen to Tech: he loves to throw filthy questions at me, partly for shock value, partly because he wants to know the answer.

But tonight, he had a surprise in store.

My back had been turned for a few moments as I shook my arse, and it was then that I heard the kind of groan every sexually active woman recognises. I turned in time to see Tech slump in his chair with the glazed eyes of a sated man.

Customers are *not* allowed to touch themselves, but this dirtbag had found a way around that.

'Did you cut a hole in your pants pocket so you could *fondle* yourself?!'

He nodded reluctantly.

'And did you just do what I *think* you did?'

The accusation caused an even more hesitant nod topped with a deer-in-headlights expression.

'You dirty fucking animal! Ejaculation in a strip club is *against the law*—it's a form of sexual assault. I'm calling the police!'

This was an empty threat because, in all honesty, who can be bothered with a lawsuit you probably won't win? If the cops were contacted, they'd appear empathetic and probably press charges if I insisted, but they wouldn't want the paperwork and they'd secretly think I provoked the assault. If it went to court, any judge would read out the offence condescendingly: *This man covertly fondled himself while you were bending over naked before him? With your genitalia on show? With the expectation that he control himself?* It would be looked upon as a waste of the court's time.

A friend of mine was held down by a man during a lap dance as he stuck two fingers in her vagina. She called the police and had him charged, and the whole thing went as far as court. However, moments before the trial was to begin, the judge asked her for a private word in his chambers. He basically told my friend to fire her solicitor and save herself time and money, as he would not be finding the man guilty, since she'd enticed him in the first place.

Tech didn't know about any of this. 'No, Sunshine! *Please* don't. I can pay!'

'You think I can be bought off? I'm not a *prostitute*!'

'Of course not,' he said shrewdly, soothingly. 'It would be my way of apologising. How much would it take to show how sorry I am?'

I had a choice here. I didn't *feel* sexually violated—I felt furious and disregarded. And, I wondered, would I make myself into a victim by taking the matter further? I suspected so. Court cases can take months or even years. The last thing I wanted was to live with that over my head. No, I would not allow that to happen. I would remain in power with a pay-off, only I'm calling it a compensation tip. I decided to get the damages up front.

I mentally calculated my bills and how much I'd like to put towards savings this week. I had to keep my goals in sight, reminding myself that in the long run, none of this will matter. Not the fine I was about to enforce, nor the unfortunate fact that this pig had just come in his pants. And it would be nice to give Aliah some money to get by, since last I'd checked she was still sitting at the bar staring at nothing.

'How much have you got?' I asked Tech. 'Apart from what you've already given me.'

'About four hundred dollars?'

'Liar. Make it six hundred. And you're on a five-month ban from this club.'

'But—'

'Suit yourself. We'll just call the cops.'

Tech swiftly agreed this was indeed a satisfactory arrangement, paid up, and scuttled out in a snappy manner.

I was attempting to erase the memory by skolling champagne when I saw Guy walk in. At first I decided not to get involved. But then Aliah began crying hysterically, so I went over to the bar where they stood. 'Guy, maybe you should give Aliah a bit of space?' I was trying to be nice and impartial, because he *had* paid for my birthday party. But hoes before bros, right?

'No, we have to work this out now,' he huffed. 'Aliah exaggerates every little situation.'

I could not believe my ears. 'Well, I think she might be justified this time round.'

He ignored me. 'Please, honey, stop being infantile! Let's go grab your things from Sunshine's apartment and get you home so we can talk.'

Aliah was gobsmacked, as was I. By the look he wore, Guy had seriously thought he would strut in here and smooth everything over.

'*I'm* infantile?' Aliah blazed. '*Your* next girlfriend is probably being born as we speak, *you cradle-snatching cunt*!' Then her voice cracked. 'Make him go away, Sunshine, *please*.'

I pointed to the door.

'I'm not going anywhere,' Guy insisted.

'Really?' I smiled. 'Because that big burly bouncer in the corner is quite partial to human taxidermy. He practises in his mum's basement. People allegedly disappear from here all the time.'

Guy became the second man to make a speedy exit.

I told Sebastian I was taking Aliah home, and for once he didn't argue: a sobbing stripper wouldn't make him any money. He followed us to the change room, shuffling uncomfortably, perhaps thinking he should say something supportive. But empathy isn't his strength, and he was saved the trouble by Soleil entering behind him. 'So, I was just thinking, Sebastian, I'll go home early on the nights it isn't busy. I need sleep-induced biorhythms as part of my skincare regime.'

'How is that different to the way your skin is affected on a busy night?' he asked, sounding baffled.

'Duh,' she said, 'busy nights inspire adrenaline, adrenaline releases endorphins. And everyone knows they're good for the skin.'

Soleil had made up the most extravagant bullshit I'd ever heard, instead of admitting that she got bored when it wasn't busy. Sebastian looked like someone had stuck a stiletto up his arse.

It was the first time I saw Aliah smile all night.

HIGHLIGHT: Thinking about being a benevolent stripper and sharing Tech with Soleil.

DOWNSIDE: Bouncer too busy filming himself with glitter monobrow on TikTok to 'escort' Guy down the stairs.

20 July

Thanks to the number of people who kissed me at my party, I have come down with a ferocious flu. I look like a germ-warfare victim after a particularly nasty apocalypse. My skin is ash under my tan, my eyes are red rimmed and my cheeks are hollow—and not in a sexy way. Heat is rushing through my bloodstream.

'There's no way you can work in this state,' Aliah sympathised, placing a cool hand on my burning forehead.

Over the past week we've become quite close. Overwhelmed by sympathy for her predicament, I've sat up each night with her till the early hours. I wish there was more I could do, but no words yet invented can comfort a pulverised heart.

Within the rare moments she forgets her pain, little pieces of Aliah surface, and I've found her to be a kindred soul. We share an inappropriate sense of humour and insecurities about whether we're good people, along with a tendency towards laziness.

To give us ample girl time, Jim has kept staying with his friend from work, Jack. Each day Jim drops by to catch up with me properly. When he came home midmorning, he took one look at me with my raging flu and whipped up a chicken-vegetable soup. He even seemed worried and was apologetic about leaving me when he had to dash off to work, but he still hasn't properly apologised for the lack of gifts and attention on my birthday.

I think we're due for another talk. We love each other, but there seems to be a ravine between us that we're both too lazy to jump. We've grown complacent. Otherwise, why would I even be looking at Orion?

'Can't you explain to Sebastian and Hugo that you're really, *really* sick?' Aliah fretted.

'I tried when I rang them, but they didn't care. If I died, they'd stand my coffin up on stage until they found a replacement.'

I'll have to shove my snotty face in theirs so they can see for themselves that customers will want to pay me to go home.

12 p.m.
FFFFFUUUUUCCCCCKKKK!!!!!!

I am hyperventilating. I am ENRAGED. I am *fucking crushed*!!!

I need to stop pacing. And crying. And drinking straight vodka.

My world has imploded.

Can't write properly yet.

1 p.m.

Drunker, but not calmer. I'm fuming and in utter, utter, *utter* disbelief. But have stopped shaking enough to write.

I officially *hate* men.

I went into work at nine so Sebastian could see the state of me. He pretended not to, even as he looked in my scarlet-hued eyes and grimaced at my hacking cough. He said, 'There's only four girls working—and *you're* one of them.' When managing nights without Hugo in attendance, which is thankfully frequent, he becomes more defensive. He fears facing us alone.

I stared at him in shock. 'You're joking, right? *Look* at me! If I were an animal there would be buzzards circling, waiting for me to collapse. I need to be home in bed!'

'Bad luck. Don't care. I've only got four girls. If you leave, you go for good.'

Not an option, since it's the only decent club in town.

Every girl in the place was aghast at his cruelty.

'Sebastian!' Aliah went running after him. 'She's *truly* sick! You can't make her stay.'

'I can and I am.'

Jade was just as appalled. 'Let her go, for Chrissake! We can handle it.'

'Nope. Not another word.'

I wondered if I had enough savings to hire a hit man.

Since there were only three living girls and one half-dead, the dance roster was split into quarters: each dancer was on stage for fifteen minutes, with forty-five minutes off.

Yes. Sebastian was forcing me to perform on stage too.

During my reprieve, I took the opportunity to lie down in the change room on my fluffy: a stripper term for a small sheepskin rug that we use to avoid direct contact with the stage.

At ten forty-five, after a fitful nap, I ventured out to slurp water from the bar.

'Hey, Sunshine, how're you going?'

I turned to see my only normal Regular, Will, tapping me on the shoulder.

'Oh shit,' he said. 'You look terrible!'

'Thanks.' I smiled grimly. 'I have a virus. Sebastian won't let me go home.'

Will shook his head in awe and, God bless him, handed me four hundred dollars. 'Make it up to me another time,' he said with a grin. 'You don't look capable of anything other than accepting charity tonight.'

'I'm not.' This time my smile was grateful.

I cherish Will, the only Regular I actually like. He's funny, honest and empathetic by nature. He frequents strip clubs because he loves exotic dancers—just *adores* us. He says he likes and respects our entrepreneurial streak and bold personalities, and that regular women pale in comparison.

We met the night he came in for a lap dance and promptly fell asleep in his chair after catching two planes to attend a business meeting in town. I woke him gently and told him to come back another time, ideally after a nice long nap. He apologised profusely and paid a hundred dollars anyway. Little did he know, he'd given me *three* hundred-dollar notes stuck together.

Will had left the club by the time I discovered the extra cash, so I chased him outside still dressed in a bikini and handed it back. He looked at me, flummoxed, then took the money and walked away.

Next time he flew in from Brisbane, he came looking for me. 'I've never met such an honest stripper,' he said. 'I didn't know they existed. Thank you for giving my money back, you've earned yourself a lifelong friend.'

And what a friend he'd turned out to be.

'Thank you, Will. My boss is such an arsehole. If I had a million dollars—and got rid of this flu—I swear I'd open another strip club just to piss him off.'

Will regarded me for a moment. '*I've* got a million dollars.'

'*Do* you?' Of course he did. Why wouldn't he, as a businessman and the owner of cafes and bars and trucks and racehorses?

'Maybe we should have a serious talk.'

'Indeed we should—but it'll have to be another night, my brain is crème brûlée.'

Back in the change room, I slid down the lockers and curled up into a sick ball. Half an hour later, Aliah came flying through the door. 'Your Regular, Will, just scared the shit out of Sebastian by using words like "Workplace Health and Safety" and "Duty of Care" and, best of all, "Lawsuit"! Sebastian almost crapped himself and said you can go home.'

I barely had the strength to smile as I got dressed. My phone beeped a text from Jim as I was leaving: *Worried about you. Am in town. Coming in to see how you're doing. You still at work?*

I didn't reply; if Jim was on his way here, he would find out soon enough that I'd gone. And since he was out on the town, he wasn't drinking with friends at our apartment as he sometimes did while I was at work.

I could go home and die in peace.

As I walked out the door, Sebastian called my name. 'Aren't you forgetting something?'

'Like slashing your tyres? I'll do it when I'm better.'

'Ha-ha. I meant your *fee*.'

I stood there gaping. 'You can't be serious. You're going to *charge* me for sleeping on the floor for two hours?'

'You show up, you pay. That's the rules.'

I wanted to murder him. 'I didn't make a cent,' I told him, confident he didn't know about Will's tip.

'Then pay with a credit card.'

Is Sebastian really Satan in disguise? What if I *hadn't* made any money?

I gave him his fee and had only one thing to say: 'I'm going to get you one day.'

He rolled his eyes. 'Whatever.'

He didn't believe me. Good. The enemy should never see you coming.

After I gave the cab driver my address, I ignored his chatter, then felt bad and gave him a generous tip for putting up with a snotty bitch, literally.

There was music playing down by the poolside of my apartment block, which made me cringe—the resort is full of partygoers who try to enlist any passer-by to join the festivities. So I bustled past, preparing to wave politely and decline the invitation.

But I stopped dead and stared instead.

Jim was in the pool.

With his dick in a brunette.

The horrified look on their faces would have been comical, if not for the searing pain that sliced my chest.

I stayed calm. Leaning over the pool fence, cold rage running through me, I stared them down. 'She doesn't look like she charges much by the hour,' I said scathingly. Not my best insult, but all I could manage at that moment.

My insult had a ring of truth, because this girl was plain, *really* plain. With a big nose. If she were a hooker, she'd have to receive government subsidies.

'It's not what you think,' Jim had the audacity to say.

She had the intelligence to stay quiet.

I folded my arms and waited. 'Great. What is it, then? I've got all the time in the world.'

Jim's face flushed red. His eyes darted all over the place as he tried to think, squirming to find some kind of escape.

A noise in the far corner alerted me they weren't alone. Jim's apprentice chef, Jack, was in the shallow end, trying to camouflage himself as pool granite—with *his* penis in a blonde.

My eyes narrowed into burning slits. A mutual infidelity session: what a fucking warped way for them to bond. 'That doesn't look like your wife on the end of your dick there, Jack,' I said in a voice laced with threat. 'I've been meaning to catch up with her. Do you mind giving me her number?'

By now, great tides of nausea were threating to spill the bile from my stomach. But I wasn't going to vomit in front of these people. I stalked upstairs to the apartment, thanking the Lord there was a latch-chain inside the door so Jim couldn't follow.

I needn't have worried: they stayed frozen in the pool, too stunned to move. It was my shrieking over the balcony that snapped them out of their paralysis. They all shot from the water and scuttled for their clothes—butt-naked, of course.

'You are *pond-scum*,' I shrieked at Jim. 'And you're no better, you *brunette whore*! I hope you see my face the next time you screw my *ex-boyfriend*, and think of how plain yours is in comparison, *you fucking troll*!' My taunts were flimsy, pathetic and egotistical. And somewhat presumptuous, given my flu-ravaged appearance. But those were the only words I could think of to make myself feel better and make *her* feel like shit.

I threw everything Jim owned over the balcony and into the swimming pool. Including his chef knives and laptop.

The neighbours rushed to their own balconies and got out the popcorn.

And Jim, the lying, cheating bastard, took off in the car. With *her*. With *our* car.

Now my head is spinning in disbelief at his cold, conniving betrayal. His text hadn't meant he was coming to check on me at work; he'd been checking up on *where I was*.

The fact that I *am* better looking than *her* gives me no relief at all. Because that means it was a flaw *inside* me that compelled him to look elsewhere.

I've just called Aliah to come stop me from having a meltdown. 'I'm on my way,' she said without a second thought.

I, on the other hand, have the depths of hell to think about. How long has it been going on? Who is she? Does he love her?

I'm going to vomit. Then I'm going to drink the rest of my birthday liquor. Even the crème de menthe.

DOWNSIDE.

22 July

My friends have gathered as though a death has taken place. They keep staring at me with anxious eyes and making me cups of coffee I can't drink. My stomach is in knots. This *is* like a wake.

Tara ripped open a packet of chips and apologised for the noise. Aliah bursts into tears each time she meets my eyes. Charlie is strangely quiet, perhaps thinking about the time her boyfriend cheated on her. But she forgave him, and I won't be forgiving Jim. Not in this life, and not even if we were reincarnated.

'I'm sure we know a contract killer—we *must* do,' Jade blurted.

'You're not helping,' Tara admonished her.

'I think Jay cheated on me once with a prostitute,' Candy revealed.

'*Not* helping!' Tara barked.

Why, why, why? Yes, we'd been a track short of a train wreck in the past, I get that. But the love and respect between us had returned. Or so I'd thought.

Why not just pull up your honesty socks and simply say, *I'm not happy anymore*? Even if you don't want to admit, *I now feel the way about someone else as I once felt about you.*

I'll tell you why he didn't break up with me first: men are fucking cowards who lie, even if the truth will create a much less dramatic situation. He should have finished things with me before he even *allowed* himself to become involved with someone else. But no, he preferred to creep around in the dirty shadows. Knowing Jim the way I do, I realise that it probably gave him a sick little thrill. He was always shady, I just chose to ignore it. Now my heart has been demolished by his duplicity.

All the tentative inquiries he made lately—'Are you going to leave me? Would you ever cheat on me?'—were a reflection of his own guilt. The guilty ask you the questions they're really asking themselves.

He sent me a text straight after he ran away last night: *Are you going to dramatise this the way you dramatise everything, Drama Queen?* At first I was shocked by his repetitive use of the word 'drama', then I re-read it and *seethed*. He was like Guy, turning his guilt into defensive indignation. Lying, philandering, disloyal *bastard*!

My phone just beeped again, and all the girls turned to stare.

We need to talk.

No. I don't think we do.

'Honey, is there anything we can do for you?' Belle asked gently.

I nodded. 'Take me out and turn me into a human jellyfish.'

HIGHLIGHT: I have mixed drinks about feelings.

DOWNSIDE: What if he doesn't bring the car back?

OPPORTUNITY SUCKS

26 July

Three whole days of debauchery. Health kick? What health kick? I can hardly seek oblivion from a banana smoothie, can I?

The days have passed in a roller-coaster haze. At first I was wounded and victimised. Now I am apoplectic.

Somewhere in the week, I went to work. Apparently I was in such an unapproachable state that even Sebastian and Hugo left me alone. I have a vague recollection of being incredibly rude to customers, and all the masochists lining up to have a dance.

'You have a beautiful body,' said a German.

'Shut up. Speak to me again and I'll perforate your skin with my spiked heel.'

'Does that cost extra?' he asked, then suggested I kick him in the nuts.

I staggered out around three a.m. with a fistful of cash and wandered over to Coconuts nightclub to spend it on cocaine. A blur of bars, parties and drama followed. Strippers and drama go together like ham and burger.

'Can you believe Comedian is here?' Jade asked me at some point in Coconuts during the night.

'I'd be surprised if he wasn't, he's here every night.'

'With his *wife*?'

Why do men cheat? I know of two girls with whom Comedian has had sexual relations while *married*. And that's not to mention his relentless pursuit of me and all my friends. He stared as I walked by with a terrified look that said, *Please don't tell on me!* I was so disgusted, I didn't bother. Shame on his wife anyway, for letting the bastard out every night and not suspecting anything.

Shame on me.

Jim has called and texted over a hundred times. I've ignored every one.

Gossip spreads fast in this neck of the woods, so everybody knows of my misfortune.

Pedro, the manager of Coconuts, pulled up a bar stool and gave me free shots. 'Come and hang out with my friend and I—he said he knows you.'

Lo and behold, it was the rock god I'd met in Newcastle. 'Pedro told me what happened,' he said sympathetically. 'Sometimes we need a catalyst on the page in order for us to turn to a new chapter. Want a line of coke?'

I nodded and stared at him, incredulous that *he* was giving out relationship advice. He wouldn't know fidelity if it took a leak on his head.

But I was thankful to get away from the nightclub when he suggested my friends and I come to a party in his hotel room: a sumptuous, five-bedroom suite with views of the Pacific that would take me a thousand lap dances to afford.

Quietly stationed in the corner with a bottle, I let my friends' irrational chatter wash over me while I stared into space.

'No, you're not getting the point,' Jade said to Tara. 'The apple on the cover of *Twilight* is symbolic of the forbidden apple in the

Garden of Eden. Bella knows she shouldn't be with Edward, but she can't help herself.'

'Well, that big red apple should have been a *big red flag*. And not only because he wanted to drink her blood!'

'What about the passion?' Jade asked. 'Don't you think it's romantic? They don't want to live without each other. That's why it's a classic. I think it's timeless—'

'Are you *listening* to yourself? She loses her self-worth in a co-dependent relationship! Is that what you'd teach your daughter, if you had one? That losing the love of your life is so mentally damaging that your only options are suicide, adrenaline addiction or severe depression? Or would you teach her that no man should be her reason for existing?'

'That's not the point.'

I was idly impressed—until the next debate began.

'How can you say that fried dim sims are the equal of steamed? Steaming keeps the moisture in, and enhances the taste of both pastry and cabbage.'

'You're insane. Who wants cabbage in their junk food? Fried dim sims beat steamed ones every time because of their crisp saltiness!'

I wandered away from their drug-fuelled bickering, and was cornered by Jay. 'Your boyfriend is a *prick*!'

'Thank you for that, Sherlock. But he's no longer my boyfriend.'

'Good! Fuck him! You know what, Sunshine? You're a cool chick and you deserve the truth.'

I looked at Jay with a mixture of trepidation and dawning awareness. Jay is a man's man who would never rat on Jim. Unless he had his own reasons.

'Did you two have a fight?' I asked.

'The bastard has owed me money for months!' Jay exploded. His eyes were popping out of his head from overindulging on speed. 'And you want to hear something else? The girl he's fucking is a waitress from his work. Did you know that?'

I shook my head, forcing down bile.

'Yep, he's been sleeping with her for a whole month! That time he said he was going camping with the boys? He went on a dirty weekend with her instead.'

My head started reeling again. Four years together, and I suppose I should be grateful he didn't fuck her right in front of me. 'So he's actually *seeing* her?' I managed to whisper. 'Who is she?'

'Her name's Lucinda, and she's married!' he announced triumphantly, not caring about my agony; clearly, he only cared about dumping Jim in as much trouble as possible.

Candy appeared between us. '*Stop it!*' she snapped at her boyfriend. 'You do this every time you have a fight with someone, spill their dirty little secrets!'

But I didn't care why I was being informed. 'No, Candy, he's right, I need to know.'

'See?' he fired back. 'Sunshine's happy I gave her the truth. If you'd found out about Lucinda, wouldn't you have told her?'

'Of course. But not the way *you* just did, dickhead.'

'Well, somebody had to tell Sunshine. Charlie knew, and *she* didn't say anything!'

Candy and I turned together, horrified, to stare across the room at Charlie.

First she smiled at us. Then her expression melted into panic. My so-called friend looked exactly like Jim had after being caught.

'I've only known for two weeks!' she blurted, so high on speed she was unaware how bad this sounded.

'So every night at work in the past fourteen days, and every coffee, phone call and shopping expedition we had together, you *knew* and didn't tell me?'

'I was leaving it up to him!'

'*Thanks*—did you think he'd get around to it before I caught him with his dick in Lucinda?' I asked bitterly.

'I didn't know what to do. When I heard about *her*, I rang Jim and warned him that he had two weeks to tell you, or I would.'

'*Sure* you would have,' Candy spat. 'Jesus, where's your fucking loyalty?'

Charlie was shamefaced as all the girls stared at her in disgust. I'm not sure who felt worse out of the two of us, but I think I'd rather be cheated on than feel the acidic disapproval of five girls who specialise in grudges.

'I have to get out of here.' I jumped up and took off before anyone could follow.

As I walked the lonely, balmy streets back home, my phone rang. My old friend Harlow was calling—the very same girl who'd told me about the money in Darwin. 'When are you getting your arse to Japan, Sunshine? There's more cash here than a political bribe!'

HIGHLIGHT: Sushi.

DOWNSIDE: Jim broke into the apartment and stole my stun gun— probably so I couldn't use it on him.

28 July

Here I sit at the airport. I don't do things by halves. I packed up what I needed, then gave the apartment keys to Aliah and told her it was all hers. I feel bad leaving my friend in the midst of her own ordeal, but my sanity requires selfishness.

'I don't want you to go,' she said, 'but I understand. I would too if I were as brave as you.'

She had no problem with me storing the rest of my things at the apartment. As I left, she went downstairs to the resort reception and told them she was taking over—and that under no circumstances was Jim allowed near the building. Ha! Let's see him get his own place without me and his blackened credit history.

Then I swung by the travel agent, who warned, 'You know how much it's going to cost, buying a ticket to Japan *today*? We only have business class available.'

'I don't care. I'd like a flight before lunchtime, please.'

'I'm sorry, I need to ask . . . Have you thought this through? You seem a bit . . . drunk.'

A *bit*? I would have impressed an AA meeting.

'Next flight out, please.'

'Okay then.' She fiddled with her computer. 'But it's highly irregular—'

'Nope. Highly irregular was the time I served homemade moonshine at a dinner party and all the guests developed hives the size of dinosaur eggs—except for me, who drank the most. This is not irregular, it's *rash*.'

She didn't quite manage the pre-lunch flight: my departure is scheduled for 2.30 p.m.

I hope Jim finds out via nightclub gossip.

HIGHLIGHT: Saké.

DOWNSIDE: In alcohol's defence, I've done some pretty stupid shit while sober too . . .

30 July ....

No, I did not think this through. Though it *is* pretty here, with delicate countryside and spire roofs everywhere you look. But it is also *weird*.

My arrival was an omen. Only one officer manned the twenty immigration desks, so I had my passport stamped a good six hours after landing, with nothing to look at while I waited except for bleak walls and signs I couldn't read.

By the time I left the airport, the buses to Roppongi and Shinjuku—the areas where I was planning to work and live—had stopped running. I texted Harlow in a panic. When she didn't answer, I remembered she was at work, so I used my translation app to help me find an alternative bus route to take me close to the city.

That app has quickly become my best friend. Harlow said the Japanese speak some English, which is not true—nobody I've met so far knows a speck of it.

I bombarded Harlow with voice messages even though I knew she couldn't answer; I was keeping her updated on my where-abouts so I couldn't go missing without a trace. When she was finally able to call during a break, she promised she was sending someone to meet my bus.

After I disembarked, a greasy-looking British guy—who no doubt doubled as a pimp in his spare time—met the bus with a placard boasting my name. 'Are you Sunshine? Hi, I'm a driver for the agency.'

'What agency?' I asked as I shook his hand.

'The one that Harlow signed you up with—we organise jobs and accommodation for you.'

'Oh. I didn't know she'd signed me up for anything. How does that work? Do you take a commission or something?'

He looked at me like I had 'bimbo' tattooed on my chin. 'Of course.'

The question may have sounded stupid to him, but I was flying blind. I knew nothing about being signed up to an agency or what that entailed, and zilch about Japanese strip clubs except that there's money to be made because Japanese men love Anglo women, especially blondes. Apparently.

We drove through Tokyo until he parked outside a shabby brown building and led me up to a tiny studio apartment on the fourteenth floor. 'No men allowed in your room—unless the club okays it.'

What the hell? Why *would* they? And more importantly, why would *I* okay it?

Just before he left, Greasy Guy gave me a key and piece of paper with something scrawled on it. 'You'll find a street full of restaurants and convenience stores around the corner. And I've written your address in case you get lost.'

I dropped my suitcase on the floor, sat down on the single bed and looked around. Not that there was much to look at. The white walls had turned beige with age. There was a clothes rack, a bar fridge, and a toilet and shower the size of a postage stamp. Also, there was a black-and-white television playing programs in Japanese. I grabbed my handbag and decided a walk would be much less depressing.

The first thing that hit me was the humid air, flavoured with Asian spice. Flashing lights in red, blue, yellow and pink announced the restaurants, convenience stores, bars, dentists, pet shops and nail salons. Deafening music that sounded cartoonish dominated the atmosphere, blasting out of cars and taxis, and from the giant arcades on every corner.

I lingered outside one, watching Japanese youths indulge in a serious-looking dance-off, performed on a vast flashing disco floor, while a legion more went head to head in air-guitar competitions. Why were their parents letting them play in arcades at four in the morning? Why weren't they home in bed?

Why wasn't I?

Staring up and down the neon street, I was hit by a rush of grief that knocked the air from me. I felt as though a sadistic giant had uprooted my life and thrown it into the unknown. I winced at memories of the good times Jim and I had: lying on tropical beaches, exploring big cities, cosied up warm on couches by open fires—places and things we'll never see together again.

I wandered around until the tears stopped, then stood in front of a restaurant with a hundred wind chimes hanging over the veranda, fittingly called One Hundred Wind Chimes. Inside, there were only two customers and an ancient-looking chef.

'*Konbanwa*,' he said, a word I quickly looked up on my translator.

'Good evening,' I answered in English.

I had a bit of trouble describing the crab roll I wanted to order. But when he held up his hand like pincers, we were both on the same page.

Then I bit in and promptly squeezed the filling down my white Sportsgirl shirt. It looked as messy as my life.

'Saké?' he asked sympathetically.

This time there was no miscommunication.

HIGHLIGHT: Tried to fold my napkins into paper plane origami to create illusion of not giving a flying fuck.

DOWNSIDE: Translation app turned 'More Saké?' into 'Me Sucky?'

31 July

I was woken by somebody rapping on the door. Harlow stood there grinning, then pulled me into a bear hug. 'I haven't seen you in forever!' she enthused. 'I love your new boobs! You'll be a hit here.'

'I hope so.' I smiled at my dry-humoured yet vivacious red-haired friend.

'Course you will! Now get dressed and come with me. The club is waiting for you.'

'What for?' I asked, pulling on some old True Religion skinny jeans—size six, I may add. Heartache and treachery: the sure-fire diet.

'You've got to audition.'

'I thought I already had a job?'

'You do,' Harlow confirmed. 'But you still have to audition.'

'That makes no sense!'

She stopped to grin at me. 'The Japanese are sticklers for rules that barely *ever* make sense to Westerners. You'll see.'

'Okay. But what's this agency you've signed me up for?'

'It's really hard to get in the strip clubs if you just walk in off the street, especially if the clubs are full. That's why I had to sign you up—agency girls get first placing.'

I nodded, only vaguely reassured.

I followed Harlow up the street and then down five levels to a train station, a confusing labyrinth of the same flashing lights, arcades and cartoon music I witnessed last night. Harlow led me past a thousand sushi bars and one-stop convenience stores that sold everything from seaweed milkshakes to glue guns.

Next, we passed through the red-light district. She told me there are over three and a half thousand 'sex facilities' comprising love hotels, peepshows and strip clubs in a small quarter-of-a-kilometre radius.

'Wait,' I said, stopping dead with my mouth hanging open. 'Is that porno cinema *seriously* advertising a threesome with vomit? Girls throwing up on each other is supposed to be *sexy?*'

Harlow glanced at me with a mixture of pity and mirth. 'It's a different world here.'

'One where spew is erotic, evidently.'

I was impressed, though, when we reached the huge, shimmering club. From what Harlow told me, Eighth Wonder is the oldest strip club in Japan, and ultimately the best in the country.

There were African hawkers—Harlow mentioned they were Nigerian—at the front door, trying to entice every male passer-by into the club with free passes for the evening. They didn't look at me with much interest.

Inside the club I found a breathtaking spectacle of wealth, no dark and dingy corners here. The chandeliers, marble tables and chesterfields would impress any run-of-the-mill millionaire.

I was given the once-over by a bored-looking Russian man. I presumed he was the manager, but Harlow told me later that he's only an agency liaison for the club.

'Just tell the DJ what song you want played, then take it off,' he said with a yawn.

'My clothes?'

'No, your nail polish,' he said sarcastically.

So I did a bump and grind around the pole to Ricky Martin's 'She Bangs', an old-skool favourite. The Russian sighed and said something about already having too many blondes, then ordered me to return by seven. Like almost every other strip club staff member I've known, he was as welcoming as gonorrhoea.

Not that anyone seems to work for the club—all staff appear to be employed by the mysterious agency.

HIGHLIGHT: Sashimi will have me emaciated in no time.

DOWNSIDE: Just as well, because the oil they put on a Big Mac here tastes like Chinese five spice.

1 August

I'm in a state of confusion, and culture-shocked to go with it. If I were thinking straight, I would probably loathe my situation.

Harlow had been rostered on earlier than me, so I had to find my own way into work. After getting lost among the deep bowels of amusement arcades, and brushing my way through plush-toy prizes and Hello Kitty merchandise, I finally found the right train.

When I rushed through the door of Eighth Wonder, there was no sign of the Russian. I was greeted by a huge Nigerian man who shouted, 'Where have you been?!'

'I got lost, and—'

'I don't want to hear it!'

Then why did you bother asking, dickhead?

'You're fined! Twenty dollars! Now go get ready for work.'

In the change room I found myself amid thirty girls who could make up a United Nations. I spotted Harlow, who told me that the big Nigerian man's name is Lance, and introduced me to dancers from Israel, Hungary, Italy, Sweden, Ireland and so forth—I will never remember all their names. Interestingly, only three Asian girls are working at the one time.

Out on the floor, I bought myself a drink for an eye-watering twenty bucks.

'Next time, have a customer buy it for you,' the bartender advised.

Oh, really? Thank you for suggesting I shouldn't part with twenty of my hard-earned dollars for one glass of stale-tasting piss. Next time I'll try to remind myself.

A blonde from the Czech Republic sat down and introduced herself as Constanta. 'Is this your first night? Mine too! Have you heard that the Yakuza own this club?'

I shook my head while warning bells pealed in my head. Note to self: do *not* get tangled up with Asian mobsters.

I was again questioning my impromptu departure from Cairns when a plump Japanese man with glasses approached and asked for a dance.

The private room, like those in Australia, was all lowlights and lounges. I began the lap dance, and the man instantly showed his appreciation by lunging for my nipples—*with his mouth*!

'*What are you doing?!*' I screeched, pushing him away.

There was shouting and drama as Lance came running in. 'Why did you push him? I'm fining you another twenty dollars!'

'He *touched* me!' I shouted.

'It's a *touching* club!' he yelled back. 'You don't have to let them touch with their mouth. It can be hands only, but you'll make less money that way.'

Oh God! Touching? *Where?* On what bits?

I was wondering why the hell Harlow hadn't told me, and how much a ticket back to Cairns would cost that very night, when Lance interrupted my panic attack. 'You were also tenth on the roster to arrive, and you cannot do a lap dance until the other ten girls have found one first. I'm fining you another twenty dollars!'

'I'd have known that if you'd gone through the rules with me before work, instead of assuming I'm telepathic!' I snapped, and earned myself an enemy on the spot.

Back in the main room of the club, a group of Japanese businessmen came through the door looking cold and superior, with some of them missing a little finger: a sign of being a Yakuza member, from what Google tells me.

'You!' Lance barked at me. 'Do not approach them—you are too much of a wise-arse.' I didn't need telling twice.

In Australia, even when the state laws permit customers to touch exotic dancers, many managers—including Sebastian and Hugo—don't allow it. Not for the sake of us strippers, but because it's virtually impossible to tell an intoxicated man to 'only touch above the waist' and not have him grope your arse when your back is turned. But at Eighth Wonder, the customers are permitted to touch tits, stomach, thighs and arse. And as Lance said, it's up to you whether they touch with their mouth.

I've worked in a few touch clubs, mainly because the money is outrageous and because I'm brilliant at switching off. But it is far from my favourite thing. Touching dances can be sickening in the way your body unconsciously responds, while your mind rejects the very idea of being turned on. One time I became all hot and flustered after performing a dance, and then vomited in sickened shame. But it's something you must deal with if *you* make the choice to work in a touching club. You don't have to let anybody squeeze your boobs, but it's triple the money if you do. When it's only my breasts being touched, I can normally separate my body from my mind.

Now I'd either have to get a whole lot better at switching off, or fork out for another plane fare. Hopefully not another business class fare. And tonight I barely made two hundred dollars after the agency took out my rent, club fee and ridiculous fines.

I don't want to think in depth about what I've done. If I jumped on a plane home now, would it cause Jim to smirk?

Probably.

What am I *doing* here? Why doesn't life come with an instruction manual?

HIGHLIGHT: Constanta shared her sneaked-in flask of vodka.

DOWNSIDE: Wonder if my mum's usual offer to slap me into next year still stands?

6 August

I could very well be in a place called denial, but I'm still praying things will get better once I grow used to this country. Some might roll their eyes at me in judgement. But who in their right mind would have stayed in Cairns? Who wouldn't have run, if every tree, beach, road and rock, every street, restaurant, person and place reminded them that life as they knew it was over? And if I'd remained in Cairns there would have been more details to come. The thought of unravelling the whole sordid story of him and her—the excuses, lies and apologies—seemed too much to bear.

I will admit that I was hasty. I'd done barely any research on Japan, but I thought the unknown, without expectation, would provide a better distraction.

I may have been wrong about that. I'm finding it hard to get my head around this culture. There's a mix of old customs and new fads, which the youth practise religiously. I've seen Buddhists chanting in front of a massive TV screen that shows a cartoon image of the Dalai Lama, and geishas playing guitar in a park. The Harajuku girls prance around in clothes that look as though Minnie Mouse crashed into a schoolgirl. Vending machines are everywhere, and they sell everything you could possibly want: pork buns and fried chicken, somehow served hot from the machine; bunches of lettuce grown in artificial sunlight; eggs, mobile phones, birthday cakes, books, dildos and used schoolgirls' underwear. Yes, you read that correctly—*used*.

As Harlow and I walked through public gardens with bonsai trees and miniature temples, we chatted about the scene back home.

'How's Amber doing?' she asked.

'Amber from Tassie?'

'No, the other Amber.'

'You mean Tattooed Amber?'

'No, the thinner one who does great pole tricks . . . I think she's from Perth.'

'Oh, *blonde* Amber! She's doing well.'

There are a lot of Ambers in the stripping world. And Aprils and Summers, and Skys and Rains. There are quite a few gems: Sapphires, Diamonds, Rubies and even an Amethyst. And exotic creatures: Tigers, Cheetahs, Phoenixes and Kitties. Plenty of weather conditions, like Misty, Stormy and Cloudy. There are, of course, a selection of fruits: Cherry, Berry, Peaches and Apple. And confectionery: Candy, Lolly and Caramel. And generic sexy names: Lolita, Tiffany, Chanel, Lulu, Sasha and Brigitte. Almost all exotic dancers adopt a stage name. Many do so because they don't want their loved ones to find out they're stripping. Most girls also seize the opportunity to shuck off given names and wear the more glamorous title they've always wanted. It helps to name your alter ego. I became Sunshine for a few reasons, one being I'd never heard the name used before and suspected it would prove memorable to clients. The second was that I wanted to embody a pseudonym that would put customers automatically at ease. And the third? To remind myself that there is light inside me, even on the darkest and most despairing of nights.

After a teriyaki lunch, Harlow took me to a shop I just had to see: Freak Brothers. A prerequisite for employment was blue dreadlocks. The store sold alien and marijuana paraphernalia, with a buffet centrepiece that offered dried peyote and Australian magic mushrooms. I brought a see-through soap with little green Martians for my grandmother.

Then it was time for more sushi, another labyrinthine train ride, and a further round of inconsistent and bewildering rules at the most puzzling club I've ever worked at.

Lucky me.

HIGHLIGHT: Over-the-counter sleeping tablets.
DOWNSIDE: I now whisper to myself 'What the fuck?' at least 125 times a day.

8 August

I avoided Lance to the best of my ability, but he kept an eye on me. Perhaps he's nursing a personal grudge. And from what I've seen, I can't expect the special treatment he reserves for certain girls; I'm simply not regarded as good-looking enough to stand out. There are some Slavic girls here who make Claudia Schiffer look dowdy. I suspect that some of these unimaginably beautiful beings have sex with both the staff and the Yakuza patrons. For money. Probably great amounts.

It's not true, however, that the Japanese love blonde strippers. Eight years ago it was a reality, or so I've just heard; apparently, the *real* Western stripper explosion took place almost a decade ago. Back then, a treasured blonde exotic dancer could expect to take home two grand a night from lap dances alone. Now blondes are so commonplace, they barely earn a second glance in Tokyo.

I must be doing something right, though. No sooner had I sat down tonight with Constanta, than a Japanese businessman approached me to ask for a lap dance. Which I performed.

Shortly after—surprise, surprise—Lance came stalking over. 'He didn't buy you a drink before you had a dance. I'm fining you twenty dollars!'

'Pardon me?'

'The customers must buy you cocktails or champagne before you dance for them. We expect you to try to hustle a whole bottle of Dom! How are we supposed to make money if you're too lazy to make it for us?'

'It might be an idea if you sit down with me and go through *all* the rules ... ?' I said politely, instead of the insults I dearly wanted to hurl.

Lance looked enraged, and Harlow came over to save me. 'Give her a break, Lance!' she cajoled. 'My friend is still learning.'

He gave her a gruff nod but couldn't help a retort. 'Try and learn faster. And make sure you fill in a work information form before you go home tonight. We need to know your age and passport number.'

'No problem.' I shrugged lightly.

He suddenly stared at me with narrowed eyes. 'How old *are* you, anyway?'

'Twenty-eight.'

Lance shook his head in disgust and walked off, as though I'd announced that I'd forgotten to shower for three weeks instead of merely reciting my age.

'What's his problem?' I asked Harlow.

'Oh, in Japan they think you should be wearing incontinence pads and drawing a pension by the time you're twenty-two.'

'What, so I'm too *old*?'

'Practically ancient.' Harlow giggled, and I would have been severely offended if she didn't have two years on me.

'Why didn't you warn me?' I whined. 'In fact, why didn't you tell me all the rules before I started?'

'Because they make them up as they go. Nobody *knows* the real rules. They vary from girl to girl.'

'Meaning?'

'Meaning, you're treated a lot nicer if you sleep with the high rollers. But always refuse, no matter how much they offer—they're likely to be Yakuza.'

'I figured as much.'

'And stay away from any proposal to work in the "soaplands". They're bathhouses where the girls are expected to soap up the customers and jack them off.'

'I'll try to refrain.'

'Or anybody who asks if you'd be interested in *enjo kōsai*, compensated dating. It's just a form of expensive prostitution. Girls who get themselves tangled up in that shit could go missing and wind up in some Mexican brothel.'

'Harlow, why did you let me come here?'

'It's not as bad as it sounds. Hang in there, Sunshine, the money can be great and it's a wild experience once you get used to it.'

HIGHLIGHT: Found a nice little Englishman to buy me drinks. Club made $250 in champers thanks to me.

DOWNSIDE: Not ancient enough to avoid getting my period. Had to ask a monk filling in at a convenience store desk where to locate tampons . . .

13 August

I've mastered the art of Japanese public transport, at least. It would have been marginally easier to learn ancient Sanskrit.

Follow these directions: walk to end of street, go down five levels, pass complex bursting with jackpot machines, a million fluffy toys and a billion sushi bars. Get on train. Go four stops. Get off train. Walk up two levels past identical extravaganza, along with endless neon lights and ever-present cartoon music, then jump on north-bound train. Disembark, stroll by weird McDonald's, complete with McNoodle Bar, and arrive at club for another fun-filled night.

Sarcasm intended.

I've been getting to work early so I can be ticked off the roster and begin hustling for a dance. So I'm learning fast. In saying that, I've also picked up quite a bit of Japanese through a language learning app. I can now order at sushi bars without drama, understand the train station announcements, address the families that mostly run the convenience stores.

I've also become a quick study at leaving my shame at the door and begging the first customer I see for a drink. I'm not making enough to spend my cash on cheap champagne that tastes like cat's piss. Or fifty bucks on a cocktail—yes, *fifty* dollars for *one* cocktail.

Whenever possible I stay out of Lance's way, while he watches me closely.

If it were up to me, I would bail out and go the fuck home. But the decision belongs to my pride. I don't want to hear Jim's explanations, or how Charlie saw fit to keep the truth from me. Her betrayal is as bad as his. Plus, I want to appear to both of them as though I'm an unruffled jetsetter, partying around the globe. And I remain reluctant to part with another six grand.

This is where my ability to switch off comes in handy—I've always been good at compartmentalisation. Tonight, I was overjoyed that the club was busier than a mardi gras. There were patrons everywhere. Japanese, Russian and Israeli businessmen. The ever-lurking Yakuza. Some Iraqi royalty. A few Australian magnates. A couple of English web billionaires. Just your average weekend at the most popular strip club in Japan.

Since I hadn't done anything wrong, Lance was champing at the bit. 'You need to put on extra eye make-up,' he barked as a flimsy excuse to rattle me.

I had to use the public bathroom mirror, as there was no space in the change room with fifty dancers on the roster.

As I walked into the girls' toilets, I near fell over in shock. Not only was my make-up fine, but there, sharing the mirror, stood one of the most famous pop tarts on the planet. I tried not to gape, for I could not *truly* believe she was there. I knew her face as well as I did my own.

What on earth was she doing in a strip club?

'Oh, hey there,' she said.

I opened my mouth but no sound came out. I admit it, for the first time in my life I was starstruck. She was beautiful in a larger-than-life way, looking just like she did on TV, and *standing right fucking here*!

I tried not to keep staring as she gazed at herself in the mirror.

'Hey,' Pop Tart said, 'you got a toothbrush handy?'

'Sorry, no.' I actually did have one back in the change room, but sharing—even with incredibly famous people—is bad hygiene.

'Are you sure? I'll give you five hundred bucks for it . . .'

Damn! I couldn't confess now, or she'd know I'd lied.

'Fuck!' She stepped into the toilet cubicle. 'I hate doing it this way. My manager is always looking for cuts on my knuckles.' And Pop Tart stuck her fingers down her throat.

When she'd finished retching, I asked her if she'd like a towel, taking one from the plush pile.

'Thanks, that's kind of you. Sorry you had to see that. This fucking coke is supposed to be the best appetite suppressant, but all I do is fucking eat.' She sniffed a few times, cleaned the streaky make-up from her eyes—perhaps Lance had a word to her too?—and ordered me to do a line with her.

Who was I to argue?

'Do it quick, though, so it doesn't melt,' she urged. 'Every part of this fucking cubicle is heated, even the toilet-roll holder.'

'How weird is it,' I said in a strained voice as cocaine blasted my nasal passage, 'that the toilet seats here are heated, even in summer?'

'I know, right?' she hooted. 'Fucking wacked country. Someone sent a solid-gold dildo to my hotel room as a gift.'

'What about the vomit porn? Have you seen that yet? Three lesbians throwing up on each other?'

She giggled and clapped her hands over her mouth in disbelief. 'No *way!*'

Two beefy bodyguards came bustling through the door. 'Are you okay?' one asked anxiously.

'*For fuck's sake!*' Pop Tart screeched. 'What have I told you about interrupting me in the john?! You're gonna have a lot longer wait for me to OD before you write a bestseller about my life. Now step off and leave me alone, fucking retard.'

'In Australia, we say *fucktard*,' I revealed as she offered me another line.

'*Fucktard*! I love it!' Pop Tart stopped to consider me, and I was taken aback at the weirdness of her being a stranger yet so familiar. 'Out of curiosity,' she said, 'why do you do this for a living?'

'Because I get to party like a rock star?'

'That's what *I'm* talken 'bout!' She grinned. 'I *love* lap dances! How much for one, and what are the rules here?'

'You can touch boobs and arse,' I said, leading her back into the main room.

'But no pink parts?'

'No pink parts, correct.'

However, she seemingly couldn't help attempting a clandestine grope. I had to slap her hands away before they could dart between my legs. 'Behave yourself!'

'I'm sorry, I just love vagina! I can't help myself.' In case of any lurking undercover paparazzi, she quickly added, 'But I'm not a lesbian.'

I smiled. 'Well, try to control yourself. You'll get me into trouble.'

'What if I tell your boss you were rude to me, would you let me touch to stop that happening?' she asked with a naughty grin.

'Um, not really, no . . .'

See? This is why I'm annoyed by celebrities—even the ones who share their drugs. They have such a sense of entitlement.

'I'm just kidding.' She giggled. 'You're kinda awesome.' Then she handed me a five-hundred-dollar tip.

Pop Tart then forgot all about me as she discovered the pole on the main stage. She had the crowd captivated within minutes, while I hid my tip in case management made up a new rule and decided to take a percentage.

A little Japanese man with hair growing out of a mole on his cheek tugged on my arm. It disgusted me—both the tugging and the mole—but, by the way he kept twirling it, I sensed he found the hair inexplicably attractive.

'I buy you drink, then go for lap dance?' he asked, aware of the way things are done around here.

'Sure.'

'You married?' he asked on the way to the private room. 'I got plenty money. I make ramen cups!' He mimicked the act of eating noodles.

'Oh! I see, you manufacture noodle containers!'

'Millions!' he said proudly, sitting down. 'You can dance now.'

'Sure thing,' I agreed, doing my usual hair-tossing, pose-striking, arse-shaking moves.

Noodles suddenly looked a bit forlorn.

'What's the matter?'

'I no like dick being squeezed by fingernails. Painful, yes? But I like you. You can squeeze.'

'Why would I want to do that?'

He visibly relaxed. 'Last girl did.'

Sick puppy.

'Then we'll stay away from dick squeezing, okay?' I smiled. 'This dance is about you. We'll only do what makes you feel comfortable.'

So the freak put his head against my stomach, licked my belly button and called me 'Mother' in Japanese. I cringed because I wasn't sure if I'd remembered to wash my belly button, and because this little dude was a warped fuck.

'Hey!' His face suddenly lifted from my stomach. 'You want some cocaine?'

'No than—' I noticed that Lance was looking my way while nodding profusely. 'Sure,' I said to the patron, 'why not?' Clearly, another rule I'd missed was the one about accepting illegal narcotics gracefully.

HIGHLIGHT: I'll make better mistakes tomorrow.

DOWNSIDE: Lance scolded me that I act like I don't give a fuck—wasn't happy when I told him I'm not acting.

15 August

'Hello?'

'Sunshine!' Candy hollered down the phone. 'Are you okay?'

'No! They sell used school-girl underwear in vending machines here. And their D-cup bras are equivalent to an A-cup back home, so I can't get any proper support!'

I heard Tara wrestling the phone from her. 'Honey, what's going on? Are you alright over there?'

'Not really.' I sniffled.

'Come home,' Tara said firmly. 'Just get on a plane and fly back. I'll lend you the cash.'

'It's not that, I have enough to buy a ticket. It's just . . . I came all the way here, spent all that money, and I've barely given it a chance. Not a *proper* chance, because I haven't let myself really see Japan without being miserable. I have to give it a go.'

'Okay,' she said slowly. 'I get that, but I *know* you, and it doesn't sound like the real reason. You normally run a million miles from misery.'

'Yeah, that's what I just did.'

'This is all about Jim, isn't it?'

'Yes and no. I suppose. I do want to give it a chance here, and I'd be fucking mortified to come home. Jim will be laughing his arse off if he finds out how unhappy I am and what a stupid mistake I made jetting off. Plus, every time I even think about facing him or Charlie, and hearing their excuses, I feel sick. I'm not ready.'

'*Fuck Jim!*' Tara spat his name. 'Just come back. You need your friends—we'll get through this together.'

Jade wrangled the phone from Tara. 'Hi, sweetheart, you alright? We're all worried about you. Hey, is it true that the Japanese make Midori-flavoured condoms?'

Tara snatched it back. '*How* is that helping, Jade? Listen, Sunshine, are you there? You need to get on the next flight home, okay?'

'I can't . . . not yet,' I told her, without fully knowing why.

'Alright.' She sighed. 'But we're here when you need us.'

'Thank you, I love you for it.' I tried not to cry. 'Wait, Tara, before you go . . .'

'I'm still here.'

'Have you heard anything more about Jim? Or about Lucinda?' I really am a glutton for punishment. 'Tara, can you hear me? Why aren't you saying anything?'

She took a long time before answering. 'I'm sorry, Sunshine, they're a proper item. She left her husband for Jim.'

I'd half expected it, but I still felt sick. 'I've got to go.'

'No, Sunshine, please don't!'

'I have to get to work.'

'Oh, honey, I feel terrible. I wish you weren't so far away.'

'I can't talk about it anymore. I'm hanging up.'

'Okay, babes, I understand. I'll try calling tomorrow. Oh, and Candy sends her love, and she said that a guy named Orion has been asking about you. Love you, bye!'

'What? Wait! Are you there?! Don't hang up!'

Damn it!

HIGHLIGHT: The only way I'd miss my ex would be if my aim wasn't straight.

DOWNSIDE: If I died and went straight to hell, it would take me a week to realise I wasn't at work anymore.

STRANGE FRUIT

I'd done something right in Lance's eyes—he actually smiled at me as I walked through the door. He seemed almost impressed. Perhaps, I thought, I'd run over and killed a homeless man without knowing it, or tortured a puppy while sleepwalking.

'The man you danced for a few nights ago, he left you a present,' Lance announced.

'Which man?'

'He owns a ramen manufacturing company.'

Oh, right. Noodles. With the long hair growing from his mole. And mummy issues. And cocaine.

Lance handed me a beautifully wrapped gift box with—drum roll—a square cantaloupe inside. I stared at him in bewilderment. 'Very expensive,' he explained. 'The fruit is grown in a square specifically to fit the box. They cost about sixty.'

'Yen?' Around five bucks.

'No. Sixty American dollars.'

For a *cantaloupe*?

'Only second to a square mango—they cost a hundred,' Lance

added. 'You're doing better than I expected. You are on your way to collecting your first Dohan.'

It was the first time he'd ever been amicable, so I didn't want to ask. But I had to. 'Dohan?'

'Yes, a customer who favours you. By the time this month is up, you are required to have two.'

Okay. Right. This shouldn't be too hard . . . like obtaining the Australian equivalent of a Regular.

'They must come in here straight after dinner, twice a week, and buy a minimum of two bottles of champagne for you.'

'Why can't they come in whenever they want, like at midnight?'

Lance looked at me like I'd just wandered out of a village named Idiot. 'Because *you* are required to have dinner with them, and still turn up to your shift on time. Talk them into an expensive restaurant. Bring the receipt—and the Dohan—to work with you. It's also your job to convince the Dohan to stay and drink in the club for at least three hours. Likewise, you must spend one weekend each month with them—Mount Fuji is nice, you should go there with one of them.'

I started to feel ill. 'Like a date?'

He didn't like the word. 'Like a *Dohan*,' he said cryptically. 'And if either of your future Dohans want you to finish a shift early and go someplace else with them, make sure they pay an "early fee" before you both leave.'

'Leave where?' I asked suspiciously.

Lance shrugged. 'How should I know? Karaoke bar, hotel room . . .'

'Am I supposed to *sleep* with these men?' I bleated.

'Not my business. But charge a lot if you do.'

For the millionth time, what the *fuck* am I doing here? It's not getting any better. And yet I continue to hang on, tenacious and ludicrously stubborn. My fear of facing life back home has just escalated into world-class stupidity. I am a global village idiot.

As Lance left me to my thoughts, I slumped in a chair, shell-shocked.

Constanta sat down next to me. 'Hey, are you okay?'

'Do you have a Dohan?' I asked.

'No, but I really need one. If I don't have two by next month, I'll be fined every week until I do. I can't afford to have any extra money taken away, I'm already paying back the agency.'

'For what?' I asked, pulled out of my reverie.

'The agency paid for my airfare to Japan. I had no choice. My mother is going blind, and my father lost his hand in a mining accident. It's up to me to support them. I'm the oldest of six sisters. There's little work in the Czech Republic, so I came here to dance and send money to my parents. We'll lose our house if I don't. Everything I make goes back home—after the agency take their cut for the plane fare and my accommodation.'

My problems suddenly seemed paltry if the worst things I had to endure were gift-wrapped cantaloupes and refusing sex with a Dohan.

I asked Constanta, 'How would a Dohan make things easier?'

'They tip big—*really* big,' she informed me. 'I might even meet a businessman boyfriend. Then my family could move into a bigger home. There were nine of us in a two-bedroom house, and I'm the only one who has left.'

'Would you have to sleep with a Dohan to make a lot of money?' I inquired.

'Probably. The agency kind of expects it, especially from the girls who have had their plane fare paid for.' Constanta suppressed a shudder, but her eyes still shimmered with tears. 'I miss my family so much, it's horrible here. I hate my nipples being licked.'

Oh my God, you actually let them lick your nipples?! I almost blurted in disgust. But I didn't think revulsion from a co-worker was what Constanta needed at that moment. I gave her hand a sympathetic squeeze. 'Couldn't you dance in the Czech Republic instead?'

She shook her head. 'It's not nearly enough money compared to Tokyo. But even if I wanted to go home, I couldn't—they have my passport.'

'What?! *Why?*'

'I won't get it back until I've paid my airfare, plus interest. Five thousand US dollars.'

I sat there aghast. I couldn't even imagine being *forced* to stay here.

Constanta suddenly looked fearful. 'Please don't tell them what I've told you.'

'Of course not!'

'It's not all bad,' she said, trying to pacify both me and herself. 'I can make plenty of money here if I work hard, and there are girls in a much worse situation than me. See Renata over there?'

I nodded, looking at a six-foot-tall brunette with doe eyes and cheekbones that could slice focaccia.

'Her own mother signed her up to the agency against her will. Renata didn't even *want* to be a stripper. Her mum was a prostitute who became too fucking fat and lazy to work, so she's now living off her daughter. Renata doesn't even *see* a cent, it all goes straight to the agency and her worthless bitch of a mother.'

I had no words.

'And Svetlana, the blonde on stage? She and her sister were orphaned as little girls, until a pimp took them in. He sent Svetlana here to make him money because there was barely any work as a hooker in her town. She likes it better dancing, but he's told her that if she doesn't send him all her cash he will hire out her sister to the men back home. Her sister is only twelve.'

When a customer interrupted us to take Constanta for a dance, I almost grabbed him by the shirt so I could beg him to tip her extra.

Left alone, I felt ashamed. It's my stupid choice to be here. *And my choice to go home whenever I want, to my blessed country.*

Why am I acting all woe-is-me? Why do I feel the worst thing I have to face is a cheating ex? What a spoilt little bitch I am.

HIGHLIGHT: Australian citizenship.

DOWNSIDE: The sixty-dollar cantaloupe was overripe.

19 August

I'm still pissed at Harlow about the Dohans.

I confronted her this morning when she knocked on my door. 'Why didn't you fucking tell me?' I asked her.

'Oh, relax,' she said in her dry, nothing-is-ever-serious way. 'You don't have to have sex with them.'

'That's not what Lance insinuated!'

'Don't listen to him, there's plenty of ways around sleeping with them. Just be inventive! I do! Think of a Dohan the same way as a Regular back home. You have dinner with them in Australia, don't you?' she asked.

We do have dinner with customers, *very* occasionally, in Australia, but only if it's a major-spending Regular who only visits a few times a year. It can mean the difference between earning hundreds and earning thousands. And there's no uncomfortable insinuation for sex, since you've got to go to work straight after your seafood platter. There's only two Regulars I personally have dinner with while in town, and I make sure I'm already drunk by the time I arrive. Most strippers dine with at least a couple on an infrequent basis. Probably because infrequently is about all we can take. But Harlow was still trying to convince me it was The Done Thing over here.

'And Dohans can be awesome,' she went on. 'A friend of mine, Violet, hustled a car and a two-carat diamond from one of hers. I'm telling you, Sunshine, just stick it out till you get used to it, then the money, presents and fun will start rolling in.'

I stared at her, unconvinced.

She had the audacity to laugh. 'Look at that sour little face on you, it looks like a cat's arsehole! You've always been too analytical, hon, that's your problem.'

'Yes—being rational is such a flaw.'

'Okay, enough moping!' She clapped her hands. 'We have a day off to enjoy. You're going to meet two of my friends from other clubs, and we're going to have an amazing night out on the town! I'm buying you dinner.'

'They're not Dohans, are they?' I said dryly.

'Ha-ha! Very funny.'

Once again, I trailed after her through myriad blaring arcades and a maze of train stations. This time we travelled into the middle of Tokyo. At an intersection that reminded me of Times Square there were thousands of people, just as many Westerners as Asians. Futuristic high-rises dominated the streets like alien giants invading the night sky. I was mesmerised by massive placards framed in blazing lights, advertising the usual brands—Coke, Nike, Burger King, Apple—in a larger-than-life manner that was new to me. And I had never before witnessed a cartoon chihuahua breakdancing on a screen ten storeys high, seemingly for no good reason.

We met Harlow's friends on a crowded corner. One was an Irish girl called Kate, the other the infamous beneficiary of a car and two-carat diamond, Violet. Both had the cynical humour and blasé indifference that comes with seasoned-stripper territory. No naive, inexperienced dancer would survive here—*I'm* barely surviving here.

The huge buffet restaurant Harlow chose was surprisingly cheap by Japanese standards. It was up on the twelfth floor of a high-rise and looked out over the lights of Tokyo. Unlike in Australia, where a smorgasbord is one price and you indulge until you're full, this spread charged by the hour: fifteen dollars for the first sixty minutes or thirty dollars for three hours of eating, or forty dollars including cocktails. No prizes in guessing which we opted for.

I was salivating and surprised when I saw the food before me. In fact, I couldn't even see where the selection ended. There were sections of African, Asian, European, South American and Middle Eastern food. Even Australian cuisine was on offer, and they do indeed consider the meat pie our contribution to the culinary world—but also, strangely, baked beans with hotdogs. If none of that grabbed your fancy, chefs lined up to mix you a stir-fry or barbecue a rump steak in your honour.

As I piled my plate to a gluttonous level, I noticed one of the chefs injecting a pineapple with a liquid. 'They're injecting sugar syrup,' Violet told me, 'because the Japanese don't think fruit is sweet enough.' I'd seen so many crazy things, I barely batted an eyelash.

The girls were nice enough dinner companions but had a merry laugh at my expense over my fear of Dohans. And Japan in general.

I was slightly more at peace when they took me to a ten-storey department store that sold . . . well, everything. Even pet lizards. And Jesus figurines that sang. I splashed out on some make-up and perfume, and a bikini made entirely of glittering cubic zirconia for the reasonable price of five hundred American dollars. What a bargain. But hey, if I'm soon to have two creepy millionaire Dohans . . .

Smashed on lychee daiquiris, the four of us headed to a karaoke bar. The patrons were predominantly Japanese and wore French-artist attire, complete with black turtlenecks and berets. They also completely fucked up popular English songs by replacing any word they didn't know with one that rhymed. I sat nursing a strong saké as geometric-patterned lights weaved across my face and marijuana smoke hazed the air, while I listened to Kylie Minogue's 'Confide In Me' become 'Residing Bee'.

It occurred to me that I will never fathom this country. I am never going to get used to it or fit in at a later date.

At that moment, I felt the same way as Scarlett Johansson's trapped and disillusioned character in the movie *Lost in Translation*. I realised the movie summed up Japan perfectly to a foreigner like me.

It's the perfect place for discovery, diversity, adventure with a difference.

It is not the right country for running away from problems.

HIGHLIGHT: Taught some Japanese karaoke patrons proper lyrics of a Kylie Minogue song.

DOWNSIDE: Couldn't be bothered to correct 'sparing his life from this warm sausage tea' in 'Bohemian Rhapsody'.

23 August ··

OH *FUCK*! I've landed myself in serious shit!

Maybe I should be writing the message: *If you are reading this, I have been murdered!*

Okay. Deep breath. Here goes . . .

I got really drunk at work last night, unavoidable when drinking is a job requirement. (Oh, you can fool the customers into buying you *fake* cocktails, which the club has specially prepared in marked bottles that contain no alcohol, but who the fuck wants to sit around drinking chemically dyed water all night?)

After midnight, I found myself with a group of Yakuza. I turned to the one seated closest and asked if he liked the song 'Turning Japanese', failing to notice his cold-shark stare as he answered in flawless English. 'No. That song is about masturbation.'

I went on to ask him what the Yakuza do with their little finger once it's cut off, and I suggested there might be a niche collectors market for it on eBay.

I had no idea that I wasn't even supposed to *know* the Yakuza existed, let alone identify them. But I clearly hit the nail on the head, because Yakuza-man asked Lance to remove me from his presence. Obviously terrified, Lance didn't even bother to shout at me. In fact, he seemed quite concerned and said I'd better stay on the other side of the room.

Good one, Sunshine, just go ahead and piss off the Japanese mafia . . .

But it gets worse. *Much* worse.

During my time on stage, I swung upside down on the pole and heard a *crunch*.

Hobbling over to Lance, I asked to go home so I could pack my rapidly swelling knee in ice.

'No.'

'But—'

'*NO.*'

Me being me, I just walked out anyway. I thought my injury more important than Lance's wrath, and I was in too much pain to care about repercussions.

An hour later, as I lay in bed praying for the painkillers to work their magic, the door to my tiny apartment was flung open. A Nigerian man I'd never seen before stood in the doorway, breathing heavily. '*Are you Sunshine?*' he yelled.

I nodded, too frozen to scream.

He stomped through the threshold, slamming the door behind him.

'How did you get a key to my room?' I whimpered, noticing the electronic pass in his hand.

'We have a key to every agency girl's room, it's policy! The club just contacted me. Who the fuck do you think you are, leaving without permission? You Australian girls! Always so arrogant.'

'I couldn't help it,' I bleated. 'I hurt my knee—'

'You think we care about your knee?' he spat. 'The agency cannot make money *if you're not at fucking work making it for us*! If you need a doctor, we will bring you to our own and recoup the medical expenses from your earnings. It will cost you four hundred US dollars to see him. Or a hundred-dollar fine for leaving the club—make your choice!'

I had visions of being carted away to a backstreet butcher and leaving with only one leg. 'I'll take the hundred-dollar fine.'

He nodded angrily. 'Be at work on time tomorrow,' he said with a warning in his tone, then muttered, 'Fucking Australians.'

I wanted to say, *Piss off, I wear heels bigger than your dick.* But I had the feeling that would be hazardous to my health.

And his tirade wasn't finished. 'The businessman you insulted tonight thinks you're wayward and unpredictable. He does not trust you, neither does the agency.' He went on in a sinister tone, sounding like a character in a thriller movie. 'We have decided you must sign a three-month contract. We'll need your passport as insurance that you'll work for us during that time. You can have it back at the end.'

Not a chance in hell, is what I thought. What I said was, 'I don't have my passport here. It's in a safety deposit box at the bank.' If *he* could use sentences like a character from a thriller, so could I.

He gave me one more incensed look. 'Bring it with you to work tomorrow.'

Even though I was already lying down, I slumped in relief as he walked out, slamming the door again for intimidation purposes.

Definitely time for me to go. Bye-bye, Japan.

But then I remembered something that made me gasp. Yes, my passport was hidden safely here. But in my haste to exit the club last night, I'd only grabbed my costume bag and stuffed my money in the pocket of my jeans. I'd left my purse in a locker at work ... *with my bankcards*! There was no way I could get a flight out tonight without them.

I would have to return to the club and retrieve my plastic money. But I didn't want to bring my passport there, nor did I relish leaving it unguarded and easy to find.

Where to hide it? The apartment didn't have an air conditioner or even a vent.

Then a light bulb illuminated in my mind.

After flinging myself from the bed and throwing on clothes as fast as my knee would permit, I hobbled down the street and into the first all-night convenience store I saw. There, I bought a metre of linoleum, some super glue, a Stanley knife and a tape measure.

Once back in my pokey room, I sat on the floor and measured the bottom of the bar fridge. Cutting a perfect square from the linoleum, I made a false bottom for the fridge then glued it into place with my passport inside.

HIGHLIGHT: Could perhaps work for a secret government agency after this . . .

DOWNSIDE: Hands won't stop shaking enough to pour the saké I also got from convenience store.

24 August

I rang the travel agent in Cairns, the one to whom I'd been an utter smart-arse when I'd requested an immediate flight to Japan and she'd told me it was highly irregular.

Now I wished I hadn't been so flippant. I felt *so* stupid.

I felt even worse when she wound up being lovely and helping as best she could. She listened for a full hour as I recounted my story while sobbing uncontrollably. 'I'm going insane here! They have a whole festival dedicated to the penis!'

'Listen, Sunshine,' she interrupted, gentle but firm, 'the computer has stored your credit card number but not the CCV number on the back. We *need* those digits to get you out of there.'

Just my *goddamn* luck, being the type of person who never remembers those three little digits on the back of my card . . .

'The earliest flight I can put you on is tomorrow midnight to Brisbane,' she continued. 'Every direct to Cairns is fully booked for three days, so it's the closest alternative. Are you fine with that?'

'Does Buddha have a weight problem?'

'Good. Now, go to work tonight to avoid suspicion, do your shift, then get the hell out of there!' The worry in her voice alerted me that I wasn't being overly dramatic.

'Have you heard of this kind of thing happening before?' I asked, holding my breath.

She was silent for a moment. 'Yes . . . but now isn't the time to share. Just ring me back with that code when you get to work. Call my mobile, I'll be waiting up for you.'

'Thank you so much.' I sniffled. 'You're a lifesaver. I know that helping me outside of work hours is highly irregular—'

'No, highly irregular is the time I took acid and rang the animal shelter to ask if they had a god for sale instead of a dog. The receptionist just happened to be a Jehovah's Witness and promised she indeed had a great god for me, free to a good home.'

HIGHLIGHT: Actually, penis festival might have been interesting . . .

DOWNSIDE: How the fuck I can remember all eight ingredients of a Long Island Iced Tea, but not my three-digit CCV, is beyond me.

25 August

You will not *believe* how it panned out . . .

I'm trying not to have a meltdown. I need to keep it together. I will proceed to write as a person who is *not* on the verge of losing contact with ground control . . .

I felt my covert actions were perhaps a little melodramatic, even after hearing the travel agent's ominous tone. But I was proven wrong when I got to the club and saw them waiting for me: Lance and the fuming Nigerian man from last night.

'Where is your passport? Did you bring it?' they demanded.

I feigned nonchalance. 'Oh. I'm sorry, I totally forgot. The painkillers I took for my knee made me sleep all day. I'll have it for you tomorrow.'

'No,' said the man from last night, '*I'll* come by at midday and accompany you to the safety deposit box.'

Right, I thought. *Good luck with that.*

'Sure.' I pretended to smile.

Once I was in a bikini and ready to face work, Harlow grabbed my hand and led me to a couch. 'Why are the agency guys glaring at you?' she asked, looking more unsettled than I'd ever known her to be.

'I can't explain while we're here. But to cut a long story short . . . First I pissed off the Yakuza, then I hurt my knee and went home without permission. So that Nigerian over there broke into my room and asked for my passport. Is he still staring this way?'

Harlow nodded. 'Jesus, Sunshine,' she whispered, 'I've heard of things getting out of control in Japan, but not to Australian girls.'

'I'm leaving for the airport straight after work.'

Harlow shuddered. 'I'd do the same. Oh, Sunshine! I'm so sorry. I feel like it's my fault.'

'Don't beat yourself up.' I gave a little shrug. 'I would have gone to the Arctic Circle if you'd asked me at the time. You know I'm not easily swayed into anything, it's my *own* fault for not thinking clearly. And it's probably time to face the music at home anyway.'

Harlow nodded, near tears. 'I just wish it had worked out for you here, you've had such crap luck lately. Is there anything I can do to help?'

'Act normal. Don't get nervous or emotional in front of them—'

We promptly fell silent as Constanta came over. 'Hi there. Hey, what's wrong? Why do you two look so jumpy?'

Harlow and I glanced at each other. 'I don't think we're doing a good job at "normal",' she said. 'We'd better try laughing.' The two of us went into a round of faux guffaws, and while it made Constanta stare at us like we were escaped lunatics, it also made both the Nigerian men look away.

I couldn't bring myself to tell Constanta about my plans, not when she was stuck here.

After a clandestine call to the travel agent with my credit card code, I imitated myself working on an ordinary night. I even sashayed through the crowd and laughed at jokes.

How many more hours until I could flee from my mistake?

When it was finally time to collect my bag at five a.m. and catch the train home, I had to order myself not to run.

Harlow came back to the apartment with me. Where we both stood speechless in the doorway.

One side of my room had been changed to the other, *everything* switched with clinical precision: the bed, the clothes rack, the television, my suitcase. Even the photos of my family and friends that were stuck above my bed.

Thank God my passport was still glued safely under the bar fridge.

'Why would they *do* this . . . ?' I whispered.

'I'm guessing just to mess with your head. *Jesus*, I can't believe I'm seeing this.' Harlow sounded as much in a daze as I was.

A daze I swiftly whipped myself out of. I threw everything into my suitcase in a nanosecond. 'Hey, Harlow, are you okay?' I asked, snapping my fingers in front of her bewildered face.

The sound broke her trance. 'I think so . . . Shit, why is this happening? The club used to be so much *fun*!'

'So was John Wayne Gacy, apparently. Look, Harlow, I really have to go, but I hate leaving you. Are you *sure* you'll be fine?

What if they take it out on you because we're friends? Maybe you should come with me.'

'No, I've been here on and off for years, I can handle myself. I'll finish up my contract for the month and get the fuck out of here too.'

On the street, I hugged her tight before we hailed a taxi. There were plenty around for seven in the morning. I didn't like leaving her, but I also trusted in her confidence and resilience.

'See you in Cairns!' she called as I blew her a kiss goodbye.

My travel agent had advised I check in at Narita Airport, about an hour away, rather than the closer Haneda; if the men were searching for me, they would surely look there first.

Arriving at the terminal nearing nine that morning, I had fifteen hours to kill. The airport sold Western-style McDonald's, and there was a bookstore with novels in English, which I hadn't been able to find in Tokyo. I bought a Big Mac and Stephen King's latest, then snuggled on the floor using my suitcase as a pillow. It was the most peaceful sleep I'd had in well over a month.

Sayonara, Japan. I'm so sorry it didn't work out between us.

HIGHLIGHT: Always buy a bigger bottle at duty free than you think you'll need—better to be safe than sober.

DOWNSIDE: Online boarding pass predicts choice of teriyaki or ramen on the plane.

UNSOLID GROUND

For the past two days I've slept, eaten as much Australian food as I could without exploding, and watched more English-speaking television than is sane. I'd given the girls and my mum a quick call to let them all know I was fine, and safe back on the Gold Coast—where I planned to reside for a little while—before going to ground.

I'm relieved yet shocked. Disbelieving and numb. Self-loathing and bitter. How did I put myself in that predicament on a whim? I'm just not ready to think it through.

The best thing for me will be returning to work. My job has always acted as a distraction for me. Strippers are required to forget about our problems and dramas, and put on our carefree alter egos for the night.

Plus, I've always had a fondness for the Gold Coast.

I didn't want to stay in Brisbane, where my plane landed, so after disembarking—and taking a personal moment to get on my knees and kiss the tarmac—I hired a car and drove an hour down the road to this tourist hotspot. The Gold Coast is comparable to Miami—without the elegance and Cuban influence, yet it has its own tropical charm. A colourful, shiny city of skyscrapers built to frame a stunning stretch of coastline: what's not to like?

I still can't believe I'm here, and safe. I keep wanting to kiss the dry Australian air. Sometimes I think I must be involuntarily doing so, since the passing tourists cross the road when they see me coming with my lips puckered.

I couldn't hide in a hotel room for the rest of my life, so I went to see the manager of a club named SexSanity. I've worked there before, but Vincent didn't remember me. I didn't mind: I'm sort of in the mood to lay low. Nor was I surprised—if I had Vincent's kind of coke habit, I wouldn't even remember I *had* a club.

'Want to start tonight?' he asked me.

'Does Jesus get around in a loincloth?'

He smiled and told me to come in at eight.

HIGHLIGHT: Anonymity.
DOWNSIDE: Anonymity.

1 September

Well, okay, I needed a place to clear my head without interference, but I'm not used to being *entirely* invisible.

The Gold Coast is a mecca for tourists, given that it was designed to be glitzy and has surrounding theme parks the size of small planets. The holiday-makers barely notice me as I wander by like a lobotomised wraith—all their attention is drawn to the whirling lights and colours, the scenery, and the aromas drifting from the crowded restaurants. I envy their seemingly trouble-free existence.

Since I haven't worked here in over two years, the line-up has changed and I'm considered the new girl. I don't know any of the dancers, and none of them know me; this means nobody will talk to me for at least a week. It isn't personal, just a rite of passage. But Gold Coast strippers seem marginally less friendly than a jilted bride on Valentine's Day, and a bit more predatory than a tiger shark sensing your period blood in the water. At my arrival they glared for a moment, then ignored me. Up until that point I'd thought I wanted to be left alone; now I'm thinking I could use a friend.

SexSanity was already crowded by the time I started work. Amid the blaring music, half-dressed women and leering men, I instantly felt relaxed.

A would-be gangster bought me a glass of champagne (at the reasonable price of A$7, rather than ¥2200), and we chatted away about his would-be drug empire. Gold Coast customers consist of quite a few wishful gangsters, as well as sunburned tourists who've escaped from the hotel room while their wife is sleeping. (Ladies, this happens on holiday more than you'd care to think about.) They'll only stay around half an hour and avoid getting dances from girls wearing glitter or strong perfume.

While I was talking to the hoodlum, a weathered Irishman interrupted to ask for a dance: a nice, normal, non-touching lap dance.

After that, as I was making my way to an older, wealthy-looking gentleman, a tall blonde stopped me in my tracks. 'Stay away from my Regular, new chick.'

And finally, I felt like I was home.

HIGHLIGHT: Looks like I have a pipsqueak gangster, a weathered Irishman or an ageing surfer as potential new Regulars.

DOWNSIDE: Also lurking were a toothless teacher, a mammoth parolee, and a swim coach with a golden shower fetish . . .

3 September ....

After all these years, my kind never fail to amaze me.

There I was in the club office before my shift, filling out the employment sheet as usual, when a psycho-drama broke out. A great big juicy one involving the manager, Vincent, and two strippers named Gigi and Raven.

Gigi came bursting into the office in a fit of rage.

Gigi: That *bitch*, Raven, is back from Melbourne wearing *my* bracelet, the one that went missing last time she was here! She stole it, I know she did.

Vincent: Are you sure?

Gigi: Yes, I'm fucking *sure*! It's no coincidence that it disappeared when she did. Now she's back and it's on *her* fucking wrist.

Vincent: Hang on a tic, let me get her in here.

There was a short break while Vincent apprehended Raven, and I tried blending into the office wall so I wouldn't be asked to leave.

Vincent: Raven, step into my office for a moment, would you? Gigi says you're wearing her bracelet, and that you stole it last time you were here. Is that true?

Raven: No.

Vincent: Are you sure?

Raven: Yes, I'm fucking sure. I bought it in Melbourne.

Gigi: I'm calling the police. And I've already rung my brother— who bought it for me. He has the receipt as proof when the cops get here.

Vincent: Okay, let's all calm down. Raven, you heard Gigi say she's calling the police—

Raven: A million fucking times in the change room. Like an autistic parrot.

Gigi: Fuck you! *Cunt!* How *dare* you—

Vincent: Girls! Stop! Please! Let's act like adults. Raven, talk to me. You know the police are about to be contacted, are you sure there isn't anything you'd like to say . . . ?

Raven: (arms crossed moodily) Alright. *Fine.* I stole the bracelet.

I noted that Raven appeared to have no remorse and was quite matter-of-fact.

Vincent: (looking relieved) Great! Well, not great. But let's just give the bracelet back, and we can sort it out among ourselves without the police getting involved.

Raven: I can't do that.

Vincent: Why not?

Raven: Because I swallowed it.

Vincent: *What?* Why? How? With your *mouth?*

Raven: No, Vincent, with my arsehole. Of *course* with my mouth. What else was I supposed to do? The stupid bitch was screaming about cops. I panicked, *okay?*

Unfortunately, just as Gigi started screaming and Vincent reached for his coke stash, he remembered I was there. 'Why don't you finish that in the change room, Sunshine?'

Damn it! How was I supposed to survive without knowing what happened next?

I managed, with some difficulty, to drag myself away and work the busy crowd. Right up until midnight, when I headed into the change room to swap my outfit and came across a forlorn Raven, sitting all alone.

'Are you okay?' I ventured.

'Not really.'

I was unsure what to say next. Asking somebody how they planned to retrieve a swallowed bracelet seemed a bit personal.

If the truth be known, though, I was happy to be talking to someone other than Vincent and the customers. Tendrils of loneliness were tugging at me.

Because I'm the new girl, I haven't been able to approach dancers for conversation—that would make me seem needy. I'm expected to do my time alone until the girls warm to me.

In the first week at a new club, I always want to fly under the radar anyway. New girls are fresh meat so tend to do exceptionally well. Earning a mini-fortune over a few nights, especially when the other girls aren't raking it in, is not the best way to endear yourself, so you try and keep it on the low.

You should also be sure of the roster and what time you're assigned to the stage: any changes made during the night should be relayed to you by management. Never believe a dancer unless you know her well; she could very well be trying to make you late for a podium or even miss one entirely. This will land you in trouble with management and earn you a twenty to fifty-dollar fine, payable to the dancer who was left up on stage and who probably worked out the scam in the first place.

If a dancer is eager to chat away with you on the first night, she is either new as well, or an outsider at the club—in which case you don't want to talk to her if you ever want the Clique's approval, or you'll risk being tarred with the same brush as the outcast. There are two types of seasoned dancer who will talk your ear off without knowing you. The first sort is lonely because nobody gels with her, while the second will monopolise you because she wants to tell you how amazing she is and share her supposedly extensive, irrefutable knowledge of the stripping world; she knows far more than you, even if you've been dancing longer. When this kind of obnoxious bitch decides to single you out, you'll find it's preferable to be ignored.

Eventually, over the next week or so, one of the SexSanity dancers will ask how I'm going and where I'm from. Probably not any Clique girls, though: they need to be sure I'll fit in and won't give them any trouble. Only by weathering their cold shoulders with quiet pride will I earn my cool stripes.

But the waiting process is a lonely one. So it was nice to chat with another girl, even though I worried she might be a lunatic.

'Did you get into much trouble?' I asked Raven.

She sighed. 'They're not calling the police anymore. But Vincent had a meeting with the other managers. He told me he didn't know what to do, because he's never dealt with anything like this before.'

No shit, Sherlock.

'So he made me take a laxative. And ordered me to wait here until it takes effect.'

Or perhaps lots of it. 'Oh. And . . . has it?'

'I don't think so. I don't need to do a number two yet.' She sighed again.

'Well,' I said, not really knowing what to say, 'I hope it happens for you soon. It can't be much fun, waiting here all night. I'm guessing Vincent won't let you work?'

'Nope. Bastard. According to him, it's my punishment.'

I didn't think it appropriate to point out his punishment was a more desirable one than a criminal record. 'That sucks,' I said.

'Thank you. Your name is Sunshine, right? I heard Vincent say so.'

I smiled. 'Yep. And you're Raven?'

She nodded. 'Well, thanks again, Sunshine. It's nice to meet you.'

'Same here. I'm so sorry to leave you alone, but I'd better get back out there. Just sing out if you need anything, okay?' I added, doing one last check in the mirror.

As I went to walk through the door, she said tentatively, 'Um, Sunshine? Do you think you could grab me a shot of tequila?'

'Coming right up.'

Lunatic or not, I fetched the poor girl a drink and even paid for it, just for taking the trouble to learn my name.

HIGHLIGHT: Have ignored every one of Jim's 237 phone calls.

DOWNSIDE: Got an invite from another of the girls—not a Clique member—to grab something to eat after work at a fucking *sushi* bar.

10 September

After working at SexSanity for ten days, I'd gotten to know a few of the girls. They'd even invited me for coffee and McDonald's after work. But I'd stayed away from the girl who goes for *sushi*—it's not Japan's fault, but I'd rather eat clipped toenails.

Halfway through my shift tonight, a tall brunette sat down next to me. She was so stunning in features and strong in confidence, I knew she was the leader of the Clique. 'Hi. I'm Tigerlily. I think we have mutual friends—you're Sunshine, right?'

I tried not to show my gratitude at her sudden friendliness: acting too eager is viewed as very uncool.

'Would you like to join me and my friends for a shot?'

I nodded, a little suspicious. The Clique normally take a few weeks to warm up. But I followed, reminding myself to sashay slowly and not skip enthusiastically.

The Clique introduced themselves and regarded me with interest.

'We've heard about you,' Tigerlily said. 'Is it true you glued a stiletto to the roof of a manager's car?'

I nodded. 'In Darwin.'

They hooted and high-fived.

A curvy blonde was beaming my way. 'I heard you stole a politician's drugs out of his briefcase and sold them back to him for double the price?'

'That was *years* ago!' I snickered at the memory. 'I can't believe you heard about that—even *I'd* forgotten it happened!'

The Clique were acting tremendously friendly, none more so than their leader.

'You mostly work in Cairns, right?' Tigerlily asked.

'Yep.'

'Is it good money there?'

I considered lying: nobody wants their goldmine stripped bare. But I decided not to be an arsehole.

'Really good,' I confessed.

'And the party scene, is it insane? I spoke to my friend, Ally, from Perth. She said you and your friends pointed her in the direction of some really good drugs while she was in Cairns. She told me the dancers there are party demons.'

I was no longer suspicious of Tigerlily's motives. I vaguely remembered Ally, who had no doubt told Tigerlily that I'm part of a Clique myself, and possibly that we have the capacity in Cairns to make life uncomfortable for strippers who've been unfriendly to one of us. And that we have access to party drugs and like to have a good time. I'm guessing Tigerlily has a trip to the far north planned.

'Did you come here from Cairns?' the curvy blonde, Birdy, asked.
'No, Japan.'

There were oohs and aahs of interest.

'How was it there?' Birdy inquired. 'I was thinking of working at Eighth Wonder in Tokyo.'

The room suddenly swam. Sweat beaded on my forehead. 'Um, it's . . . it's . . .'

Tigerlily peered at me worriedly. 'Hey, are you okay, Sunshine? Shit! She's gone white—someone get her a shot of tequila, quick!'

HIGHLIGHT: Vincent also shared his valium stash with me.

DOWNSIDE: My silver necklace has gone missing. Am afraid to ask around at work.

14 September

For days I haven't woken up screaming that a giant chicken teriyaki is coming to get me, which is a good sign. Spending my afternoons at the beach with girls surreally similar to my friends back home has made me myself again.

Yes—I made a mistake going to Japan. Move on.

Yes—I landed myself in a situation that could have hurt me badly. But it didn't.

And yes—I was cheated on and betrayed by my boyfriend of four years. Deal with it.

I will no longer cringe at the missing zeros in my internet banking. I will accept I put myself in a dangerous situation, not just because my mum screamed it down the phone at me, but also because girls *do* go missing around the world every day.

But no more disdain aimed at myself—I refuse to be pathetic a minute longer.

I've considered exploring the tropical island of Guam, or the other stripping meccas of Paris and New York. But I'm somewhat sour at the idea of returning overseas.

I'm well aware I'll have to return to Cairns at some point. There are issues that need addressing, and all my best friends and most of my belongings are there. Plus, it *is* my adopted home. But how long will it be before I want to go back?

Another question I've been asking myself of late is: how much longer do I want to go on doing this work? As I myself have proven time and time again, the stripping lifestyle can be a trap. Eventually I'd like to do something where I'm using my brain in a more professional, less calculating and manipulative way. And I'd like some normalcy too.

I have seen strippers who wake up one day and they're forty. Now don't get me wrong, age isn't the problem—by that time they're brilliant at what they do, and regular botox and fillers ensure they remain beautiful. One dancer I know is nearing forty-seven, and not one twenty-year-old can compare to her beautiful face or incredible body. Keep in mind that celebrities like Jennifer Lopez, Kylie Minogue, Gwen Stefani, Halle Berry and Elle Macpherson are into their fifth decade.

But what about when an exotic dancer has spent her best years living a stripper lifestyle without any kind of back-up plan? The problem is the *scurry* to secure something else. You might still be stunning, but if you're inching towards fifty and haven't given thought to the future, your options grow limited. Plenty have bought homes and other real estate but have not even considered an alternative career path until time is running out. And at forty-five or above, most ex-strippers don't have the patience or inclination to go back to uni.

Of course, one way or another most *do* forge an occupation elsewhere, usually as hairdressers, beauticians or yoga instructors. But it's best to avoid uncertainty and worry as much as possible, and it's difficult enough out there on the job-seeking front for a person with experience, let alone an older woman with a big gap in her employment history. What are strippers supposed to say they've been doing all those years? And how can you job hunt without skills or references?

Of course, any person can make up a CV. Aren't most half fiction anyway? But imagine a truthful one from our line of work:

A highly manipulative, sexually suggestive individual with experience in pole tricks. Adept at twerking. Has a talent for making sales and ensuring repeat business, and a keen eye for both weaknesses and wealth. Able to work efficiently either alone or with an alter ego.

Think I might look at starting my own business before I'm thirty . . .

HIGHLIGHT: Could probably add 'experience with the intellectually challenged' to my CV.

DOWNSIDE: Jim has moved in with Lucinda in Cairns instead of a Taliban area in Afghanistan.

17 September

Urged on by Tigerlily, I paid to see a psychic today. The woman told me I wouldn't get out of stripping for a number of years, but I would indeed wind up in a normal and 'happy relationship'. I told her that was a complete fucking oxymoron, and if she could see into the future why the hell couldn't she just give me lottery numbers? Charlatan. Who believes in that crap? What friggen stripper ends up in an ordinary relationship?

As you can see, I am completely myself again. It felt just like old times when I went out with the girls for dinner before work, and the bill was paid by the owner—who sat with us, of course.

During my shift I found myself getting along like bacon and eggs with a gorgeous patron who turned out to be a world-famous artist. And something exciting occurred to me. All the time I'd spent sad and dejected, it had never once crossed my mind that I'm a free agent now: free to flirt, free to have sex with other men, and free to feel emotions for somebody new without any guilt over what it would do to Jim. Destroy him, I hope.

And though that would prove most satisfying, my realisation wasn't fuelled by revenge. I felt *interest* in the artist. It was so good to *feel* something positive and warm again; it seems I'm coming back to life.

Admittedly, I was a little put off that I'd met him at work. But as though he'd read my mind, the artist quickly explained himself. 'I hope you don't think I come to these places regularly. I'm an old friend of Vincent's, just visiting the Gold Coast. He insisted I come here. Now I'm glad I did.'

'Me too.' I grinned. 'Where are you visiting from?'

'Cairns, at the moment.'

'No way, that's where I'm normally from! Who'd have thought? I presumed somebody like you would live in London or Los Angeles.'

'You know what, Sunshine?' he suddenly said. 'I want to give you a painting. Please, *please*, go into one of my galleries and choose one—tell my staff I sent you. And when you get back to Cairns, I'll take you out for a seafood platter and lots of champagne. Okay with you?'

I couldn't keep the dumb grin off my face. His paintings are worth over fifty thousand dollars, but my smile was mainly caused by the thrill I felt: that mysterious, whirling natural high when you truly *like* somebody, and they like you too.

HIGHLIGHT: Friends, flirting, sarcasm and attitude are so much cheaper than therapy.

DOWNSIDE: Might have been premature in shouting at the psychic.

20 September

I've never been called a prude, but really, it was all a bit much . . .

The evening at work began in a perfectly normal manner. I sat at a table with my new friends, raised a glass, and thanked them all for welcoming me in and helping to re-establish my confidence. They responded with a toast in my honour, their newest group member, and thought a round of shots would complete the moment.

Then another round. And another.

I was feeling quite drunk and weepy. Without these girls, the journey of getting over Japan and Jim would have been much longer. Spending time with the like-minded is the best way to get your shit together. 'We're all mad here,' said the Cheshire Cat happily.

Our little BFF party fizzled out at the arrival of a handsome, household-name athlete, who had everyone in the place sitting up in their seats. Usually I would rather watch snails copulate than view sport, but even I recognised him. He walked in with a rowdy group of equally tanned, equally good-looking friends. There's something irresistible about Californians. Is it their pathologically upbeat attitudes and glowing facades? Like they've had an enema flushed with sunshine.

Californian was nice enough but had that air of superiority acquired from the whole world telling him how wonderful he is. And, of course, the dancers were no exception. They fawned and cooed over him, turning up the sexually suggestive banter and coquettishness to maximum wattage. Californian sat there, as if on a throne, and accepted the reverence as his due.

His friends carried on like they were just as important. Speaking from experience, often the entourage behave worse than the celebrity, and this time was no different. His merry band of outdoorsy types were soon touching up the girls, and outdoing one another with crude jokes and dirty propositions. Californian, with a slight smile, did nothing to deter them.

I loathe the way celebrities sit around without giving anything of themselves away, but expect *you* to perform and win their approval—as though they're saying, *Show me if you're interesting enough for a slice of my precious attention.*

At least Californian wasn't cheap, as so many famous folk are. Why would you spend money on yourself when the world is more than happy to give you freebies—cars, clothes and limitless drugs—just for the honour of your presence? Californian, however, did shell out for him and his posse to have lap dances. Beforehand, he looked each girl over with a lazy, critical eye, deciding on the lucky prize winners. I was one of the dancers he pointed to, along with Tigerlily, plus two of her Clique members, Birdy and a redhead named April. Oh *joy.*

Twelve of us—six girls, six boys—piled into the private room.

For Californian's comfort, any dancer or customer who wasn't part of the prestigious group was ordered out of the room by

Vincent, who also insisted upon a round of shots on the house. And, hell, why didn't we just keep the bottle? It was only a thousand-dollar decanter of Courriere XO, after all.

The lap-dance room took on the atmosphere of a bucks party.

'Look! My girl's better than yours! Her boobs are *real*!'

'No way! Did you see the *size* of the tits on mine? Who cares if they're natural?!'

'You both lose! My stripper is better looking than Angelina!'

We dancers giggled and fluttered our eyelashes—insults are inconsequential where millionaires are concerned. And it was rare for the private room to become a shindig with gorgeous men, a celeb thrown in for good measure, and free alcohol to boot.

The room had crimson-velvet walls and low lighting that cast dark, steamy shadows as the laughter intensified and the drinks flowed. Californian began throwing money around like confetti—either as tips or to extend the lap dances, I wasn't sure.

When the plush carpet was laden with scattered cash, I wondered why nobody was bending down to pick it up.

I found out soon enough.

The guy I was dancing for seemed nice enough, in a remote kind of way. I was sitting on his lap with my boobs in his face, but his eyes were peeping elsewhere. Swinging around to see what had stolen his attention, I saw that Tigerlily had done a naked handstand in front of Californian's face, and he'd responded by sticking his tongue between her legs. He went to work on her clitoris with the first bit of enthusiasm I'd seen from him all night, while Tigerlily moaned and thrust her vagina in time with his licking.

I wasn't sure if I was more surprised by the sight, or the fact that she could orgasm upside down.

My lap dance had fizzled, as me and my guy gaped while we looked around the room.

Birdy was stroking a particularly great-looking guy's crotch, while he sucked on her neck and slid a few fingers inside her. April helped him out by leaning over and lapping at Birdy's vagina, as the guy April had been dancing for unzipped his pants and thrust his cock in Birdy's mouth.

Soon there were fingers and mouths and dicks and pussies all over the place, getting a workout. Vincent popped his head in and took in the scenery, along with the money lining the floor, and shut the door firmly to the public. Of course, if Californian hadn't been who he was, neither Vincent nor any other Australian strip club manager would have allowed this shit to go on.

I had no inclination to join in, but I guessed that my new friends were assuming I would. Instead I was bored, annoyed and uncomfortable.

My guy suddenly gave me an inquiring look, as his erection sprang up against my leg.

I extracted myself from his lap. 'Sorry, orgies are not my thing.'

'This is not an orgy,' he informed me. 'Twelve people only makes it a luncheon.'

'Well, enjoy the hors d'oeuvres.'

HIGHLIGHT: Disease free.

DOWNSIDE: Unfortunately sure I'll never orgasm in anything but missionary.

21 September

Time to go home and face the music.

I rang my travel agent to get me on a flight to Cairns this morning, which was much less expensive than a Japanese whim.

'How are you feeling, after everything that happened?' she asked.

'Annoyed in general,' I said with a sigh. 'But more like my old self again.'

'I'm happy for you. I was worried . . .'

'I know. I could tell from your voice, mostly by the things you *didn't* say. What other stories had you heard about Japan?'

'My co-worker had to arrange a quick flight for a girl who'd been stripping in Tokyo. One night, the dancer was drugged, then woke up naked in an empty room with a video camera pointed at her and an open condom packet next to the bed. She couldn't find the condom anywhere. She has no idea to this day what happened while she was passed out.'

A shiver went through me. Oh, I had *indeed* dodged a bullet. Never again will I be the idiot who produces the gun in the first place.

HIGHLIGHT: Home.

DOWNSIDE: Jim has neither left town nor been struck by lightning yet.

I CAME, I SAW,
I MADE IT AWKWARD

I have returned to relationship Armageddon. My friends and I have all landed as single peas in the same freaky pod, each with our own special traumatic break-up.

The girls met me at my former apartment, since Aliah has graciously invited me to be her flatmate again. All my best friends were present except Charlie, who has been blacklisted by the group. As we sat together in the living room, Aliah giggled and said, 'I got drunk and told Charlie she wouldn't know loyalty if it shivved her in the shower.'

'Cold,' I said.

'I wasn't that inventive,' Belle said, 'I simply called her a two-faced bitch.'

'I'll drink to that.' I lifted my glass in a toast; it was filled with the hell's brew of a mojito that Candy had mixed.

Lord knows she needed a drink too. She and her boyfriend, Jay, have finally parted ways—he pissed on her clothing one too many times. 'I could never really get the smell out,' she confided.

Belle is still embroiled in her ongoing custody battle.

Jade told me she'd been seeing a Canadian whom she'd liked a lot. Until he'd told her he was returning home—to his pregnant girlfriend. He revealed this sensitive information during a romantic dinner at The Pier, a collection of bars and restaurants on the Cairns marina. Jade responded as any ordinary stripper would: she threw his backpack, containing his passport, over the railing into the sea. Unfortunately the tide was out, leaving nothing but an expanse of mudflats. So Jade flung herself over the rails, into the mud, and stomped on the Canadian's bag until it was a sodden, irretrievable mess.

Tara isn't faring much better—she's fallen into utter obsession with the DJ, who is more vain and detestable than Joffrey Baratheon. 'He told me I should repeat Year Twelve and use a stronger moisturiser, and that I could lose a few inches,' she revealed with a drunken, forlorn hiccup.

'From *where*?' I said indignantly, gazing over her size-six body. 'Your heels?'

'Wait, it gets worse,' she said. 'The last time he came over, I was nice enough to have a dozen oysters and a bottle of Moët waiting. After he ate them all and drank the bottle, he said he'd suddenly developed the flu and had to go home. But later I found out he'd gone straight to Coconuts and spent the night drinking with a blonde. I haven't heard from him in two weeks.'

Aliah is doing better than any of us. When she'd learned that Guy was dating the seventeen-year-old he'd cheated with, she had realised that she could likewise do as she pleased. My flatmate is seeing a young man whom she described as 'Made by Mattel'. 'He's just like a Ken-doll. His IQ is about equal to the temperature in the North Pole, and his collapsed consonants make a hillbilly sound eloquent. But his body is so mouth-watering, nothing else matters to me. Actually, I said I'd meet him at Coconuts—does anyone mind if we go out?'

Does Kim Kardashian like a camera?

HIGHLIGHT: Allergic reaction to mint in mojito has given my lips a bee-stung look that I usually pay six hundred dollars for.

DOWNSIDE: Jade was wearing *my* white Rip Curl slides when she jumped in the mud.

24 September

Small towns are proverbially terrible for gossip. Half of Cairns heard I'd been eaten sashimi-style by a Nigerian serial killer, and the other lot were informed I'd had my little finger auctioned off on eBay.

Ken-doll, listening in on the rumours—and as stupid as Aliah promised—commented that he had 'no idea that sushi was made from real humans, or originated in Africa'.

The bright side was, all the bar owners and managers in town shouted every round of drinks to help anaesthetise my trauma.

The girls and I visited four bars before drama broke out. Only ten minutes after we ventured into Coconuts, Candy threw a drink over Jay. And as we all know, he very much likes to reveal information told to him in confidence as a means of revenge. He probably has a mile-long list on poor Candy to last him years.

Since I happened to be standing next to the pair, sniggering at his vodka-drenched face, he kindly included me in one of his exposés. 'You wouldn't gang up with her if you knew the truth!' he shouted. 'Candy's not your real friend—ask her what she knows about Charlie.'

Candy yelled, 'Shut up, Jay, you fucking troublemaker! Stop twisting things! I didn't know *anything* until *you* told me.'

'What now?' I asked, long suffering.

Jay gave a cruelly triumphant grin. 'Charlie and her boyfriend went out for dinner with Jim and his new girlfriend. The four of them have been spending time together. I filled Candy in on it, but she didn't bother to tell you. So do you still think my bitch of an ex-girlfriend here is your *good* pal?'

'Drop dead, you drug-addled twit—the best thing I ever did was delete you from my life,' Candy snapped, grabbing my hand to pull me away. 'Don't listen to his version. I *was* going to tell you as soon as you got back to Cairns. I just wanted to wait for the right moment and not blurt it out like my intellectually damaged ex did.'

'But it's true?' I asked. 'My supposed friend, Charlie, *really* went out for dinner with the girl Jim screwed behind my back?'

Candy nodded. 'I also heard Lucinda's been over to Charlie's for coffee. Why do you think none of us will talk to her?'

See? This is *exactly* the kind of thing I didn't want to come back and face.

I felt sick. And decided to meet with Jim. May as well get it out of the way.

HIGHLIGHT: When something in your life goes wrong, throw your hands in the air and shout, *'Plot Twist!'*

DOWNSIDE: You have to know what the fucking plot is first.

29 September

I met Jim at an all-night cafe late this evening and asked him to tell me the truth.

He said, 'I promise, Sunshine, the night you caught us was the *only* time. She's just a friend. I've barely seen her since, except at work.'

I wasn't sure what nauseated me most: the lies, the clichés or the bad coffee (it's impossible to get a good double-shot cap in Cairns in the middle of the night).

I stared at him until he squirmed, while I decided on the best and most devious way to extract the real story. We girls are unfortunately required to become inventive while interrogating philanderers.

'Your phone bill came to the apartment, after I kicked you out,' I said, lying through my teeth. If he'd been seeing her it was common sense that he'd been ringing her too.

He tried a defensive strategy. 'She came on to *me*! I swear I didn't hit on her. From the moment I started working there, she was all over me like cheese on pizza. I didn't know what to do! I felt sorry for her.'

'You felt sorry for the waitress, so you *fucked* her? What a beautiful start to a relationship. *It all began with a mercy hump . . .*'

'It's not a relationship!' he yelped. 'I've only seen her at work.'

'What about the time the two of you had dinner with Charlie and her boyfriend? Let's not forget about that, hmm?'

His face took on a panicked sort of guilt. I could not believe I'd once seen him as a laid-back, charismatic Jim Morrison type. Now the illusion had lifted, all I could see was the skinny, ugly, shifty person he truly is.

I realised that bullying him wasn't helping. I needed to get him cosy enough to tell me what I wanted to know: the gory details. I wasn't quite sure *why* I wanted to hear them, I just felt it would help me move on.

'Jim,' I said in a beseeching manner, 'you and I weren't just in a relationship for four years, we were *best friends*. If you ever loved me, ever had any respect for me, you'll be honest with me. Please, I *need* to know.' *You know me better than anyone*, my expression read. *We have a history nobody can take away, so you can tell me* anything. Years of stripping had taught me how to arrange my facial features better than any method actor. 'Pure honesty between us, okay?'

Jim finally sighed and relented. 'Okay, it began soon after I started working with her, about three months ago. But I've only been seeing her now because I'm so lonely without you.' Then he started to whine. 'You were always out with the girls—you never seemed to have time for me! And I hate you being a stripper.'

I only just managed not to lunge across the table. He'd never minded the ocean-front apartments, the fine-dining restaurants or the five-star resorts my money had brought him. But if I'd heard correctly, he held my career largely responsible for his wandering dick. What bullshit!

Why do men always manage to convince themselves that they're blameless?

I had a few more cards to play. 'What about the dinner party with Charlie, how did that eventuate?' *Tell me, arsehole, how one of my so-called good friends saw fit to eat at the same fucking table as you, without inserting a fork through your hand.*

'I was having a drink with Lucinda at Coconuts—she was already there, I didn't take her out or anything! Then Charlie walked in and started chatting to us. She said Lucinda was a cool chick, and we should all get together ... They got along well ...'

'So Charlie arranged it?'

Careful now, Sunshine, I told myself. *Do* not *take his eye out with a teaspoon.*

He nodded.

I decided to up the stakes and bluff my hand. 'I know all about Melbourne and Sydney too, Jim.'

His eyes desperately darted around as they'd done when I'd caught him in the pool. 'What do you mean?' he answered, his tone saying, *Oh shit, not that too!*

'I know you played up on me, because I stole numbers from your phone and rang them. They all turned out to be girls. The waitress from Sydney, the receptionist from Melbourne . . .' I knew of no such dalliances. I was thinking back to things I'd seen but looked straight through. All the times he'd made somewhat flimsy excuses for not coming home. And the way certain female co-workers had looked at him, and how they'd looked at me: smug, with an amused sort of pity.

Jim was clearly contemplating how much I had on him. He decided it must be a lot. 'All those girls . . . I swear, Sunshine, they didn't mean anything!'

'How many were there, exactly?' The edge was creeping back into my voice, and it took everything I had to keep my tone light. 'Honesty between us, remember?'

'Around twelve or fifteen, I think. But listen, Sunshine, I did it for you. There were things I wanted to do sexually . . . dirty stuff that every man loves but doesn't want to do with the girl he plans to marry. I never wanted to degrade you, so I found another way. That's how much I respect and love you.'

Oh God. Fifteen girls, give or take, behind my back. While I was bundled up on the sofa or hard at work, wishing him a good night with the guys, he was getting down and pornographic with women. For four years.

Some might say I deserved this. What had I expected? What man would take a girl seriously when she gets naked for other dudes every night?

But strippers rarely cheat in a relationship. Every night we work, we come face-to-face with would-be philanderers. Our job doesn't urge us to stray—we see too many men seeking something else, someplace else. It isn't us strippers who can't stay faithful, it's the men who blindside us into thinking they're nothing like the guys we deal with at work. And perhaps we sometimes wind up with those very same guys, not recognising them for what they are because we can't spot the difference anymore.

I'd never suspected I lived with a monster who cheated on me and degraded women.

The fucking idiot was looking at me softly, like he understood this was quite a blow. But he also looked content, as though I would thank him for his honesty.

I'm not sure how he missed my eyes narrowing. I was so furious I could barely see. Angry blooms of red clouded my vision. 'Did you use a condom?'

'I don't remember.'

'So you spent our entire relationship *screwing* other girls, *and you could have killed me with a disease along with it?*'

He flinched as the kraken was released. I stood up like a piston, then I rummaged for my coffee and threw it in his face. '*Fuck you!*' I screamed, trembling in anger. 'If you *ever* contact me again, I'll pay somebody to kick your balls so hard, your *future fucking children will come out bruised*!'

HIGHLIGHT: Left him with the cheque.
DOWNSIDE: Coffee I threw was cold.

2 October

There isn't a woman on the planet who can't envision the aftermath of a friendship group finding out that one of them has done something unspeakably disloyal. Judgements are passed, alliances declared. Last night the Pacific Club became a war zone. Charlie couldn't have been more scrutinised if she'd marched in a rally to support animal testing.

My friends and I sat at the other end of the bar doing what girls do in a state of ultimate bitchiness: shoot acidic glares, make snide comments, and giggle loudly and pointedly enough that the victim has no doubt the animosity is aimed at them.

Charlie sat with her head high, but her body language was stiff and twanging with nerves. Then she got off her seat and made a move.

I admit I was impressed when she approached our unfriendly pack. I doubt I would have had the balls under the same circumstances.

'Can I talk to you alone, Sunshine?' she asked.

'Nope.'

'Please?' she wheedled. 'We've been good friends for years—doesn't that mean anything?' She sounded a bit like me with Jim the other night, which made it easy to see through her. Never try to manipulate a manipulator.

'Not particularly. You forfeited any friendship privileges the minute you invited Lucinda over for coffee.'

'I was trying to get information for you!'

'Bullshit!' Tara spat in disbelief as she stalked off.

Charlie barely watched her go, her eyes still beseeching me. 'I promise you, Sunshine, that's exactly what I was doing. I thought if I spent time with her, I could uncover the whole story for you.

I knew you'd want to know how long she and Jim had been seeing each other, how it started, if it's serious, all those things! I was trying to learn who this Lucinda character is. I even found out she's married. See? I bet you didn't know that!'

'Actually, I did, but thanks all the same,' I sneered, acting like a complete and utter bitch because I deserved to.

'Sunshine, you *know* me, I'm not lying.'

I almost caved, but shook myself firm. 'Charlie, I could have believed you if you'd only spoken to Lucinda once, but throwing a dinner party for her *and* inviting the bitch over for a coffee is going too far. What you *should* have done is strangled her with a G-string. And why the hell are you still spending time with Jim anyway?'

'He's a friend of my boyfriend! I can't control that.'

Tara reappeared. 'Don't believe a fucking word this liar is saying. I just went to the change room and had a look at her phone.' My friend produced Charlie's iPhone like evidence in a trial. We all stared, riveted, even before Tara had revealed anything. It was bound to be something shocking, since Charlie looked as though she'd just been arrested for public exposure.

'Look, everyone!' said Tara. 'Charlie has a new BFF—she and *Lucinda* have been texting each other every day. Check it out.'

Charlie lunged for her phone. But Tara was taller and faster. She evaded Charlie while reading the texts out loud in a mocking, bimbo-like tone.

6.15 a.m.

LUCINDA: You're *so* my favourite person right now! Apart from Liam Hemsworth!

CHARLIE: OMG! I *love* him! Miley never deserved him! You are so my favourite person too!

11.47 a.m.

LUCINDA: Am in Myer. Should I buy a Kardashian handbag? Or is that too lame?

CHARLIE: No, it's super-cool! I would *so* buy one!

LUCINDA: I'll grab one for you! They're on special!

CHARLIE: OMG! I love u so much!

10.20 p.m.

LUCINDA: Are you at work now?

CHARLIE: Sure am, whassup?

LUCINDA: Quick question. Do you ever dream you're flying. And then you wake up and can't move? OMG! Just happened to me! Scary!

CHARLIE: OMG! Happens to me all the time! Supposed to mean your spirit is astro-travelling! We must be soulmates! Geddit? Lol!

LUCINDA: *Love* it! My BFFSM! Want to come over in the morning for eggs benedict?

CHARLIE: I'll bring the coffee! Decaf soy, right?

'Decaf soy?' Belle spat. 'What's the fucking point?'

'And what kind of crazy bitches text at six in the fucking morning?' Tara added.

'Since when is a Kardashian handbag cool?' Jade shuddered. 'Are you insane?'

'So,' said Aliah, 'let me say this out loud . . . just so I can make sense of it. *You're* going to have breakfast with the girl who fucked Sunshine's boyfriend behind her back?'

Charlie couldn't meet my eyes. Then she walked away quickly, to save me the trouble of thinking up a comment that would scar her for life.

HIGHLIGHT: Charlie's bad choices mean she will appear in public with a handbag designed by a *reality* star.

DOWNSIDE: Keep your friends close and hug your enemies closer . . .
so you know what size hole to dig.

6 October

Sebastian and Hugo hadn't been around much since my return, because they were taking care of other businesses I neither know nor care about. I'd only seen one or the other each night at opening and the end-of-shift collection of money. But now the Dickhead Duo are back full-time. May the heavens weep for me.

'Hey, Sunshine! I was told you had a terrible time in Japan? Heard it was the worst experience ever! Lucky you didn't end up on a sushi platter, huh? Ha-ha-ha!' said Sebastian.

'Closer to the truth than you know, thanks for reminding me. Would you like to bring up my grandfather's funeral as well?'

He looked at me blankly. 'Why would I do that? Did he die in Japan?'

'Never mind.'

'Okay. Did you lose weight over there, or have you got that anorexia thing?'

'Sebastian, have you ever met anyone who actually likes you?'

'My wife.'

'Is she medicated?'

Another blank stare—when Sebastian doesn't understand sarcasm, he simply pretends it didn't happen. Then Hugo took over and asked, 'What's going on between Charlie and your nasty little group?'

I was surprised he'd noticed: Hugo's observational skills are usually unremarkable. Then again, the air in the club has been so thick you could have sliced it with a nailfile.

I decided to feign ignorance. 'What do you mean?'

'Looks as though you're all picking on her. I don't trust you girls. When a group of strippers get together, it's like a coven. Ha-ha, get it? A coven of strippers?'

Yes, just like witches. Truly, the man's wit knows no bounds.

But the Dickhead Duo's limited knowledge of women ensures they'll never understand that any group of girls can turn coven-like, whether it be at a club, an office or in a fucking hot-air balloon. Though it probably *is* more rife within these ebony walls.

I hope Charlie is happy with her treacherous choice. And her new Best Friend Forever. The two-faced cow.

'Two-faced cow,' Aliah whispered in my ear, seeming to read my thoughts as she glared at Charlie across the room.

Her loyalty made me smile. 'Thanks for being on my side. You've turned out to be such a good friend.'

'Are you kidding? You saved me from the non-drinking nerds *and* gave me somewhere to live when my ex-boyfriend's dick went walkabout. I couldn't buy you enough alcoholic beverages to thank you for all you've done.'

'Aw, shucks. You had me at, "I hate that bitch too."'

I love my flatmate. Even if she is seeing a Ken-doll who told me last night that *The Curious Case of Benjamin Button* was his favourite autobiographic movie.

Charlie, meanwhile, is looking unsure of herself. While she pretends to be distracted by work, she can't help glancing our way each time we erupt in laughter, to see if she's the cause. If she hadn't done what she had, I'd feel sorry for her. But honestly, what *was* she thinking? My grandmother once told me that trying to fathom another person's reasoning—when they behave in a way you would never dream of—is as possible as solving world peace by chewing jerky.

I suppose I'll never understand why Charlie chose Lucinda over me. I'm even more intrigued by how Charlie couldn't foresee the way her actions would alienate her from our Clique. Strip clubs are notoriously lonely and demoralising, and after a particularly harrowing night of groping and insults, you need the sympathy and understanding of those close to you. You *need* your friends. I can't imagine working in a club where I'd lost them all.

After musing half the evening away, I decided to get off my arse and go find some money. Within minutes, I came across a young man who seemed rather normal. He worked in the fresh produce section of one of the main supermarkets in town.

Our lap-dance room was almost at capacity when we walked in. The dancers were in various stages of undress, swishing and swaying, as I found a seat for him.

No sooner had I turned my back did he reveal a true fondness for his job, though he might have been better suited to the deli section than fruit and veg. Because it seemed the only thing he wanted to freshly produce was his sausage.

First, I gaped at the specimen rearing from his jeans. Then I laughed my arse off at its vulnerable size. 'Hey,' I announced to the entire lap-dance room, 'who here wants to see a man with a champignon where his penis should be?'

Every girl in the room stopped, gaped and guffawed.

I can't imagine anything more mortifying for a man than a roomful of beautiful women laughing at his dick.

This young man was turning as pink as his little wiener when Hugo and a bouncer arrived to see what all the ruckus was about.

'What's going on?' my boss asked. 'Why has everyone stopped dancing?'

'Because the smallest cock on the planet has put in a surprise appearance,' I explained.

Hugo's face displayed a montage of shock and outrage. 'You *dirty little bastard*! You're out of here, and banned for life!'

My boss took hold of one arm, and the bouncer grabbed the other as they frogmarched the sausage-flasher to the front door where they threw him out, none too gently. Only thing was, nobody had thought to make him tuck his cock back in his pants. So my last (and lasting) image of the little pervert is of him running away with his deflated member bobbing in the breeze.

HIGHLIGHT: Best friends do not judge one another. They all sit together and judge everyone else.

DOWNSIDE: Didn't know penises came in size zero. Please God, make sure my next boyfriend comes in L. Or at least M–L.

12 October

Authentic happiness has been an abstract concept for too long. I awoke today thinking it was time to alter this.

I spent the morning with Aliah at a spa, where we indulged in massages, seaweed wraps, facials and manicures. I didn't let it bother me that we had to get a cab to the spa, since Jim has kept the car.

I then decided to enlist someone other than me to work on my self-image. And after paying the most sought-after hairdresser in Cairns an indecent amount, I emerged with my honey-coloured lion's mane gone, and a sleek white-blonde curtain in its place. Next I obtained an extra-dark spray tan, and lastly I invested in a pair of sky-blue contact lenses. The overall effect is not dissimilar to an alien ice queen who has swum in Willy Wonka's chocolate river.

Step one of changing my life ticked off: a sexy, interesting new look.

Step two was finding someone to appreciate it. And I had that someone in mind.

I told Aliah about my magical meeting with the famous painter on the Gold Coast.

'No *way!*' she squealed. 'Oh my God, I can't believe he told you to pick one of his paintings, and asked you out! He's so gorgeous. We have to go to the gallery and choose one right this minute.'

As we wandered the shiny, spacious showrooms, looking at every option, my heart was set on an oil painting of sunset over the ocean. I then became embarrassed at the thought of approaching the flawlessly groomed receptionist and asking for a free artwork.

Luckily, Aliah had no such reservations. 'The artist has personally invited my friend to choose a picture for herself. We'd like the sun setting over the sea, please.'

The receptionist smiled coolly and announced in a condescending voice that she'd have to ring Painter to seek his approval. After she'd done so, looking a bit put out, she explained to me and Aliah that, yes, Painter wanted me to have the picture, but it was on exhibit for another few weeks. He'd phone me as soon as it was ready; he'd like to present it to me himself.

'How lovely!' Aliah trilled. 'Maybe he's going to be your new boyfriend.'

Hmm: rich, gorgeous, generous *and* talented. Wouldn't that make a nice change?

Before work, Aliah and I met up with the girls at a restaurant for a bite to eat. My mood was all butterflies and rainbows from the number of compliments I received about my hair. The restaurant manager even announced he was creating a brand-new shot for me and naming it 'White Hot'. It turned out to be a concoction of Kahlúa, cream and lychee liqueur, which tasted absolutely revolting . . . but it's the thought that counts.

The conversation turned to my rendezvous with Painter on the Gold Coast, and my apparent good fortune in the gallery today.

It didn't get the reaction I was looking for.

Candy was staring at me in sympathy. 'I hate telling you this—after all you've been through—but Painter is even worse than Jim. He's a lowlife dog.'

I slumped. 'Why?'

'I went over to his house once because he wanted to paint me, and when I went to the toilet I found a camera hidden in a vase—the *freak* was watching me pee. I heard later that he has hidden cameras in every room.'

I drooped some more. The shine was off my day.

Belle leaned over and squeezed my hand. 'Honey, it's his MO. Painter will offer a pretty girl one of his pictures, but you have to go over to his house to pick it up. Then he expects you to sleep with him for it. He did it to me when I met him in Sydney. He's done it to all of us.'

My friends nodded solemnly.

'Did any of you get your painting?' I asked.

'No way!' Tara exclaimed.

'Not a chance!' said Candy.

'Absolutely fucking not!' Belle snapped.

All the girls turned to Jade, who'd found a sudden interest in her cocktail. 'Um . . . It's hanging in my lounge room.'

HIGHLIGHT: Great hair, at least.

DOWNSIDE: Hope nobody finds out that bloody hideous drink was named after me.

14 October

Maybe in my last life, I was a sniper who went up to a bell tower and wiped out fifty of the world's most promising college students. Perhaps I clubbed seal pups for a living, or it could be that I ran a backstreet abortion clinic. Whichever it is, the universe seems to be splitting its pants at my expense. Lucky me, the cosmic joke.

Yes, I may have an amazing white-blonde curtain of hair, but my ex is a pervert. The whole Japanese strip club scene is perverted. Now my prospective new love interest has turned out to be a pervert. What did I do to make fate turn on me so ruthlessly?

I'm also irritated that Jim took the car, and could freely do so because it was bought in his name, even though *my* money paid for most of it. The upside to this is the thought that I can buy a *new* car—the kind he could never afford in his wildest, wettest dreams. But for the moment I have to catch a cab everywhere I go.

My exasperated and slightly bitter mood is beginning to show.

As I arrived at work, Hugo asked me if I'd had a haircut. 'No,' I snapped, 'I just dyed the ends invisible.'

'Pity they can't colour your saddlebags see-through too,' Hugo retorted in his bitchy way.

Then I behaved despicably towards one of my Regulars, who may be warped but is harmless. The unfortunate soul grew up on a farm, hundreds of miles from civilisation, without television, newspapers or magazines. His schooling was conducted via a two-way radio, and he had no contact with women and girls aside from his mother and sister. Farmer became sexually maladjusted—you see, he's hopelessly attracted to his sister.

Yes, it's grotesque, and my private judgement is harsh. But other than a therapist or a priest, strippers are pretty much the only people anyone can admit this kind of twisted shit to. Not that Farmer is forthcoming with such delicate information—he doesn't exactly shout from the rooftops, *I want to bang my sister!* Each time I'm dancing for him, it slips out like a bout of Tourette's. 'You're so pretty. I love seeing you naked, because you give me such naughty thoughts . . . Sis.' Even if I hadn't known of his family history, the shamed melancholy on his face would have given away his faulty carnal wiring.

Usually while this exchange happens, I pretend it isn't. Tonight, however, I snapped at him to stop by an asylum for evaluation before he comes to see me again.

I instantly regretted it. Not only is Farmer my highest-paying Regular, but he also travels hundreds of miles from the farm he inherited and is running alone, just to come and see me. This lonely man has very few social skills and no other means of getting a woman to instantly drop her pants.

On the other hand . . . am I experiencing an awakening? Is this what every man is like deep down? I don't mean they all have a depraved yearning to get it on with a sibling, but does every man have debauched secrets?

What I'm trying to say here is, will I ever meet a normal man?

Now I'm sitting here with my own yearning, although it's just for my days in Darwin, when my biggest problem was deciding whether I should put a conditioning or protein treatment in my hair.

Well, it seemed that was my biggest problem. Jim was probably playing up on me back then too.

HIGHLIGHT: Hairdresser has come up with a moisturising and protein treatment in one!

DOWNSIDE: If this year were a drink, it would be colonoscopy prep.

31 October ··

To forget about the lack of sane men in my life—and my life in general—I've been working as much as I possibly can. The silver lining is the money I'm saving, although some of it is spent at the bar at Coconuts. Admittedly, they may as well set up a fold-out bed and port-a-shower for me, with the amount of time I spend there.

I have a new philosophy. Worrying is like a rocking chair: it gives you something to do, but it doesn't get you anywhere. Vodka, however, takes you exactly where you want to be.

I haven't even been bothered to go shopping. In saying that, I was forced to venture out today to buy a Halloween costume. Believe it or not, this night requires a lot of thought for those in the stripping industry. Why? Because women and men do *not* fantasise about dress-ups in the same way.

Our patrons are only impressed by certain generic costumes. In a word, their fantasies are basic: nurse, cowgirl, French maid, policewoman. They do like lingerie, of course, but even a Playboy Bunny outfit hasn't gained me much attention on Halloween in the past. And customers hate it when we become creative. They have no interest in a witch, fairy, zombie—or giant pumpkin. Most men find none of these things sexy, and many a stripper has learned the hard way with an empty purse to show for her troubles.

Charlie, continuing her spate of bad judgement, dressed up as the Queen of Hearts. The costume had such a huge round, frilly collar that my initial thought was, *At least the bitch won't lick her stitches.*

Halloween also brings out the freaks.

A little before eleven o'clock, I found myself at the bar having a conversation about complex carbohydrates with a man dressed head to toe in armour. The knight in shining aluminium wanted a lap dance but couldn't sit down without a custom-made throne. We decided to attempt the feat by placing him in a corner, where I could shimmy against his jousting stick while we remained standing. Stranger things have happened . . . I think.

This bizarre encounter gave me a bird's-eye view of the lap-dance room, so I found myself looking straight at Aliah's naked body writhing for another customer.

It struck me as strange, and ominous, when he suddenly shot bolt upright. 'How much for a fuck?' he hollered.

Aliah couldn't do more than blink in surprise. We sometimes encounter this charming proposition at the bar, but I hadn't before seen any patron interrupt a lap dance in order to scream it.

'We don't do that . . .' Aliah stammered.

'Why the *hell* not?' he shouted, growing more agitated as he took a menacing step towards my friend. 'A whore who degrades herself by showing her body should let men do what they want. You deserve to be raped, you fucking cock-tease.'

Aliah's eyes filled with tears as she bolted. I was absolutely floored myself—it's rare for anyone to say the word 'rape' around us, let alone condone it so vocally.

I could see the bouncer running after Aliah to the change room. The abusive bastard, left behind, bent over to fish his drink from the floor, no doubt ready to knock it back and make a fast getaway.

Pandemonium broke out with no security present. Girls were shrieking in outrage and pointing their fingers. Customers were out of their seats and shuffling nervously. And so I took the opportunity to stop the bastard from escaping without a lesson.

As he was leaning down to grab his Scotch, I stepped on his tie, trapping him in a chokehold as he tried to rise. His face turned magenta as I glared down at him until the bouncer arrived, took over—with a cloaked jab to the kidney—and hoisted the filth down the stairs.

Mentioning rape to a stripper is just as bad as trying for a grope. There is little more frightening or degrading to us.

In the change room, I hugged Aliah tight as she cried all over my naughty nurse outfit. My poor, poor friend—what a humiliating and terrifying thing to go through. And a frustrating one, because nothing can really be done about it. There aren't any laws against insulting a stripper, and the piece of shit hadn't directly threatened her.

Aliah was still sobbing huge gulps when Sebastian and Hugo came hurtling through the door. '*Was it you who choked him?!*' Sebastian yelled at her.

A touch of concern might have been nice. And pigs might also learn to mix cocktails while tap dancing.

'No!' she shouted back. 'But I wish I had!'

'I choked him for her,' I answered calmly. 'And will tell the police so, soon as I call them.'

We had no real intention of calling the law, but Sebastian and Hugo, like most club managers, are extremely anxious around cops. Sebastian took it down a notch at the mere mention and became surly instead of irate. 'No need to get the police involved. I mean, he only yelled a bit and took a step towards you, right? He didn't actually grab you?'

Aliah and I gaped at him. 'Are we to understand a man shaping up to a woman and saying she should be raped *isn't* a serious violation?'

Sebastian went on the defence. 'It's serious when you go around choking customers! You could get the club in trouble.'

I raised an eyebrow. 'Serious as the trouble *you* could get into if we called the Fair Work tribunal tomorrow? I know we're subcontractors and all, but I should think they'd frown quite heavily on the boss downplaying verbal abuse.'

He looked as though I'd tasered his testicles, then he turned his helpless fury my way. 'You know, Sunshine, you were much nicer when you were *fat*.'

'Fuck *you*.' I'd had enough of this night, this week, this year. Throwing my bag over my shoulder, I stormed out of the club before realising I wasn't exactly dressed in respectable streetwear: my naughty nurse outfit ended somewhat short of my buttocks, and the built-in push-up bra gave me the kind of cleavage I could have used as a dinner tray. But I'd be damned if I was going to walk back into that change room.

Spying the coat rack behind the reception area, I reached over in a rush and grabbed the first thing I saw: a garment resembling a fuzzy purple onesie. Not caring to inspect it, I stepped in and zipped it up as irate tears stained my face. Then I stomped onto the street to hail a taxi or book an Uber.

Where I ran directly into Orion.

'Hey!' he said, then frowned as his eyes travelled down my body.

My eyes followed suit.

No. No, no, *no*. This could not be *happening*! Why, oh *why*, had I not left my naughty nurse outfit on?!

Without a word, I jumped into a cab and sped away.

I can forget about anything happening between me and Orion— any interest he had in me surely withered and died tonight. And there's no way I can ever face him again, not when he's seen me standing in the middle of a busy street, tears streaming down my face, dressed as a Teletubbie.

HIGHLIGHT: Could have been a Wiggle.

DOWNSIDE: Tinky-Winky outfit was awful staticky material, so hair was standing on end like a shock-treatment patient.

3 November

Whenever I think I'm too old to do this job, I shall look back on this day and giggle. Just a little bit. Praise the Lord I'm twenty-eight, not eighteen with underdeveloped instincts.

It's all about Generation Z, otherwise known as Post Millennials or Zoomers. Spawned somewhere between Britney Spears's rise to fame and the Columbine High School massacre, these youths can behave as though everything should go their way. Plenty are naive to the perils of the real world, as they're used to receiving a hundred likes or retweets on social media because they changed their lipstick colour.

In their sweet ignorance, they never take my word as gospel that a young hot guy does not have lots of money to spare. 'But he's so cute, Sunshine! What if he turns out to be, like, a gorgeous millionaire?!' They refuse to believe that there is more chance of the Twin Towers reassembling themselves.

Although teenage strippers watch me and my older cohorts dance on stage, they still miss the point. In their eyes, at our advanced age we're almost ready for embalming, so what could we possibly know that their generation doesn't? Well, for starters, our patrons are mesmerised by sensual undulations, so it's best to dance like a snake on heat. Of course customers are impressed by pole tricks, who isn't? But tricks are only good for an occasional wow factor. Spend your entire fifteen minutes on stage looking like an aerial contortionist, and you can bet your diamond-flecked nail polish that your audience will grow bored of the gymnastics.

Recreating the complex choreography of Beyoncé or Ariana will get you nowhere money-wise either. But do you think Gen Z listen?

Girls today, honestly.

So it should have come as no surprise to me when a group of Lolitas asked my advice on a particular matter, then ignored it completely. (Askhole: a person who asks for your opinion, then does the exact opposite of what you advised.)

A film crew, lead actor in tow, were having a few days off. The actor in question is recognisable enough to have a fanbase in the next galaxy. I'll call him the Dude. As he walked through the door of the Pacific Club, I was not only unimpressed but indulged in a bit of eye rolling to prove it. Yet the Dude was not only perfectly behaved but also made sure every dancer in the club got a tip. The film crew, on the other hand, were ghastly; all night they displayed appalling conceit, overwhelming misogyny and general rudeness.

But the crew then invited all of us dancers to a party after work. The big bash was to take place on an exclusive private island, one that charges the reasonable accommodation fee of ten thousand dollars per night. The film crew wanted a handful of gorgeous girls to top off their luxurious tropical holiday.

My antenna for trouble was twanging on high-alert. I told the teenage dancers not to go—my friends and I certainly wouldn't be accompanying the Dude's badly behaved posse. But did the Zoomers listen when I warned them to steer clear? Of course not. Like Sebastian, they're still enthusiastic about fame and easily impressed by it.

So off to the island they went.

My group of friends had gone for a quick drink at Coconuts before Aliah and I headed home. I'd only been asleep ten minutes when my phone rang. To begin with, I thought it was a prank call. Then I realised someone was hysterically crying on the other end.

'S-s-s-unshine! H-h-h-elp us!' Great gulping gasps from a childlike voice.

'Calm down, I can't understand you. Take a deep breath and tell me what's happened.'

The nineteen-year-old stripper, Rosaleigh, got her voice under control. 'We're at the police station—*all of us*! Can you please, *please* help? I think we're in big trouble!'

What could I do but come running? The sisterhood recognises no age group.

'What have they got themselves into?' Aliah yawned in the Uber on the way there.

The five teenage dancers, acting like starstruck groupies, had been under the impression they would engage in a hot and heavy session with the Dude. Once they'd arrived on the island via private catamaran, the girls and film crew indulged in a spot of skinny-dipping. However, the Dude—no doubt having seen it all before—got bored and went to bed. The girls were stranded with only the leering film crew. These chivalrous men demanded the dancers have sex with them—all *fifteen* of them—or security would be called. They threatened to report the girls as intruders on a private island who were hoping to entice a movie star with nudity and drugs.

And they were good as their word. When the girls said no (one smart choice, at least), the crew hid their clothes and called the authorities. Once security arrived, the clothes miraculously turned up with a few grams of coke in the pockets—the movie business must pay well if they can afford to throw away a baggie or two of Colombia's finest.

Security then handed the girls over to the cops, who came down hard on them without listening to their side of the story. The powers that be do *not* like a side order of scandal attached to celebrity visits in the region: naked groupies don't go well with tropical-haven tourism campaigns, no matter how good-looking the groupies.

Lucky for all involved, one of my Regulars just happens to be a solicitor. Even more fortuitous, he's one of the few I can actually tolerate. Solicitor isn't abnormal, just a dirty middle-aged perve.

I whipped out my phone, wondering how rude it would be to call him at six in the morning. Then I decided I didn't much care.

'Sunshine, what a sexy surprise!' he drawled in greeting. 'I heard you're back in town. I hope you've called to tell me you're not wearing panties?'

'Nobody says "panties" anymore, except Ron Jeremy. I'm ringing because I need your help.'

'Please say it's a twisted bra strap you're having trouble with.'

'Wish I could, but you'll be happy to know public indecency *is* involved, along with five teenage strippers.'

'My favourite thing! I'm on my way!'

HIGHLIGHT: All sick days covered by teenage groupies forever.

DOWNSIDE: Definitely felt my advanced age though, after groupie-saving sleep deprivation.

4 November

You'll be pleased to know the police didn't have a leg to stand on, since one of the dancers remembered the name of the catamaran that took them to the island. The cops looked at the ship's log of guests, which contained the strippers' names, along with footage of the film crew having a wild time with the girls in the Pacific Club. And I'm not sure how the cops ever believed that five teenage girls had swum to an island in possession of cocaine, without getting their clothes or the drugs wet.

All charges were dropped on the proviso that the dancers resist the urge to share their story with *People* magazine.

Sebastian was in a particularly foul mood after the police interviewed him and went through the club's security cameras. Unfortunately, he now chose to remember I'd stomped out during my shift a few nights earlier. 'How dare you leave whenever you feel like it! Next time, ask permission before you go strutting out. If you're rostered on for a shift, you *finish* that shift! You hear me, Sunshine?'

Yes, dickface, loud and clear.

But for once, I sort of agreed with Sebastian. If I'd stayed in the club, I wouldn't have been traumatised by Orion catching me crying in the street, dressed as Tinky-Winky. I want to die of shame each time I allow myself to think about the look on his face. He has no doubt taken the safe bet and gone back to his normal nurse.

Sebastian continued to rant at me. 'You bitches think you can walk all over me. Not one of you has respect for me, or this club!'

I agreed with him there too. Poor Sebastian. Some people just need a sympathetic pat. On the head. With a hammer.

But I had no blunt instrument handy and couldn't be bothered to think of a reply. So I nodded politely till he finished, then sat myself at the bar.

I felt suddenly exhausted, as though the year was catching up with me. But no matter how opposed I felt to working, I was already there, undressed, with a face covered in war paint. And

I would most certainly have got the sack if I'd walked out the door again. I made myself go forth to seek dances.

On a quiet weeknight it can be difficult to make much money. I have a philosophy though: never panic until one o'clock, as your luck can change. There might be a string of small fifty-dollar dances or perhaps none at all for the first half of the night, then you'll be run off your feet with hundred-dollar shows. The club doesn't have to be busy; sometimes you only need that one big fish. It's not uncommon to have made a paltry twenty dollars when some high roller walks in with a thousand bucks to spend on you. And it's always easier to make money after midnight, because the customers are more intoxicated by then—extracting money from a drunk is child's play.

Never panic till one.

So it was with joy that I found an easy, shit-faced target near the end of the night.

'Can I give you two hundred for a dance?' he slurred.

Of *course* you can! Come right this way!

I had already made a few hundred before I led the drunken twit into the lap-dance room—that I promise you. It's why I was gobsmacked by what happened next.

After groping for his wallet, the drunk dropped it on the ground. On polite instinct, I bent down to help him retrieve it. But as he lurched and fumbled, then finally picked up and opened the wallet, I could see there was no money inside.

I sat down in shock, G-stringed arse on the carpet, as he began yelling that I'd stolen his non-existent cash.

Sebastian came running in. 'What the hell is going on?' he shouted.

'She stole all my money!' the drunk hollered. 'This *whore* pickpocketed me!'

And Sebastian actually stared at *me* with a question in his eyes.

'Of course I didn't!' I scoffed. 'That's ridiculous! He had no money to start with!'

'How do you know that?' my boss asked suspiciously.

'Because it was obvious when he fumbled with his wallet . . . Oh Christ, why am I even being asked to explain myself? This is stupid. Check the fucking cameras!'

In a continuation of the bad luck I've landed this year, it so happened we'd been seated in the security camera's one blind spot. All that could be seen was the wallet being dropped, and both of us on the floor rummaging for it.

Sebastian was swayed . . . in the drunken liar's direction!

'You can't honestly believe I'd steal from a customer?' I gaped. 'We were only on the floor a few seconds. How could I have had time to scoop up his money, fold it neatly and tuck it into the slot on the side of my shoe?'

Sebastian ignored me and looked at the drunk. 'How much did you lose?'

The man wasn't as intoxicated as I'd judged. Those stilettos are made of clear perspex, and the wily bastard could see two green hundred-dollar notes inside one of them.

'Two hundred.'

Sebastian looked down at my shoe. 'Give it back to him.'

'I beg your pardon?'

'You heard me, Sunshine. Give him back his money.'

'But—'

'*Do it now or I'll sack you on the spot!*' he bellowed.

I had no choice. Sebastian can get away with this treatment because this is the only decent club in town, so the evil drunk left a happy man.

I had no words when I faced Sebastian. I just stared in silent fury.

He squirmed but managed to sound self-righteous. 'Whether you stole it or not doesn't matter. I couldn't have the police here twice in one night, it looks bad for the club. I did you a favour in the long run. What if that customer told everyone in town our girls are pickpockets? Then we'd lose all our clientele!'

'So, you don't care if I'm a thief, you just threw me under the bus to ensure your club remains busy?'

For once, Sebastian had the grace to look embarrassed—but not remorseful. And because he couldn't face his own behaviour, he couldn't face me and walked away.

Only a few leaps of thought later, I found myself smiling.

Sometimes, I wrestle my demons. Sometimes, we snuggle instead.

I am going to ruin this club.

HIGHLIGHT: Whatever doesn't kill me . . . better start running.

DOWNSIDE: Maybe *People* magazine would have paid me more than two hundred bucks for island story.

13 November

When life knocks you down, calmly stand up and say, 'You hit like a bitch'. Then proceed to hit back. And I just happen to know someone who can pack a punch.

I waited at a luxurious restaurant beside the marina, overlooking the white boats, and watched as Will—the *only* Regular I count as a friend—emerged from a particularly huge and shiny one to meet me. He looked a bit like a stout cherub with curls and a merry expression, in his work shorts and Target T-shirt. Most people wouldn't guess that he's worth close to a billion dollars.

The waitstaff did, though, as Will habitually dines there, and they bowed in sycophantic worship as he walked through the door.

I didn't blame them. I was about to turn on the grovelling myself.

'Lovely to see you, Sunshine!' he greeted, kissing me on the cheek. 'I've wanted to do lunch for a long time. And you've booked my favourite table!'

Yep. Which was no accident.

'Great to see you too,' I told him. 'I've ordered you a bourbon. Hope you don't mind?'

'Mind? I love a girl who remembers my favourite drink.'

I sure did. With pathological dedication.

Will is fascinated by the stripper world and exotic dancers in general. He has a whopping respect for our confidence and admires the fact we make our bodies sole-trading businesses.

I entertained him with stories of Japan and my break-up with Jim while we waited for lunch. Fully alert to Will's way of thinking, I didn't dare order a salad—he likes his girls flamboyant and self-indulgent. Besides, I don't mind a big porterhouse now and then. Especially when it comes to the table still sizzling from the flame grill.

But my mouth went from watering to a horrified gasp as I cut into the steak with too much force, and the whole slab went flying across the table to land on Will's lap. His pale blue shorts looked like they'd undergone an autopsy as the waiter arrived to remove the offending prime cut. Why do things always get so fucking messy whenever I'm involved?

To make matters worse, my phone was on the table between us when it dinged a text message alert. The words *Tell me you have a pocket-rocket dildo in your sexy little clutch purse?* were lit up for both me and Will to see.

I buried my face in my hands, mortified. But to my surprise, Will burst into a bellowing laugh. He couldn't stop as tears rolled down his face.

As though wanting to join in the fun, Solicitor appeared at our table with a mega-watt grin. 'Sorry to interrupt, I saw Sunshine from across the room and used her as an excuse to get away from a ghastly client.' He turned to me. 'I trust you received my message?'

'The one that's still vandalising my phone screen? Yes I did, thank you. Really, you're wasted as a lawyer—you should write love poems for a living instead.'

This sent Will off into further gales. He motioned the waiter for another seat as he invited Solicitor to join us.

'I'd be delighted.'

I wasn't—how was I going to wheedle help out of Will with my other wise-cracking Regular present?

'I'm so pleased to see you, my darling,' Solicitor said after I'd made introductions. 'I was worried you might have given in to the understandable urge to commit homicide against your bosses. I'd act on your behalf, of course.'

'I'd help you too,' Will put in. 'Sebastian and Hugo had a private detective do some digging on a good friend of mine, to stop him opening another strip joint in Cairns. The PI found my mate had committed a criminal offence in another country, which liquor licensing would never have found out about if your bosses hadn't ensured they did.'

'I could have got that licence passed, had I known,' Solicitor said.

Will shrugged. 'Too late now. My friend can't open any kind of bar in Australia after that stunt.'

Solicitor shook his head. 'I wondered why there's been no whisper of genuine competitors to the Pacific Club.'

I liked where this conversation was going—I liked it a *lot*. I just prayed Solicitor didn't spoil it by changing the subject to hotpants or anal-waxing. But I'd underestimated the man, and perhaps misjudged him too.

'Opening a better club would be the perfect revenge on such unpleasant vulgarians.'

Will looked perplexed; he had begun life as a truck driver and risen from the working class by instinctive business acumen instead of a formal education.

'He means my bosses are both vile pieces of shit,' I offered.

Will guffawed. And I saw a light go on in his head. I hadn't even had to flick the switch, as I'd come here to do.

'No need to throw insults,' Will said, 'when we can throw money instead. Weren't you and I going to have a chat about a few possibilities, Sunshine?'

'We were indeed.' I grinned happily, trying not to twerk in my seat with excitement. 'You and I planned to catch up after the night Sebastian kept me at work with a raging fever and *still* made me pay a fee. I *was* pretty close to calling Solicitor that night, but I physically put away my shank before any damage was done.'

'You can physically put away my shank any time you'd like, dear-heart,' Solicitor couldn't help put in. After where he'd just led the conversation, he deserved to blurt out all the smut he wanted.

'If *I* opened a new gentlemen's bar,' Will asked me, 'would you be okay with me being your boss? And would the other girls be okay with leaving their old club?'

'Does stepping on Lego hurt your feet?'

Will smiled and clapped his hands in delight. 'Excuse me, waiter! Can you bring us a bottle of your best champagne? And a seafood platter? I can hear my friend's stomach grumbling after she played frisbee with her steak.'

'Thank you!' I said, the grateful tears in my eyes caused by both joyful exhilaration and hunger pains.

'Let's do this!' Will enthused. 'Let's *really* open a new club.'

'Yes, not just to get back at Sebastian and Hugo,' I said, 'but as a haven for the girls too.'

'Plus it'll be a great money-maker for me! Oh boy, it's going to piss Sebastian and Hugo off that I have no prior offences.'

It was going to do a lot more than that. Nothing would cause the Dickhead Duo more fear, increasing their need for valium and giving them plenty of sleepless nights to reflect on what happens when you push a woman too far.

With unholy glee, we toasted the champagne and gorged on prawns as we worked out the particulars.

'You find me a location, Sunshine, and I'll start getting the tradesmen together.'

'Oh, I can help with that,' Solicitor offered, glowing with Veuve and enthusiasm. 'I act on behalf of most nightclub owners in town, and I recall a few of them are eager to sell, so you won't have to build from the ground up.'

Will shook Solicitor's hand across the table in thanks. 'In that case, I'd like to employ you for all the new club legalities.'

'It would be my honour. However . . .' Solicitor had a familiar mischievous look on his face. 'Only if you can guess the colour of Sunshine's underwear before I do.' He grinned Will's way.

'Pale pink silk. I pretended to drop my napkin the moment I sat down.'

HIGHLIGHT: Restaurant kitchen peeled my prawns so Will wouldn't have to wear their carcasses.

DOWNSIDE: How am I expected to keep new club a secret if someone buys me tequila?

24 November

'We're all going to be sacked, if we don't get to work in fifteen minutes!' Aliah screamed through my sleep-sodden consciousness.

All us girls were sprawled across Belle's apartment, dead to the world. We would have slept the whole night away if Sebastian hadn't rung Aliah in a fit of rage.

Throwing costumes into bags, sliding on stilettos and wiping our faces clear of last night's make-up in the Uber, we made it to work in half an hour. I prayed Sebastian wouldn't shriek at us; I knew it would spear through my head like ice-cream brain-freeze. My hangover was so mammoth, it needed its own postcode.

I've been celebrating nonstop and still have yet to tell a soul the secret, no matter how many shots, nips or cocktails are involved. And there have been countless of all the above.

Best of all, the Duo no longer has the power to irritate me. I find myself filled with jubilant spite whenever I smirk their way.

I just wish I could let the girls in on it, because they aren't faring as well as me without the promise of freedom and change. And they seem to be immersed in more melodrama at the moment than the entire year put together.

At the club we were likely still drunk from last evening's partying and simply elevated our blood-alcohol level to triple digits once we hit the bar. Luckily for us, Sebastian was in happy awe that he'd pulled six zombies out of bed and ended up with them functioning—even though our intoxication would have been apparent to an individual with prosthetic eyes. He thought it added atmosphere to the club when Jade jumped on the bar to dance, and Candy, having forgotten her bag in the rush, had nothing to wear, so decided naked was a good enough costume.

My poor Tara was spiralling on a downer, though. She sat at a table away from us, staring solemnly at her phone, so I went over and threw my arm around her. 'What are you doing, sweetheart?'

Misery overtaking shame, she showed me the phone screen: a grainy image of a sultry brunette hovering at what looked like a front door. I looked at Tara in bewilderment, and she confessed, 'I put a video doorbell at the DJ's front door this morning and connected it to my wi-fi.'

'What on earth *for*?'

'To see who comes and goes. To catch him out with other girls. Looks like I proved myself right. This pouty bitch has been pressing on the button for fifteen minutes.'

'Honey, the fact you spent money on spyware—which he'll undoubtedly find and destroy—means you know the relationship is dead as a doorbell. I mean, doornail.'

'You acted just as crazy when Jim cheated,' she reminded me, and she was right. People in glass houses shouldn't throw stones—they should have lots of parties, with naked guests.

'That's true,' I said, 'but it's time to let go and allow yourself to be happy again, okay?'

I said this not just because I didn't want to see her getting inventive with a stainless-steel cocktail shaker to perform an impromptu castration at Coconuts, but also because I truly wanted Tara to smile without distraction.

I then noticed that Candy was also looking a bit despondent. It turned out she hadn't been at the club the night before because she'd taken on a pricey dominatrix job instead. Now she was drowning her sorrows at the outcome.

'The client wanted Chinese love balls shoved up his arse. He wound up in hospital. They went up so far, we lost them.'

'I hope you made him cover the cost—those things aren't cheap.'

I was less worried by the existence of a man with a fetish for rectal pain than by my indifference to the story. It seems I've reached the point where nothing can shock me. An actor who wants me to dress up as doll while he masturbates? *So what?* A German who wants his balls pierced by a stiletto? *Big deal.* An orgy with athletes in a lap-dance room? *Been there, done that.*

I didn't have time to ponder this further, as Charlie came bouncing over. She'd gone from begging and pleading to something much worse: pretending it had never happened.

She grinned at me like she wasn't now good friends with my ex and his hussy. 'Tell me honestly, Sunshine, do you think my make-up is too heavy?'

'Depends on whether or not you're planning to kill Batman.'

Aliah, after overhearing the exchange, ran off to the change room only to return giggling a few minutes later. 'Charlie left the key in her locker,' she whispered to me. 'I've just stolen all her G-strings so I can sell them later!'

Oh God. It was all spinning out of control.

'Hey, Sunshine!' Tara hollered over the music. 'You'll never believe who's here. Come and look!'

I couldn't help grinning when I saw the patrons—finally, something positive. If one thing could lift my rock-chick best friend's spirits, it was a band who, once upon a time, were labelled the most famous *in the world*. There they stood in our little Queensland club. For the sake of Tara's happiness, I put my celebrity prejudice on hold and promised to hang with the band.

This didn't please Soleil the Penthouse Pet. She cornered me on my way over. 'Is that who I *think* it is?'

'Yep.'

'Hang on a minute. Why are you headed their way? I told our bosses from the get-go, any celebrities who come in here should be greeted by me first. They're more relaxed around other famous people.'

'Meaning you?'

'Exactly.'

I sneered at her. 'In the words of another famous witch, *you have no power here.*'

I was soon surprised as hell to find myself forming a *positive* view of celebrity hype. It seems once you get to the point where you can't be any more famous, you return to earth. After the supermodels, drugs, mansions, Ferraris and private jets wear thin, maybe all you have left is a clearer view of what's true. Maybe real people become appealing again over sycophants and groupies. That's the only way I can explain why these rock-royalty figures were so normal—except for the limitless wads of cash, of course.

Much to Soleil's fury, the band booked only me and Tara to keep them company in the club's prestigious Glass Room: a decadent space lined with cushions and mirrors that costs three hundred per hour, plus the price of champagne and the strippers' time.

As we sat on the floor like a yoga group, we discussed the perks and perils of fame. It was a much more desirable way to spend time than being groped and propositioned on the main floor. The band didn't even want us to dance for them, quite content to pay me and Tara five hundred bucks each to 'shoot the shit with ordinary people'.

Nobody entered the Glass Room while it was booked—not even Sebastian or Hugo—so I was surprised when the door opened and a dishevelled, drunken dude lurched in. I was about to call for security when the band broke into indulgent smiles. Here to join them was one of the planet's most well-known music producers, who now produced a big bag of coke. The band refused, happy with their Grey Goose.

But they'd grown bored with the strip club and wondered if we might like to escort them to Coconuts.

'Is Keith Richards the man who death forgot?' I answered happily.

Since the hour was late, our bosses—who recognised the band—let Tara and me leave early and allowed us to take Jade, Candy, Belle and Aliah along for the ride. The thousand dollars they were tipped probably helped sway their decision.

We all headed off in a haze of vodka and good cheer. But, sadly, it's as rare as Al-Qaeda being benevolent for things to stay pleasant in our presence. As we neared Coconuts, we were confronted by a chubby young woman with a sour expression and a T-shirt stained with baby sick. 'Which one of you is Aliah?' she demanded.

'Why?' we all challenged—except Aliah, who gave herself away by not saying a word.

The young woman held out a picture, aiming it at Aliah. 'Do you know this guy? He's my husband, and the father of our two children. He hasn't been home in a week.'

Yes, we knew that guy. He'd been staying with Aliah. It was the Ken-doll.

'He'd been going out a lot for the past month or two,' she went on, justifiably furious, 'then it became every night, until he stopped coming home at all and disappeared last week. He left me alone to look after two kids, so I asked around until one of his friends confessed that he was shacked up with a stripper.'

Aliah gasped in shock before her expression set as her own fury kicked in.

I patted the distraught housewife's shoulder. 'I guarantee he'll be home by morning.' After all, the cheating prick wouldn't have anywhere else to go after Aliah kicked him out of our apartment.

Aliah nodded fiercely. 'I'm so, so sorry. I had no idea. He never said a word.'

Ken-doll's wife stared at her as a tear trickled down her face. 'I've suspected he played up on me in the past, but I never thought he'd sink this low.'

Ken-doll is an incredible new level of bottom-feeder, which shows that even himbos can be bastards.

'You deserve better,' I told her. 'If you wipe that piece of shit from your life, you'll find it.'

Hopefully, I thought, after Aliah threw all Ken-doll's things out the front door, his wife would feel inclined to do the same. Right before she ripped the balls from his body and fucked his best friend.

'Wow!' one of the band members exclaimed. 'We didn't even see this kind of drama on a world tour.'

Indeed. Welcome to our world.

At Coconuts we're usually treated like slightly insane royalty. But when we walked through the door with the band and the illustrious producer, we were overwhelmed by adulation. Security ushered us to the lounge area, which was sectioned off with ropes. Buckets of champagne appeared on the tables, and fans screamed across the room trying to get the band's attention. After half an hour of feeling smug, though, we grew bored with the star treatment, so we all opted to mingle with the common people.

By the time daylight surfaced, I had drunk myself straight. The band had left with some female fans from the crowd, and I couldn't find Tara or Jade anywhere.

But at the front of my mind was the knowledge that the girls and I would be expected at work again this evening. 'Let's go home and drink water,' I suggested to the remaining Belle, Candy and Aliah. 'There's no way I can face the club tonight in the same state I did yesterday—and I don't have a spare liver to carry me through.'

Sounds like the perfect plan, doesn't it? Water, sleep, maybe some vegetables, and perhaps an alcohol-free twelve hours. However, as my grandmother always said, if you want to make God laugh, tell him your plans.

My phone rang.

I listened in horror for a few moments before hanging up.

'We need a car! And someone to drive it—preferably sober!' I shouted at the girls in panic.

'But none of us have one.' Aliah bit her lip. 'An Uber to Port Douglas will cost at least seven hundred bucks there and back.'

'At least,' I agreed. 'But I doubt we'd get one right now anyway. All the nightclubs are finishing up—they'll be booked solid. And we need to get there *fast*.'

Tara had gotten herself into a situation. Awed in the presence of rock-and-roll royalty (and paid six hundred dollars) my friend had done the producer a favour by driving his Corvette home since he was in no state to do so himself. I doubted Tara was either. But they somehow made it all the way to his beach house in Port Douglas, an hour down the coastal road.

Now she was unable to escape—he'd locked her in. Frightened by what might happen next, my friend relayed that Producer had snorted so many drugs, he'd short-circuited into something less than human. 'It's like a zombie has risen from the dead just to booty-pop. Help me!'

I rubbed my temples while I scrambled for an answer. 'Where's Jade?' I asked the others, needing all the help I could get.

'Last I saw, she was curled up asleep behind the bar. The staff were mopping around her.'

Candy, Aliah, Belle and myself stood outside Coconuts at a panicked loss.

'Quadruple the fun!' exclaimed a sleazy voice. 'Are you ladies in need of a ride?'

I'd never been so happy to hear Comedian speak.

'Is your car here?' I demanded.

'It is indeed—a *Mercedes*.' He preened.

'Have you been drinking?'

'Not a drop,' he said proudly. 'I have to film a show at lunchtime. But I *do* have some awesome ecstasy tablets left, if anyone wants one?'

'How is it you haven't flatlined yet?' I said, climbing into his car with the girls. 'You know the way to Port Douglas, right?'

'Huh? I can't take you all the way there—I'm flying to Sydney in a few hours!'

'You'll have plenty of time,' I cajoled. 'The four of us will give you a free lap dance when you get back, all at the same time.'

He immediately swung the car around and headed towards Port Douglas.

The fastest way to get there is by a winding highway. Usually the hour-long drive is a breathtaking spectacle through an emerald rainforest beside the sparkling Pacific. But today we chain-smoked without seeing the view, sick with nerves and agonised by Comedian's double entendres.

I imagined my friend molested and murdered. Or, worse, scarred for life by the sight of Producer indulging in a spot of autoerotic asphyxiation.

So I gulped when my phone rang, expecting the worst. Especially since it was a hidden number. I thought, *Oh Lord, please don't let it be the police. Or the ambulance.*

'Hello?'

'Sunshine? Hi, it's Orion.'

Could his timing be any worse? He'd called right as we drove into the gated resort that housed Producer's holiday home. 'I can't talk right now, I'll have to call you back,' I said brusquely and had no choice but to hang up.

As we stood outside the opulent house, Justin Timberlake's 'Sexy Back' blared through the tightly locked doors and shutters.

'Knock on the window and say you're security,' I ordered Comedian. 'But do it in a butch voice.'

'My voice is *always* butch,' he retorted.

'Actually, it always sounds like your stockings are on too tight.'

'I'll have you know—'

'Just hurry up and do it!'

He did a fairly decent job, and a few moments later there was some fumbling at the front door. Without waiting for Producer to peep out, I kicked the door as hard as possible. It swung open, sending him sprawling to the ground; we strode past him and made our way to the living room.

'Thank God!' Tara cried, leaping from a terrified crouch in the corner to throw her arms around me.

I returned her hug tightly while staring over her shoulder in disbelieving shock.

Producer, apparently unperturbed by being knocked to the floor, had stood back up and resumed dancing to Timberlake, dressed in Tara's blue lace lingerie and wearing her scarlet lipstick; neither complemented his grey sideburns and paunch.

I then noticed that Tara's work costumes and underwear were

strewn all over the room. A sequined G-string had landed in a soccer-ball sized mound of coke.

'He tried them all on,' she wailed. 'Now he wants to marry me in a Wiccan ceremony! Get me the fuck out of here.'

'*I'm swinging sexy sacks, yep!*' Producer sang to himself as though we were invisible, adding an arse-shake for good measure. I'd seen enough. 'Let's go.'

In a couple of seconds we'd collected Tara's things and bundled her out the door without Producer even noticing. Nor did he bat an eyelid when Comedian ran back inside and pocketed half the cocaine stash.

We stopped off for breakfast at a beach cafe, then drove the hour back home. Once there, with everybody safe and sound, we dissected the past evening, week, year. We all agreed none of it sounded healthy. In fact, we were all surprised none of us had needed CPR. Comedian missed his flight.

On hardly any sleep I have to be back at work in six hours, and so do my friends. We need a miracle—and soon I'll have one for them. I hope.

HIGHLIGHT: Soleil was removed by security for hiding in bushes outside famous band's Airbnb.

DOWNSIDE: Orion had caller ID switched off. I have no way of getting his number.

1 December

Okay. So there's a new club in the works, along with the chance Sebastian and Hugo will lose the plot. And my drinking is moderately under control now I've put myself on rations. But there are two things left to conquer.

The first is authentic happiness. I've had an emotional year, and now it's taking its toll. Everything is going okay on the outside, so the inside has decided to begin unravelling. I feel bone-tired and without valid goals, even though I have exciting things to look forward to. Perhaps I just need a long holiday—nowhere near Japan, though. Whatever the case, I know I have to find reasons to smile again.

Which brings me to my next hurdle: finding a healthy, normal relationship. A feat seemingly more rare in the stripping world than a doctor with neat handwriting.

My first attempt was an epic fail.

The girls and I were enjoying a few cocktails at the local Mexican restaurant and bar, Cacti, when I spotted a beautiful man, all sun-lightened hair and butterscotch tan.

'Check out how hot that guy is,' I shared.

'Go show him your moves,' Candy suggested.

'I'm not stripping in Cacti!'

'No, moron.' She rolled her eyes. 'I meant go get your swagger on.'

The truth was, I had no idea how. I hadn't hit on anyone in over *four years*, and I was beginning to need sex. But was I ready for a relationship?

I made it uncomplicated: I asked the striking young man if he'd like to accompany me home for an unemotional tryst without the promise of further communication. Because isn't that every man's dream come true?

'Sure,' he drawled with a smile and a Canadian accent. 'I love nothing better than going home with beautiful girls for uncomplicated sex.'

I blathered in the Uber all the way home, a mess of nerves. I kept asking him what part of the Caribbean he came from, no matter how many times he reminded me it was Canada from which he hailed.

Inviting him in, I was anxious to put it mildly. Who would make the first move? Did he have condoms, or was I expected to provide them?

What if he was a serial killer? Or worse, a *male* stripper?

But there was no need for my misplaced panic. He couldn't get it up.

'I'm sorry.' He grimaced. 'My penis is really frightened—it isn't usually approached by gorgeous women who want nothing to do with the owner.'

He went on to admit that while he loved the idea of unattached sex, his subconscious didn't. Apparently, men don't like it much when we act like them. And me being a stripper didn't help—he confided that he thought of exotic dancers as highly experienced vixens who expected eight hours of porn-star standard performance and eight inches of penis.

I couldn't be bothered telling him how far this was from the truth, and even remained polite as I showed him the door.

My booty call had been disconnected before it even rang.

At least there was no reason to share my leftover pesto and prosciutto pasta.

HIGHLIGHT: Maybe I've already found my soulmate in the form of carbs.
DOWNSIDE: Will any man ever give me the same excitement I feel when I see my cocktail on its way?

8 December

'Okay, dear-heart, it's time to stop feeling sorry for yourself and get back on the horse.' So said the Solicitor after ringing me unexpectedly.

'What are you on about? What fucking horse?'

'Does it matter? Any one that you can ride. Or be ridden by.'

'Is there a valid reason why you're calling to talk pornographic riddles at midday? And who said I felt sorry for myself?'

'I certainly would,' he said, 'if I'd gone home with someone who couldn't get it up.'

'Who the hell told you that?!'

'Small town, darling. But to ease your paranoia, your friends mentioned it.'

'They were supposed to keep their mouths shut!'

'Yes, well, six of you can keep a secret if five of you are dead, and all that. Anyway. You need to pick out your best party frock and look enchanting—I'm inviting you to a dinner party. Tonight. Lovely outdoor restaurant. I've invited some interesting characters, so you might actually meet someone without an erectile dysfunction.'

'No thank you. Not happening. You have more chance of me flashing my liver at a Hannibal Lecter.'

'Sunshine, my stubborn little sweetheart, despite the indecency I love to aim your way, I actually care about you. And I think you should come out and have a night of fun with some particularly fetching fellows. Or you could continue to test your sanity with yet another evening of gratuitous groping grubs for money you don't actually need. Why not think outside the box and embrace adventure?'

He had a point . . . despite the overuse of clichés.

'Who'll be there?' I asked.

'A few of my clients and acquaintances,' he said. 'And a dashing young professional who occasionally acts as an expert witness for me in court. Very pleasant in nature, but with an unexpectedly wayward sense of humour. Each are very decent, mature and good-looking chaps, all the things you've seemed to shun in a man.'

'Cheers for the compliment. So you're saying I'll be the only woman present?'

'Thank me later, dearest.'

'Solicitor, I can't rock up to a restaurant and be the only girl in a group of professional men. I'll look like an escort!'

'Of course you won't, sweetness, just don't wear that silky red dress of yours.'

A dinner party with grown-up, career-wise men—oh, I thought, this should go well, since maturity and I are only passing acquaintances.

But what the hell, I told myself, maybe Solicitor was right. Perhaps I'd meet the man of my dreams. And I *did* need a night away from the club to have some *fun*.

By six-thirty that evening, I was already having plenty. And I hadn't even arrived at the dinner yet. In an explosion of nerves, I'd drunk a bottle of sav blanc while getting ready, and opened another for one more glass of courage.

Staying away from red slinky numbers, I chose a boho maxi dress that didn't require a bra. It was sexy but chaste, offering only a hint of jiggle. Unfortunately, it was a bit long for my five-four frame, but a pair of towering pink wedges fixed the problem nicely.

By seven-thirty, I was only slightly sozzled when I arrived at the restaurant Solicitor had booked. I did my best not to cringe when I asked for his table.

The eatery was set in a rainforest garden, cusping the bay, and a lovely humidity accompanied the lush landscape and tiki torches. As a waitress led the way, in the light of dancing flames I caught sight of the group—and my stomach lurched.

The merry gathering included Solicitor, Comedian, Painter and Orion.

Yes, *Orion*. And Painter. Yes, *Painter*: the bathroom hidden-camera perve I'd been so taken by on the Gold Coast.

I couldn't believe I was smiling and walking towards the table. My mortification had placed me on polite autopilot. But where was I supposed to run to? They'd already seen me, and my wedges weren't made for sprinting.

'Here she is!' said Solicitor. 'You look lovely, my darling. Will you have a drink?'

Comedian roared with laughter. 'A drink? Sunshine likes to double-park her espresso martinis. You'd better order four, just to be safe.'

Oh, for the love of God, no, this wasn't happening. Comedian was winking at me, Painter was leering my way, and Orion just looked put out. And I could count on Solicitor starting on inappropriate bawdiness before the entrees arrived. This was the opposite of playing 'Your Dream Dinner Party'. (Coincidentally, my dream guests are Jesus, Jim Morrison, Dolly Parton, Billy Connolly and the Dalai Lama.) I would never have chosen three deviants and a man who made my heart and vocal cords seize in his presence.

But of course I was seated next to Orion. With Painter on my right.

'I gather you two know each other?' Solicitor asked me and Comedian.

'All the way to Port Douglas and back,' he guffawed.

'I'm familiar with everyone here,' I said, keeping my voice light.

'Good show! No need for introductions, then.'

Nope. Everyone here knew I was Sunshine the stripper, with a million mishaps to keep the conversation flowing.

But luckily, Solicitor began entertaining the group with his own adventures. Namely his new case defending a girl who'd run naked through traffic while high. I hoped I didn't know her, but more than likely I did.

Painter leaned over to whisper in my ear. 'You didn't collect your picture.'

'No, I didn't,' I answered flatly.

'It's waiting, gift-wrapped, in my living room.'

And no doubt it's collecting the grime you radiate, you sick peeping Tom, I thought as I smiled evenly.

'. . . then she mooned the policeman,' Solicitor was saying to the table.

Orion took his turn to whisper in my ear. 'You never returned my call?'

With a start, I turned to look at his bronzed beauty. The tiki torches gave his amber eyes a deep lustre, and his freckles were like sparkles of copper. My chest swelled with something molten. 'I don't actually have your number . . .'

He grinned down at me. 'That's your only excuse?'

I took a shallow breath. This man actually *robs* me of functioning normally. 'It's not an excuse, I truly didn't know how to ring you back. But I also wasn't sure you'd want me to, once you remembered the last time we met. I was dressed as Tinky-Winky.'

Orion chuckled softly, close to my earlobe. His warm breath made my skin blaze, and my stomach filled not with butterflies but a whole zoo.

'I'm just glad it wasn't Bob the Builder. Masculine women scare me. I'm more drawn to beautiful, feminine blondes who light up a room with their quirky presence.'

Quirky? Not neurotic, or freakish, or batshit crazy? Maybe, I thought, just maybe . . . there was a chance here.

But I've always been the universe's plaything. Right then, just as Solicitor finished his story, Comedian thought it a good time to ask if I'd like to accompany him to the bathroom for some coke. And at the exact same moment, a beautiful girl arrived at our table to glare at Orion.

Actually, she wasn't beautiful. She was jaw-droppingly, heart-breakingly *stunning*. All eighteen or so years of her.

'Sorry to interrupt,' she said, glowering Orion's way while still managing to dazzle everyone. 'Why did you let me sleep in this morning? I didn't have keys to lock up. You knew I had the last day of that medical conference!'

'I thought it was finished.' Orion stood to put his arm around her shoulder. 'I can email the organisers for notes. And take you out for dinner to apologise.'

'I don't need dinner, but yes, I need a summary of the speeches—so I'll hold you to that. I also need the keys. I've had to leave the place open.'

It had to be her. The normal nurse girlfriend Orion had said he'd broken up with.

Thanks to Comedian, I had two espresso martinis to knock back as I started to shake, which just added a head-spin to my shock.

Then Painter murmured in my ear again. 'I'd love to see you do your business.'

'What?' I snapped. 'You told me you weren't into lap dances. Or did you forget to keep track of that lie?'

'No,' he whispered urgently, as Orion was occupied with his gorgeous girlfriend, and Comedian debated with Solicitor about whether the bushes were dense enough to hide them doing lines. 'I meant, I'd love to see you do your *business*. On the toilet. I'd pay for the pleasure.'

Then and there, another night was added to my shit-list of evenings. I shot up from my seat, needing to escape.

'Is everything alright, dear-heart?' Solicitor inquired.

'Fine,' I said, walking away from the table. 'I'm just going to the . . . um, ladies'.' No way was I going to say 'toilet' in front of Painter.

Hadn't I known deep down that this dinner was a bad idea? At least now, I thought as I stomped towards the bathroom, Solicitor could start up all the smut he wanted without hurting my ears, while Painter wouldn't get near one again to whisper with his literal potty mouth. And Comedian could entertain them with stories about rescuing my friends from a drug-addled producer.

And Orion could get down on one knee and fucking propose to Normal Nurse.

My head spinning and my face smarting, at first I didn't see that I'd walked into the men's bathroom. But as my too-long maxi-dress got caught in my extremely high wedges, I noticed the mistake I'd made in record time.

Just as I tripped over and landed in the urinal.

HIGHLIGHT: Six blocks home to walk off my hangover, since no Uber would pick me up covered in piss.

DOWNSIDE: Still don't have Orion's number. Not that it matters anymore.

15 December

The papers had been signed, the deal had gone through, and the tradesmen were being assembled. With Will's credit card in my purse, I invited the girls to the same marina restaurant where I'd met with him and Solicitor.

I'm staying right away from nightmare-inducing restaurants in rainforest settings.

I still haven't said anything to my friends about that godawful night. I trust them with the important things, but they told Solicitor all about my non-erection encounter, so I know they wouldn't be able to resist toilet humour. Not that I would blame them—if it hadn't happened to me, it would have been hilarious. I was yet to laugh over the incident, though, and felt my next lifetime would still be too soon for a giggle.

Having arrived before the others, I placed a little red and green gift-wrapped box in front of each table setting. It was, after all, beginning to cost a lot like Christmas.

I had other presents hidden in my bag for a bit later . . .

Needless to say, champagne was already on ice.

I'd met with Will the day before and told him that my gang's colours were fading—they were either about to break apart or engage in a drive-by. Our cruel sergeant-at-arms was putting our dance fees up, and he'd demanded attendance on Christmas Eve out of festive season malevolence. My best friends were drinking even more despondently than ever. Will had agreed they needed some Yuletide cheer, so he'd given me permission to spill the sequins. He'd also given me carte blanche with his card to order the entire food and drink menu if that's what the girls wanted, in thanks for switching sides.

I could tell that the waitstaff instantly remembered me. Even though I hadn't been there in a few weeks, I'm guessing very few patrons hurl around medium-rare short loins in this fine-dining establishment. And so the staff barely raised an eyebrow as Tara arrived and dropped her handbag in the entrance, spilling an array of make-up, tampons, cheese-stick snacks (just to add insult to their truffle-infused gruyere) and extra-ribbed condoms. Thank

God it wasn't Candy: the staff would have developed an adult-toy phobia if they'd seen the collection in her bag.

Aliah had clearly popped into the marina public toilets beforehand: she walked through the prestigious restaurant doors with three feet of toilet paper stuck to her heel.

Belle arrived in ripped stockings and Doc Martens. Jade turned up in a man's shirt smelling of aftershave.

The waitstaff didn't even have to ask; they pointed all five girls straight to my table. Once all were seated, Tara picked up her Christmas gift, then swiftly put it down like it was the urinal cake I'd landed on the other night. Tears sprang to her eyes. 'Just give it to us straight,' she almost sobbed.

'Pardon?' I said, mystified.

'You're either leaving us, or *leaving* us . . . right?'

'Tara, have you been swimming in paint thinners? What are you *talking* about?'

She sniffled and motioned to the others, who all looked similarly distressed. 'We all thought you invited us here to say you're either moving back to Melbourne . . . or moving into palliative care . . .'

'Seriously, you assumed I'm terminally ill because I wanted to take you out for lunch? Or moving back to Victoria, which would make me *mentally* ill.' Tara's face was so stricken that I couldn't help throw my head back and laugh. 'Wow, you really have been bathing in turpentine. How did you come to those little gems?'

'We thought maybe you were going because you've had enough of our bosses.'

'Or made yourself ill over their bastard behaviour,' Jade put in.

I smiled at my posse. 'You're right in a roundabout way. I'm sick to death of them, and I *am* moving. But not from Cairns.'

They were puzzled as I told them to open their gift boxes.

'There's a key in here.' Belle spoke for all of them.

I nodded happily. 'It opens your new locker. My Regular, Will, had a metallic-sparkle set made up especially for us—for when we open the new club.'

There were no words from the girls at first. I knew how they felt; I'd had a similar reaction a few weeks back when it had sunk in, one of those moments when you're so overwhelmed with relief and happiness, all you can do is cover your mouth.

Then Tara burst into tears. 'You mean I'll never again have to hear Sebastian ask me if strippers make good spinsters?'

'Or listen to Hugo say it's a pity I can't move the dimples from my thighs to my cheeks?' Candy added.

'Not for much longer,' I promised.

They all shot out of their seats to hug me, causing a ruckus throughout the restaurant. Oh well, I'm sure the staff didn't expect anything less. Nor were they prepared to utter a word against us when the bill was already sitting at well over a thousand of Will's money.

The girls wept and cheered. 'Thank you, thank you, *thank you*!'

'When?' Jade asked, sitting back down and wiping her eyes.

'The agreement just went through. Will's bought a nightclub that doesn't need much more than some paint and decoration. And a stage with poles, of course. According to him, it won't take a great deal of time.'

'Let's start texting everyone!' Belle cried. 'We can take all the Dickhead Duo's customers before it even opens.'

'No!' I yelped. 'No one can know yet! You're the only ones I've told. We have to keep it a secret—you really want to be sacked and face working at one of the other shabby clubs if Sebastian or Hugo finds out? We need to keep our mouths shut until the new one opens.'

'Good point. But when the time comes, let's take everyone!'

Candy giggled. 'Except Charlie.'

I nodded. 'Except everyone who hasn't shown us respect, empathy and honesty.'

We toasted to that.

'So this Will?' Aliah asked, digging in. 'He must be a genuinely lovely guy if he's already bought us sparkly lockers and shelling out for my mudcrab.'

'Put it this way, it'll be like leaving Kanye West to work for Morgan Freeman.'

'And we'll all still be together,' Jade said softly.

'Always,' I vowed. 'Nothing will ever get in the way of our friendship. Except if anyone starts wearing blue eyeshadow with red lipstick.'

'Hey,' Aliah said, 'there's a note in my gift box too.'

'Feel free to read it out loud.' I giggled. 'You all have the same one.'

'It says, *Do you know if you text your boss to get fucked, you won't have to go to work anymore?*'

The girls roared with laughter.

'Is that how we're handing in our resignation?'

'Does the pope have a balcony?'

HIGHLIGHT: The restaurant staff didn't bat an eyelid when I produced six sets of devil horns for me and the girls.

DOWNSIDE: When I ordered the seafood platter again, staff did inquire if I'd like a bib.

20 December

I was so nervous, I could barely apply my make-up. I didn't want to wear my work war paint anyway—just some mascara and gloss would do. I wanted no artifice tagging along on my first date with Orion.

He'd had the courage to call again twelve days after that disastrous dinner. A brave move, in my eyes, to persist with a girl who keeps running away.

'I can't go out with you,' I'd said at first.

'Why?' he'd asked.

Because you're a sane, balanced, socially acceptable individual. And I'm a maladjusted screwball. Plus you have an eighteen-year-old supermodel girlfriend.

'I don't go out with attached people,' I feebly answered.

That warm-honey chuckle poured down the line. 'Just meet me for dinner, and I'll explain.'

So I accepted. I couldn't bring myself not to. Then I did a few handstands and high-fived a few strangers on the street.

I wore all white, because he represented the chance of a clean start.

Hangover free, I met him at a little tapas bar. I stared in heated delight when I first saw him sitting there, waiting for me. He appeared lit from within with hues of chestnut, gold and bronze. His face split into a smile when I bent to peck his cheek as I sat down.

My breath caught as he reached over to hold my hand. I wanted to grasp his. But I also didn't want to add him to my list of catastrophes.

'Orion, should you be on an obvious date when you have a girlfriend at home?'

He ignored my question. 'We're going to play a game, if it's okay with you—since I noted you don't mind a drink or two.'

Bad idea. Orion didn't realise that nerves and alcohol turn me into a Jackson Pollock-type diner: food and drink are sure to be festooned around the restaurant. Soon, every eatery in town would be applying a dry-cleaning surcharge as I walked in.

I'd stayed sober in preparation for this evening (and planned to order only see-through food). But I've never been able to resist a drinking game . . .

He grinned. 'I call it "Getting to Know You by Cocktail".'

Okay. I was curious. And in.

The waiter, who'd been standing nearby, approached at Orion's beckoning smile. We were both a bit stunned when Orion asked for two Cosmopolitans.

'I've never seen a dude drink one of these before,' I said, taking a generous sip.

'And I haven't drunk one up until now. I ordered a Cosmopolitan because it explains my *ex*-girlfriend. The nurse. Cairns wasn't big enough for her, so she left to pursue her career at a hospital in Melbourne. The girl who showed up at dinner the other night is my little sister, Kandis. She's an acupuncturist. There was a natural medicine conference on here, so she took advantage of attending and having a holiday with her big brother.'

'Oh . . . so no girlfriend?'

'Nope. I'm single. Your turn to order.'

'Pina Colada. Because I only like to live in tropical places.' This was also my way of letting him know that I wasn't running off to a southern city anytime soon.

'I love that drink. I once heard it described as sunshine in a glass. Which is kind of fitting.' He gave me a soft smile, and that might have been the moment my heart declared ownership.

After that there was a Screwdriver—unfortunately not due to the somewhat lusty vision I had in my head—because Orion started out as a builder with his dad's company, before studying psychiatry. Followed by a Bloody Mary, an ode to my love of horror films. An Old-Fashioned, as Orion said his friends often find his values outdated. (I hope that doesn't mean he'd like to see me in an apron and baking a sponge cake if this goes anywhere.) Then came a Mudslide, because I thought it appropriate to mention my clumsiness. (Luckily there isn't a Piss-Trough cocktail.) And then a Flaming Lamborghini when Orion shared the tale of his car accident, although it hadn't actually caught fire and had been a Honda rather than an exorbitantly priced sports car. After rolling the vehicle because he'd been drive-dancing, he'd somehow walked away without a scratch.

I was having an absolute ball as we scratched the surface of our life stories. We were going at a lovely, pleasant pace. But as every drinker knows, cocktails are lethal creepers: they seem all fun and flirty but can have you blathering bullshit in no time.

My downfall was the Japanese Slipper. 'I'm ordering this one in memory of how I ran away from Japan like a demented Cinderella,' I slurred, 'after I got myself in trouble with the Yakuza. And couldn't take schoolgirls' underwear looking me in the face anymore. I paid over six grand to fly there on a stupid whim because I caught my ex-boyfriend with his dick in a brunette. With a big nose. Then I came home and walked out of an orgy.'

The cocktails had caught up and turned me emotionally slutty, and Orion was staring at me in amazement. Or at least I hoped it was—it might have been horror, because that's definitely what the waiter, overhearing, wore on his face. When I called him over, he looked like I might inquire about endangered species being on the menu. Either that, or he wished whatever I was about to say would be saved for my therapist.

All of Orion's recollections were so ordinary compared to mine. Who was I kidding? This wasn't going to work.

The waiter was obviously relieved when I ordered a jug of water. When he nodded and made a run for it, I wondered if I should do the same. Wouldn't it be best to just end this now, without Orion wondering if he should write a groundbreaking thesis about me?

Instead I faced him and made a split decision.

'I took my friends out for lunch a few days ago, and we wore devil horns at the most upmarket restaurant in town. To celebrate my Regular finding us a new club. Because I hate my bosses. And I don't want to deal with their woman-hating tyranny anymore. In fact, I loathe Sebastian and Hugo so much that I sometimes imagine hobbling their ankles, like Annie Wilkes did to that author in *Misery*. But I didn't just orchestrate opening a new strip bar to get back at them—I did it for my friends too. So they can't get pushed around anymore either. Because I'm insanely loyal to my friends, who are all really weird and possibly mentally disturbed. I'm always working myself into a ball of stress because I make their problems my own. I cry when I see other people's tears, and I always give homeless people my spare change. Sometimes I buy them McDonald's too. And I never brag about it either. You're actually the first person I've told.'

I took a huge gulp of water and went on.

'I'd like to consider myself intelligent and analytical. But that's wishful thinking, because I'm thoughtless and rash. I want to be the kind of person who listens when people talk, rather than waiting for my turn to speak, but I'm not that either. I have a track record of acting shallow and ignorant. I intimidate people with sarcasm, then I'm genuinely shocked when they don't like me. I'm also truly stunned when I buy a lottery ticket and don't win. I gorge myself with junk food, but rather than exercise I starve myself for days to make up for it. I'm addicted to reality shows because I love watching characters I hate. I snap at people and immediately apologise, instead of learning to control my anger. I can also be egotistical, selfish and standoffish to strangers. I've had a shit year, and I think it's changed me for the worse. But I also believe we all have spells of bad luck before things change for the better. And I'm telling you this up front because you should know what you're getting yourself into. Plus, I'm crap at picking up men.'

Orion frowned, and my insides lurched. I'd taken a gamble. It might not have paid off.

Just when I thought about sliding under the table and never coming out again, I saw a ghost of a smile. 'Normally, that speech would cost you $120 bucks of my time,' he said.

'It would have cost you fifty of mine.'

He snickered and reached across the table to take my other hand, his eyes skewering me. My stomach gave a stampede, rather than a flutter. Then he motioned for the waiter. 'Two Dark and Stormy, please.'

'Are you *sure*, sir?'

'More than I've ever been of anything,' he replied, his gaze never leaving mine.

My fingers helplessly entwined themselves in his. I was unable to let go as he spoke.

'I'm choosing this drink because I used to have a toy ship as a kid, one of those expensive kit things with endless pieces. It was supposed to sail on water without falling apart. But I remember something always breaking—a little oar, a cannon, usually an intricate part that took ages to fix. And when I look back, I sometimes think that's the reason I went into psychiatry. Because the time I spent mending it never felt like a chore, it felt worthwhile.'

'I didn't say I was broken, Orion. I'm not looking to be *fixed* by anyone.'

He shook his head. 'I'm trying to tell you that the complexity was my favourite part. Yes, the ship needed help. So does every person on the planet, even if it's just in the form of friendship or kindness. But you know what I found amazing? No matter how many times the ship would break, it *always* sailed again. And sometimes, the alterations made her next voyage stronger. I was in awe. I'd sit there, up in the attic my mum made into a playroom, fiddling with the boat, thinking how bad the sail was torn, how cracked the hull was, and that she'd probably never float again. But every single time, that ship would hit the water and decide on a path for herself. In storms, wind or rain, every new passage was determined by her alone. Do you see what I'm trying to tell you?'

I nodded slowly. 'I'm the ship . . . ?'

His eyes bored into mine.

'You're *like* that ship. Whatever changes she went through, whenever a piece didn't fit the way it used to, she *owned* that change and used it to decide exactly which journey she'd take next. I used to think I'd never seen anything so fucking beautiful. Until now.'

My insides turned to liquid as he leaned in and kissed me. Unlike his ship, I drowned, swirling in sweet waves and caught in a delicious undertow. I couldn't remember the last time I'd felt so euphoric. I was animated again. And the past year evaporated.

'I didn't think you would be interested in me,' I said. 'I thought you were attracted to conventional things, like nurses and antipasto . . .'

'I'm a psychiatrist, Sunshine. On a daily basis, I have semi-rational conversations with people who believe they're werewolves or have been anal-probed by aliens. How normal do you think I can manage to be?'

'Point taken.'

'And as for the nurse . . . She was sweet, but she thought of glamour as something external. Not the way it shines naturally from inside you.'

Grinning my head off, I went in for another kiss.

'Would you like to order?' the waiter interrupted.

'Um, should we have the antipasto platter?' I suggested.

Orion went back to frowning. 'Sunshine?'

'Yes?'

'I'm not sure how many times I have to tell you—apart from the two or three times I already have—I fucking *hate* antipasto.'

'How about the Moroccan barbecue for two?' the waiter advised.

'Great,' he said.

'Awesome,' I agreed, and the waiter nodded and walked off. 'Orion?'

'Yes, Sunshine?'

'Did your mother really have an attic?'

'Yep. Why?'

'You're not going to try to fiddle with me in it, are you?'

'Only if you ask nicely.'

HIGHLIGHT: Gave Sebastian a cryptic answer when he rang to see why I hadn't shown up: 'My work here is done.'

DOWNSIDE: Spiced pork between my front teeth, but still received kisses.

EPILOGUE

···

Another year to keep a diary commences. This time as a marketing consultant in Cairns.

Last year, I was stripping for a living, which almost drove me insane, and then . . . Actually, I can't be bothered going into it. See your predecessor to bring you up to speed. But plenty of changes have happened. Hence the late diary entry.

I should begin where the year started: at Orion's New Year bash. A great party where no rock stars were in attendance, while three of my best friends were present and drug-free. Belle had met a Texan filmmaker with a helicopter and was living it up in Fiji. And Jade is cohabiting with a body builder in Melbourne.

They were all jubilant about getting out from under Sebastian and Hugo's tyranny. Candy, Tara and Aliah ended up working on the Gold Coast until it was time for the new club to open, unable to bring themselves to work at the other second-rate strip bars in town.

The fact that I've needed a break from stripping and have gone back into an office hasn't changed our kinship at all. Marketing doesn't hold the same dazzle, but I do *not* miss the night shifts;

I get rather excited about going to bed at ten (this is partly due to Orion being in it). And I do not miss my life being a cycle of drunken bouts and debilitating hangovers. Nor do I miss the dramatic self-indulgent person that the stripping world seems to make of me. I don't crave any of those things.

However, sometimes I wake around three in the morning—the time that translates to afternoon tea in the nightclub world—and feel a ghost of nostalgia for the thumping, sensual beat, the flashing strobe lights, the tinkle of ice cubes and extravagant laughter. But mostly, I miss the freedom of living without boundaries—a rock star's existence without the fame or quite as much money. But near enough.

Alas, every dancer needs a break from time to time. Luckily I took one before I started hearing voices. And my stress levels have flatlined, perhaps a bit too much. There's rarely drama in my life anymore, and I can't help yearning for it a little. But it *was* time for me to hang up my G-string, at least for a while.

Not that I have any regrets. Last year, however traumatic, adventurous, seedy, idiotic, extravagant and melodramatic, was a gift of lessons.

So what has stripping taught me?

An invaluable plenty. There is no profession more empowering yet degrading. Yes, you are sometimes looked upon by the mainstream as having less worth than others, but you're able to measure your *own* worth by what people are willing to pay for your time. There is the benefit of great profit, while it's up to you whether you become the object you're treated as. And whether or not you hand over your soul.

The job will help you develop impenetrable strength. It will hack off your shell and replace it with a glossier version. It can spur you into making changes to your appearance you always promised yourself you'd make someday. And mentally it will prepare you for almost anything. Any part of you that is shy, awkward, nervous in crowds or antisocial will be ripped off like a superglued bandaid—for the first requirement of strip clubs may be nudity, but the second is sociability. Working in a gentlemen's club will give you little option but to develop verbal skills; you can't hustle without talking the talk with everyone from the most illiterate labourer to the most jaded, world-weary millionaire.

The job will teach you flamboyance, patience, grooming, communication, confidence, artifice, foresight, sales techniques and how to hold your alcohol well. You will emerge a social butterfly with a wily, manipulative centre. Often I wonder why strippers don't all wind up as actresses or car salespeople, since our job is a combination of the two.

Stripping will grow you a resilient alter ego. It will open up a mesmerising, difficult, theatrical new world. It will challenge you to make life-changing transformations. And it will create the most amazing memories to look back on, some day.

I'm not yet ready to mentally revise last year all that much— the parts that aren't a blur, at any rate. I either get caught up in the bad memories by reliving them emotionally, or grieve for the good ones. Orion tells me this is normal, but I think it's just plain weird. Perhaps to become a stripper, you can't be entirely normal to begin with.

With his burnished colouring, Orion has become my sun—the shine on my day, the smile in my dreams. At night, I especially feel as though I've been given my own star to warm the cold and light the dark.

He never once suggested I stop dancing, that was my own decision. Orion, being the intuitive individual he is, said I was just as interesting either way, and it was nobody's place in a relationship to dictate what the other should do with their life journey. I suspect he *does* try to fix me a bit, though . . .

After three months together, we've become almost inseparable. I never knew this kind of floating elation existed. I still can't control the butterflies let loose in my stomach whenever I see him. Now I realise that love and quirkiness can blend, and that serious relationships don't have to include normalcy.

I don't think I'll ever be run of the mill, although a certain degree of seriousness *is* required of me each day at the office. And for the past few months, on nights when I wasn't seeing Orion I would stop by the new club to help Will with the renovations. He and his team of employees worked around the clock.

Tonight signified the grand opening.

I toasted Will with champagne as I looked around in wonder. He had gone with the traditional strip club red and black but had brought in artists and tattooists to liven up the walls. The mirrored ceiling and flattering lights lent it a decadent feel. Yes, the new club was a sight to behold—particularly because it would cause Sebastian and Hugo anxiety deeper than the plush carpet.

Likewise, I was thrilled to see most of the Pacific Club girls have jumped ship, including Candy, Tara and Aliah. The presence of another decent strip club in town ensures that exotic dancers will no longer have to put up with the Dickhead Duo's indifference and cruelty. For years it had been their way, or the sacked way.

There were plenty of other performers who'd come from all over the country. The club was dazzling with their exotic colours, like an aviary of rainbow lorikeets. And the atmosphere pulsated with excitement and music, the way a gentlemen's circus should.

Drinks were flowing, customers arrived in droves, lap dances were danced, and a strip club was breathed into life.

All the good elements came back to me: the communal euphoria, the glitter, the merriment, the mountains of money— *especially* the money. Try working for a normal wage after you've been in a position to name your price.

I *had* been out of the game for three whole months. Enough time to have mentally and physically rested? Perhaps.

It was fortunate I was wearing my best lacy underwear ... just in case.

Acknowledgements

It's an honour to have shared in a life-journey, stranger than fiction, with so many rare individuals, so my first thanks goes out to you witty, outlandish, glamorous, sexy Ladies of the Lap Dance. There was never a dull moment with you crazy diamonds.

Another massive thanks goes to Jess Tuckwell from Village Roadshow for wanting to bring the ladies behind the scenes into the light. And to my incredible agent, Jane Burridge, who let me blather away and then made all my dreams come true.

I'm only just learning how much work is truly involved in the creation of a novel, and there should be many names other than mine on the cover. So a huge thank you goes to Jane Palfreyman for your overwhelming talent, insight and understanding, along with Angela Handley and Kate Goldsworthy for your unparalleled editing skills.

Thanks also to Jeff Lindsay, who saw something in me—enough to mentor my path with legendary experience. Not forgetting Chelsea Wootten, Ebony McVicar, Rosie Wang, Amanda Donaldson, Lauren Gratis, Sandy Ellis, Trish Brown, Krissy Paynter and Jessica Bannock for your support throughout, and Melea Turnbull for cocktail secrets!

And of course, my family—Dad, Bev, Ross and Rach—for your unashamed encouragement. Especially my mum, with your unshakable belief in me, and words that have resonated my whole life: *I never taught my daughter to stand in the corner.*

A huge hug to my biggest advocates, my backbone, my heart, my hope: Adam and Dex, you are my true sunshine.

Lastly, to you the reader, thank you for your curiosity, and for walking a mile in my stilettos.